Royal Commentaries of the Incas
and General History of Peru

Abridged

Garcilaso de la Vega, El Inca

Royal Commentaries of the Incas and General History of Peru

Abridged

Translated by

Harold V. Livermore

Edited, with an Introduction, by

Karen Spalding

Hackett Publishing Company, Inc.
Indianapolis/Cambridge

This translation was originally published by the General Secretariat of the Organization of American States, which has granted a non-exclusive and limited license of its rights in the work to this Publisher. New Introduction, Further Reading in English, Notes, and Index copyright 2006 by Hackett Publishing Company, Inc.

For further information, please address:
Hackett Publishing Company, Inc.
P.O. Box 44937
Indianapolis, IN 46244-0937

www.hackettpublishing.com

Cover design by Abigail Coyle
Text design by Carrie Wagner
Composition by William Hartman

Library of Congress Cataloging-in-Publication Data

Vega, Garcilaso de la, 1539–1616.
  [Comentarios reales de los incas. English]
  Royal commentaries of the Incas and general history of Peru : abridged / Garcilaso de la Vega, El Inca ; translated by Harold V. Livermore ; edited, with an introduction by Karen Spalding.
      p. cm.
  Includes bibliographical references and index.
  ISBN-13: 978-0-87220-843-8 (pbk. : alk.paper)
  ISBN-10: 0-87220-843-5 (pbk. : alk.paper)
  ISBN-13: 978-0-87220-844-5 (cloth : alk.paper)
  ISBN-10: 0-87220-844-3 (cloth : alk.paper)
    1. Incas. 2. Peru—History—To 1548. 3. Indians of South America—Peru.   I. Livermore, H. V., 1914- II. Spalding, Karen.
III. Title.

F3442.V3713 2006
985'.01—dc22

                                                      2006016436

Contents

Map of Northwestern South America

Map of Modern Cusco

Legend
- Inca buildings
- Inca walls
- colonial church
- train station

N

Av. Ccollayuy
Retiro
Retiro
Retiro
Recoleta
Lucrepata
Lucrepata
Lucrepata
Tocorepata
Pumapaccha
Chiuampu
Recoleta
Tandapata
Carmen Bajo
Carmen Alto
Cuesta de San Blas
PLAZOLETA SAN BLAS
Atocsaycuchi
7 Culebras
Choquechaca
7 Culebras
Tandapata
Sacsahuaman
Colcanpata
SAN CRISTOBAL
Amargura
Tambo de Montero
Tecsecocha
Saphi
Pumacurcu
Plazoleta
Las Nazarenas
Purgatorio
Ataúd
Palacio
Almirante
Ladrillo
SANTA TERESA
Sta. Teresa
San Juan de Dios
Teatro
7 Cuartones
Arones
Meloc
Nueva Alta
Nueva Baja
Ceniza
Suecia
Procuradores
Plateros
Plaza de
Armas
Plaza
Regocijo
Espinar
Heladeros
Márquez
Tordo
Plaza San
Francisco
SAN FRANCISCO
Desamparados
Unión
Chaparro
SAN PEDRO
STATION
San Pedro
Cascaparo
Concevidayoc
SANTA CLARA
Sta. Clara
Tupac Amaru
Trinitarias
Calle Nueva
Pera
Tecte
Belén
Pavitos
Lechugal
Carmen Quicllo
Matará
Queja
San
Bernardo
San
Andrés
Cruz Verde
Medio
Medón de la Estrella
San
Blas
LA COMPAÑIA
LA MERCED
Ave. el Sol
Almagro
Loreto
SANTA
CATALINA
Santa Catalina
Arequipa
Maruri
Afligidos
Ayacucho
Herrajes
Ruinas
Triunfo
CATEDRAL
Haun Rumiyoc
San Agustín
Santa Mónica
Cabracancha
Av. Tullumayo
(old Tullumayo River)
Pampa del Castillo
Romeritos
San Agustín
Abracitos
Zetas
Limacpampa
Chico
Limacpampa
Grande
Arcopunco
Collacalle
Av. Huascar
Av. de la Cultura
Av. Huayna Capac
Av. de la Cultura
Av. Garcilaso
Av. Manco Capac
Av. Pachacutec
Garcilaso
Av. Tullumayo
Intichahuarina
Ahuacpinta
SANTO
DOMINGO
Sto. Domingo
Coricancha
Ave. el Sol (old Huatanay River)
Av. Pardo
Av. Pardo
Av. Cementerio
Ave Grau
Cuychipunco Pte. Rosario

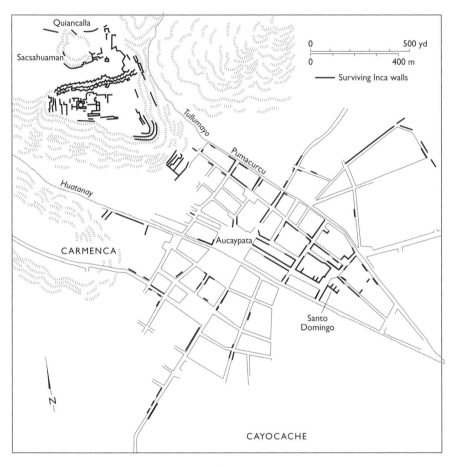

Map of Inca Cusco

Introduction

This edition is intended for people who enjoy going to strange and exotic places and getting to know new and unfamiliar societies and cultures. You may already may be traveling as a member of a college course, or you may be preparing to leave for one of these exotic places. Most travelers get more out of exploring a new and strange country if they have access to a guide who knows the world that is foreign to the traveler, and there is no better guide to the Andean past than Inca Garcilaso de la Vega. The sixteenth-century author of the texts presented here dedicated his life to explaining the history and culture of his native Andes to his Spanish contemporaries.

The Andes are one of the three highest and most mountainous areas of the globe (The others are the Alps and the Himalayas). For centuries, Andean societies have thrived in the mountain slopes, high valleys, and mile-high plains. This beautiful and difficult landscape reaches heights that people who live in lower, flatter regions often think of as fit only for mountain goats and ski resorts. In *Royal Commentaries of the Incas and General History of Peru* Garcilaso provided a guide to the lands and peoples of the Inca state, whose reach extended from what is today northern Ecuador to Chile and northeastern Argentina.

Garcilaso was born in Cusco, the center and capital of the Inca empire, in 1539, less than a decade after the Spaniards entered the Andes in 1531. His early life was shaped by two conflicts: the battle among the Spaniards over who would control Peru and its riches, and the ongoing struggle between Spaniards and the Incas, who fought back against Spanish conquest. The conflict among the Spaniards for control of the Andes ended in 1554, but the Inca resistance did not end until 1572, forty years after the Spanish arrived.

When the Spaniards marched into the Andes, they stepped into a struggle for control of the Inca state. They captured the leader of the victorious faction in Cajamarca, in the north of Peru, and killed him a year later, after he provided the Spaniards with an immense ransom. The Spaniards next fought their way south to Cusco, where they joined forces with Manco Inca, a member of the defeated faction. In 1533, Manco Inca was crowned in a ceremony in which the Spaniards occupied the position of valued allies. During the ceremony the Spanish read the *requirimiento,* an odd bit of legalistic bombast that demanded that the hearers acknowledge, without question, the supremacy of the Christian God in heaven and the Spanish monarch on earth. Manco embraced Francisco Pizarro, the leader of the Spanish force, and "with his own hand offered drink to [Pizarro] and the Spaniards."[1]

The records from this period suggest two very different stories that have been mixed together. Pizarro's actions were those of a victorious conqueror who, in his capacity as governor, proceeded to organize and consolidate his victory, while at the same time it appears that Manco was attempting to rebuild the complicated alliances that supported the Inca rule from Cusco. I suspect that Manco saw the Spaniards and their actions, violent and brutal as they were, as tools for the reprisals that he expected to make in the process of reestablishing the authority of Cusco.

But the two stories soon clashed, and by 1536, Manco decided to rid himself of his increasingly violent allies and called upon his subjects throughout the still-unsettled Inca state to join him in expelling the invaders. Manco withdrew from Cusco to meet the warriors who responded to his call, and his forces surrounded the city and attacked the Spaniards inside. The siege lasted for months, and the Indians[2] came close to eliminating the invaders, but the arrival of additional Spanish forces by both land and sea and the exhaustion of the storehouses of the Inca state after years of war and disruption forced the Indians to withdraw into the rough lands leading into the jungle regions behind the capital. There Manco and his supporters established a court-in-exile from which they harassed both the Spaniards and the Indians who submitted to the new rulers.

Even before the Incas withdrew, however, the Spaniards began to fight among themselves. A power struggle between Pizarro and his partner, Diego de Almagro, ended with Almagro's capture and execution in 1538. That event marked the beginning of endemic conflict between Spanish factions—and later between the Spaniards and royal authority—that went on until 1554. Almagro's death was followed by Pizarro's assassination in 1541 by the supporters of Almagro in revenge for the death of their leader, and the "Almagrists" were defeated in turn by the Spanish governor sent to investigate reports of turmoil in Peru, while a group of Manco Inca's warriors watched the Spaniards battle one another from the surrounding hills.[3]

---

[1] Pedro Sancho, *Relación de la conquista del Perú*, (Madrid: Ediciones J. Porrua Turanzas, 1962) pp. 67–8.

[2] The term *Inca* refers to the ethnic group that ruled the empire from Cusco, while "Indian" refers to all of the native people in the Americas. Manco's call went out to all of the groups that were part of the Inca state, a group that was considerably larger than the Incas alone.

[3] John Hemming, *The Conquest of the Incas* (New York: Harcourt Brace, 1970) p. 263.

The conquerors were unable to consolidate their control of the kingdom they had won, however, for word of the brutal violence of the conquest was carried to the crown in Spain by many—especially horrified missionaries who hoped to convert the Indians to Christianity. Convinced by arguments that the Spaniards had forfeited all claim to the new kingdom by their brutality, the crown issued an order effectively eliminating the basic institution of the conquest period: the *encomienda*.

The *encomienda* was the basis of the economic and social power wielded by the Spaniards. The institution is usually defined as a grant of authority over a member of the native elite, a *cacique* or *curaca*, and his people, in exchange for which the recipient—the *encomendero*—was charged with the responsibility for converting the natives to Christianity.[4] But the *encomienda* can also be seen as a notice to other Spaniards of the *encomendero's* exclusive access to a specific group of people, to use in whatever way he was able. That Spaniard then negotiated—more or less violently—with the *curaca* of his *encomienda* for the goods and labor he wanted. The institution made it possible for those Spaniards who held an *encomienda* to amass great wealth. Consequently, the royal orders addressed to all of Spain's American territories that effectively eliminated the *encomienda* would have ended the conquerors' control over the labor and goods of the Indians.

The ordinances, called the "New Laws," forbade the granting of any new *encomiendas* and specifed that current holders could retain legal title only to the end of their own lifetimes. Royal officials in other areas of the Americas, such as Mexico, avoided the execution of the order and eventually persuaded the crown that such extreme changes could not be made so quickly. The New Laws were brought to Peru, however, by a royal official whose arrogance far exceeded either his understanding of local conditions or his sense of self-preservation. His actions provoked an armed rebellion by the Spaniards that ended in his death. But the majority of the men who killed a royal representative sent by their sovereign had little wish to cut themselves off from Spain. The dispatch to Peru of Pedro de la Gasca, a priest-diplomat armed with full authority and a set of unspecified pardons and orders carrying the royal signature, offered the *encomenderos* an opportunity to back down, and most of them took la Gasca's offer, deserting the rebellion and swearing allegiance to the crown.

Garcilaso was a child of war, born in the middle of the struggle of the Spaniards against one another, on the one hand, and the threat of the Incas

---

[4] The *encomienda* in the Andes did not include land, and Spaniards were legally forbidden to live among the Indians.

who refused to submit to the invaders on the other. Both wars affected him personally. His father, Captain Sebastián Garcilaso de la Vega Vargas, was a descendant of a Spanish noble family, and his mother, Chimpu Oclla, later baptized Isabel, was a member of the lineage of the Inca Tupa Yupanqui and a niece of Huayna Capac, the last Inca to rule before the state dissolved in civil war and the Spaniards invaded. We do not know if Chimpu Oclla entered into a relationship with one of the Spanish invaders of her land voluntarily or if she was—like so many—part of the spoils of war, but her child, baptized by his father with the name Gonzalo Suárez de Figueroa, was raised as a young Spaniard of noble birth. The difference between the child's surname and his father's was common in the sixteenth century; the naming practice of the child carrying the surname of the father did not become standardized until the seventeenth century. Captain Garcilaso gave his son the name of an illustrious grandparent.

Young Gonzalo Suárez thus belonged to the first generation of *mestizos,* or offspring of Spaniard and Indian, in Peru. There were a number of such children, for a union between one of the conquerors and a member of the Inca elite was a time-honored way for invaders to assure themselves a larger share of the spoils than could be guaranteed by plunder alone, in addition to the simple fact that Spanish women were scarce in Peru in the early years following the conquest. Garcilaso mentions that he had ten or twelve schoolmates of the same age who dared one another to play preadolescent pranks during the violent period of the 1540s.[5] A survey of the biographies of the Spaniards present at the capture of the Inca Atahuallpa in 1532 (Garcilaso's father was not among them) reveals more than twenty acknowledged children born of a union between an Andean woman and one of the "men of Cajamarca," the conqueror-elite of Spanish Peru.[6] These children were brought up much like any well-born youngster in Spain: they were taught the basics—reading, writing, arithmetic, geometry and Latin—by a tutor before being sent to a relative or patron who trained the young man in the skills regarded as important for a potential courtier, warrior, and statesman.

The Spaniards in Peru saw themselves as the founders of a new nobility in the Andes, and they did their best to train their offspring to become the *caballeros*—the noblemen—of the land they named "New Castile," even as their control of that land dissolved in the disputes and power struggles that

---

[5] Harold V. Livermore, *Royal Commentaries of the Incas and General History of Peru,* Part II, (Austin: University of Texas Press, 1966) book 5, ch. 42, p. 1215.
[6] James Lockhart, *The Men of Cajamarca* (Austin: University of Texas Press, 1979). Calculations are based on the biographies of the subgroups that Lockhart calls "leaders," "hidalgos," "clerks," "men of affairs," and "solid commoners."

followed their spectacular initial success. The young Gonzalo Suárez de Figuera (Garcilaso) had a tutor, a member of his father's household, who taught him to read and write together with other children. He also learned horsemanship, swordsmanship, and the use of the lance—all skills expected of a son of a Spanish noble family. But while these children were brought up to think of themselves as the heirs of a new land that their fathers added to the possessions of the crown of Castile, some of them could boast of an illustrious lineage from their mothers as well, who were members of the Inca elite that had ruled the Andes for at least five generations before the Spaniards appeared in Peru. Isabel Ocllo made sure that her son not only learned the language of the Incas but also spent time with his Inca kinsmen, who were as proud of their traditions as any Spaniard. Garcilaso himself tells the story of an Inca woman, a member of one of the royal clans or *panacas,* who initially refused to marry a Spaniard she insisted was beneath her. When pressured by her kinsmen to accept the alliance, she reluctantly agreed, but when the couple took their marriage vows and the priest asked her if she freely took the man beside her as her husband, she answered in Quechua with an ambivalent phrase that Garcilaso translates as "maybe I will, maybe I won't."[7]

The boy who grew up to be Inca Garcilaso de la Vega was two years old when Francisco Pizarro was murdered by the son of the partner he had executed, and when the elder Garcilaso was forced to choose sides in the conflict that followed, the boy and his mother suffered the consequences, barricaded in their house in Cusco. The house was bombarded by cannon shot from across the street, and the family ran so short of food that the boy ran across the plaza each day to eat at the house of a neighbor. When the elder Garcilaso was later taken prisoner by Pizarro's brother Gonzalo, his son lived as a page in Gonzalo's house. After the defeat of Gonzalo Pizarro, the crown decreed that all Spaniards who held *encomiendas* must either marry or forfeit their *encomienda,* and in 1549, when the boy was ten years old, Captain Garcilaso obeyed the royal decree and married a Spanish woman rather than his Inca mistress. Garcilaso's mother married another Spaniard—one with none of the noble pretensions of the elder Garcilaso—and moved to another house with a dowry that was probably provided by the man who set her aside.

For the next decade, until his father died, the young man lived in his father's household with his stepmother, visiting his mother in her house. As a granddaughter of Tupa Inca Yupanqui, Garcilaso's mother often received the members of her clan in her home. Her son remembered that "on these

---

[7] The story is not included in this edition; see Livermore's complete translation of *Royal Commentaries,* Part II, book 6, ch. 3, p. 1230.

visits the ordinary subject of conversation was always the origin of the Inca kings, their greatness, the grandeur of their empire, their deeds and conquests, their government in peace and war," ending their reminiscences with tearful memories of "their dead kings, their lost empire, and their fallen state."[8] Specialists in oral history have noted that people tend to retain their memories of periods of particular personal or social upheaval in their lives, whether adolescence or war, and Garcilaso seems to have been one of those, for he drew in his fifties and sixties on the memories of his adolescence. He was still living in Cusco in 1558, when decades of negotiation with the remnants of the Inca state in the jungle region behind Cusco finally brought about what became a short-lived truce between the Spanish authorities and the Incas.

Throughout his adolescence, Garcilaso learned an oral tradition in his mother's home, while at his own he served as his father's clerk, writing the letters and reports that were part of his father's tasks as the appointed governor of Cusco after the end of the rebellion led by Francisco Pizarro's brother Gonzalo. But a year after formal peace was made between the Incas and the Spanish authorities, Garcilaso's father died. Shortly after, the Inca died in suspicious circumstances, and in 1560, the tenuous settlement between the Incas and the Spaniards fell apart. That same year, the young man who would later become the Inca Garcilaso left for Spain with a small legacy left him by his father "to study in Spain." The young man was twenty years old. He would never again return to the land of his birth.

In Spain, Garcilaso contacted his uncle—his father's brother—Alonso de Vargas y Figueroa, who received him warmly in his home in the town of Montilla in the region of Córdoba. The young man's first action was to go to Madrid to petition the crown for a pension in recognition of his father's accomplishments and his own standing as a descendant of the Inca nobility. The practice of seeking royal compensation for services rendered the monarch was normal, and several children of conquerors as well as members of the native elites had been rewarded in that fashion, among them Don Carlos, the son of a member of the Inca elite who was recognized as a descendent of the Inca rulers during his lifetime. Garcilaso spent nearly two years—from 1561 until early in 1563—in that pursuit. He was rejected by the Council of the Indies[9] in a particularly wounding fashion, for his father was said to have given support to Gonzalo Pizarro in his rebellion against

---

[8] See p. 2.

[9] The Council of the Indies was made up of men with experience in the Americas who advised the crown on the government of its American possessions. Its members were appointed by the monarch. Spain's possessions in America were called "the Indies" until the end of the eighteenth century.

the crown, and the young man left Madrid disillusioned and resentful and never again petitioned the court for recompense for services.

He seems to have reacted initially to his rejection by the court by seeking to return home, and was granted license to sail for Peru in 1563, but went only as far as Seville, and never embarked for America. In Madrid, the young Garcilaso met many people who had played a part in the events in Peru, among them Bartolomé de las Casas, the famous bishop of Chiapas who was remembered in Peru not as the protector of the Indians but as the man responsible for convincing the crown to dispossess the conquerors— among them Garcilaso's father—of the wealth they won by their own force of arms. Needless to say, the "apostle of the Indians" was not remembered kindly by Garcilaso in his work; he notes that las Casas gave him his bishop's ring to kiss until he learned that the young man was from Peru rather than Mexico, after which the bishop lost all interest in the young mestizo.[10]

In Seville, Garcilaso resumed his studies, working on his Latin and perhaps beginning to study Italian. That same year, 1563, he returned to his uncle's home in Montilla, where he remained with only short absences for the next thirty years. He also assumed his father's name, Garcilaso de la Vega, and by the end of the century his name appears in legal documents as Garcilaso Inca de la Vega.[11] He left Montilla twice, in 1564 and again in 1570, to serve in military campaigns—the second time in a campaign to suppress a rebellion of the *moriscos,* or forcibly converted Muslims, in Granada. He apparently served at his own expense, obtaining the rank of captain, and after his return to Montilla he began to sign his name in town documents as "captain."

Shortly after Garcilaso retired to Montilla at the age of thirty-one, his uncle died after having made his nephew his heir. In later life, Garcilaso credited his uncle's generosity as making it possible for him to retire from the world to "the haven and shelter of the disillusioned, which are corners of solitude and poverty," where "consoled and content with the paucity of my scanty possessions, I live a quiet and peaceful life, . . . more envied by the rich than envious of them."[12] The inheritance was not large, but it was

---

[10] Harold V. Livermore, *Royal Commentaries of the Incas and General History of Peru,* Part II (Austin: University of Texas Press, 1966) p. 959; Garcilaso did, however, read las Casas' history of the Indians and use it in his own work. See Margarita Zamora, *Language, Authority, and Indigenous History in the Comentarios Reales de los Incas* (Cambridge: Cambridge University Press, 2005) pp. 91–100.

[11] Francisco Carrillo Espejo, *El Inca Garcilaso de la Vega* (Lima: Horizonte, 1996) p. 36.

[12] From the preface to *La Florida del Inca* [1605], various editions. The text is cited by Livermore in the introduction to his complete translation of *Royal Commentaries,* Part I, p. xxii.

sufficient to permit Garcilaso to dedicate himself to study. There he continued to study Latin, Italian, and the classics, building a library of works of
Italian literature, history, Americana, and other books, which reveal the
direction of his thoughts by the notes he made in the margins. Having
failed to gain the recognition he sought either as his father's son or as a
descendant of a ruling house of Peru, he sought it in the model of the older
tradition of the knightly chronicler, modeling himself on an ancestor of the
same name who was both a soldier and a poet.[13] Garcilaso began his career
as a writer with a translation of a Neoplatonic text, the *Dialogues of Love*,
by León Hebreo, which he completed and dedicated to King Philip II in
1586, at the age of 51. Despite his dedication, however, it took more than
three years before the royal censors granted permission to publish the work,
which appeared in Madrid in 1590. Once again, however, Garcilaso was
disappointed in his search for recognition, for in the increasingly restrictive
climate that followed the Council of Trent,[14] the philosophical ideas of
León Hebreo were questioned by the Inquisition, and Garcilaso's translation was withdrawn from circulation.

His next project drew on a friend from Peru, Gonzalo Silvestre, who
was in Peru during the campaign against Gonzalo Pizarro, after having
been a part of Hernando de Soto's ill-fated expedition to Florida in 1538–
43. Garcilaso wrote a history of the Florida expedition, "*The Florida of the
Inca*,"[15] based on Silvestre's memories, but the approval and publication of
this work was delayed until 1605. In his sixties, Garcilaso turned to the history of Peru, completing Part I, which he entitled *Royal Commentaries*,
sometime in 1604, judging by the date of March of that year in its final
chapter. The manuscript was then submitted to the Inquisition for its
approval—standard practice in order to obtain permission to print—and
was printed in 1608 under the title of *Royal Commentaries of the Incas*. He
continued writing, and completed Part II of *Royal Commentaries* in 1612,
submitting the completed manuscript to the bishop of Córdoba before
sending it to the censor in Madrid. Unfortunately, Garcilaso fell ill before
the end of the process, and died in 1616, within a few days of the deaths of
William Shakespeare in England and Cervantes in Spain. The second part
of his history appeared posthumously in 1616–7, but with a striking
change. The crown rejected any reference to Inca royalty in Peru, giving its

---

[13] The ancestor was the soldier-poet Garcilaso de la Vega, who lived from 1503 to 1536.

[14] The Council of Trent was called in order to reform the Catholic Church and reaffirm
its doctrinal bases in the face of the Protestant threat. It met intermittently from 1545 to
1563.

[15] There is an English translation of *The Florida* by John Grier Varner and Jeanette
Johnson Varner, *The Florida of the Inca* (Austin: University of Texas Press, 1951).

approval on condition that Garcilaso's grand project—the tragedy of the grandeur and fall of the Incas—be split in two, and the Spaniards' role in the tragedy appear separately under the title of *General History of Peru,* thereby eliminating the comparison between Incas and Spaniards that Garcilaso intended.

The old adage that "you can never go home again" applies to Garcilaso in particular, because the world he left behind him in the Andes changed completely after he left it in 1560. The Andean world that Garcilaso lived in during the 1550s was, from the perspective of a member of Andean—and particular Inca—society, violent and uncertain, but at the same time hopeful. The clergy who sought reform joined the Andean elite in an effort to set limits on the amount of goods and silver that could be collected from the Indians, and then the two groups fought to reduce those amounts in a series of legal appeals to the colonial courts. A crown lawyer who knew a great deal about Andean custom and took part in the process left a vivid description of the effectiveness of this organized political offensive. As he put it, " . . . the tribute was barely set when many assured [the *curacas*] that if they were oppressed by the tributes they could get them lowered; and since some of the people who said that were the ones who would do it, it didn't take much for the Indians to believe them, particularly when they saw that the first plaintiffs got the tributes lowered by simply asking and without any other formality. . . ."[16]

The price of the alliance for the *curacas,* however, was their active support in imposing Christianity on their people, and while many of the native elite enlisted in the campaign at the beginning, the benefits of transferring their allegiance to a new deity looked less and less attractive to people hammered by waves of epidemics—smallpox, plague, measles, and the entire arsenal of European diseases—and told at the same time to reject the rituals for the ancestors and other deities that they believed brought prosperity and good harvests when properly honored and celebrated. Many *curacas* began to lose their initial enthusiasm for Christianity and return, with their subjects, to pre-European practices; the alliance between the reform clergy and the *curacas* began to fray, and by the 1560s, it became increasingly clear that the "struggle for justice" for the Indians, as some have called it, had given way to the need for Indian labor to mine the silver upon which the crown increasingly depended.

---

[16] Juan Polo de Ondegardo, "Relación de los fundamentos acerca del notable daño que resulta de no guardar a los indios sus fueros [1571]," cited in Carlos Sempat Assadourian, *Transiciónes hacia el Sistema Colonial Andino* (Lima: Instituto DeEstudios Peruanos, 1994) pp. 182–3.

As the sympathy of the crown for the Andean population declined, the Inca elite that was courted and favored during the 1540s and '50s saw its hopes of recognition and recompense from the crown as the descendants of royalty fade. At the beginning of the decade of the 1550s, the Spanish authorities put much emphasis on conciliating the Inca faction that still resisted Spanish rule. After much negotiation, the current Inca, Sayre Tupa, accepted the Spanish offer of extensive properties and a pension in exchange for accepting Spanish authority and leaving his jungle hideout. He traveled with his entourage to Lima in 1558 to meet with the viceroy and then returned to Cusco to accept the homage of the Indians there. The young Garcilaso was sent by his mother as a representative of her kinsmen, and the Inca received him with the traditional toast of *chicha,* or corn beer, which was offered by a superior in paired *q'eros*—carved wooden cups—the contents of which were drunk together to confirm the relationship. When Garcilaso left Peru two years later, the future looked bright for the descendants of the Inca.

But less than a year after Garcilaso left, Sayre Tupa died suddenly. There were rumors that he had been poisoned; the truce fell apart, and the attacks of the rebels who remained in the jungle began again. In 1564, a Spanish priest sent word to the authorities of the spread of a nativist millennial movement that held that the Andean deities were uniting to defeat the Christian God and eliminate the Spaniards, and the following year the authorities found a cache of weapons that fueled fears of renewed Indian rebellion. By the end of the 1560s, the crown decided to send a new authority to Peru to end the impasse. Francisco de Toledo, the fifth viceroy of Peru, has been credited with the establishment of the colonial system in Peru. His solution to the "Indian problem" of the sixteenth century was to destroy it. In 1572, the forces he sent attacked the rebel holdout, capturing or killing virtually all of the Indians there, and executing the last Inca, Tupa Amaru, in the plaza of Cusco. Garcilaso kept in touch with what was happening in Peru, communicating with and receiving members of the Inca elite who came to Spain, and his bitterness at the destruction of the world he grew up in is clear in his interpretation of the Andean past.

Garcilaso de la Vega has been described as shy and withdrawn, and yet he chose to write a book that, no matter how graciously and skillfully presented, took an unequivocal stand on some of the major political issues of the time. Further, the issue was one that had a very personal connection to him—not the behavior that is usually associated with a desire to remain unobtrusive. For Garcilaso proposed to tell the story of a conquest that was regarded by many in Spain (as well as among Spain's enemies) as not only unjust but illegitimate. And he offered, as the basis of his claim of expertise on the subject, not his link to the conquerors but his tie, as the son of his mother, to the Indians who were regarded by an important faction of the Spanish elite as inferior by virtue of their ignorance of the "true faith" of Christianity. Garcilaso claimed his mixed ancestry with pride, insisting that his knowledge of the language of the Inca and his Indian heritage, rather than marking him as suspect and untrustworthy, made him uniquely able to present the true story of the Incas. He made what some regarded as a defect into a name assumed with pride, writing that:

> The word [mestizo] was applied by the first Spaniards who had children by Indian women, and because it was used by our fathers, as well as on account of its meaning, I call myself by it in public and am proud of it, though in the Indies, if a person is told: 'You're a *mestizo*,' or 'He's a *mestizo*' it is taken as an insult.[17]

That pride permitted him to challenge much of what had been written about the Incas by Spanish authors, for Garcilaso could not only claim authority by virtue of direct experience, but as a native speaker of Quechua, he could also offer his version of Inca history not as a challenge to the versions offered by the official historians designated by the Spanish crown but as a correction of misunderstandings that were the product of a limited understanding of the Inca language.[18] And that ostensibly modest and humble stance not only gave him additional credibility without openly challenging the official historians, it made it possible for him to undermine the versions of Inca history and culture sanctioned by the crown without falling afoul of the censors who blocked the publication of many histories of the Spanish invasion of the Andes for centuries.

Garcilaso used his carefully crafted authenticity, his linguistic skills, and his years of careful study of the published and unpublished works on the history of Peru to construct a reinterpretation of the Inca state and its encounter with Spain that took a stand on one of the burning issues of the day: the nature of the Indians and their rights. The controversy began early in the sixteenth century, with the question of whether or not the people found in the Americas were rational human beings capable of being converted to Christianity, and if so, what would be their relationship to the

---

[17] See Part I, ch. 7, p. 88 [9:31]

[18] While Quechua was the language introduced into the territories of the Inca state when the Spaniards entered the Andes, several chroniclers, including Garcilaso himself, referred to a secret language used by the Inca court that appears to have been an archaic form of Puquina perhaps originally spoken by the Incas and later overlaid by Aymara. See Rodolf Cerrón Palomino, "Tras las huellas del aimara cuzqueño," *Revista Andina* No. 1 (July, 1999) pp. 137–61.

Spanish crown. The question was not at all an academic one, for if the Indians were found to be incapable of self-rule, as some lawyers and theologians contended, the crown could in all good conscience grant authority over them to designated Spaniards to teach them Christianity and the customs of civilization in return for their goods and labor. The issue was hotly debated both within Spain and outside of it, and was used by Spain's enemies[19] to question the very legitimacy of Spain's right to the Indies.[20]

Whether vassals of the crown, as the Indians were declared to be, could legitimately be conquered and exploited by the men from Spain was a burning subject of the day in the 1530s, as the *peruleros,* or "men of Peru," fought to confirm in the courts their authority over the land they invaded. The intensity of the struggle led Francisco de Vitoria, a theologian and canon lawyer at the University of Salamanca, to comment in a letter to his superior that "[a]s for the case of Peru, I must tell you, after a lifetime of studies and long experience, that no business shocks me or embarrasses me more than the corrupt profits and affairs of the Indies. Their very mention freezes the blood in my veins."[21] There were many, however, who were quite willing to offer arguments justifying the legitimacy of the Spanish invasion of Peru and Spain's claims to the Americas, as well as claiming that the barbarism of the Indians justified their assignment to Spaniards who would control and use them in exchange for teaching them the tenets of Christianity. The matter culminated in a great debate before the crown in 1551. The royal council that presided over the debate was unable to reach a consensus, essentially opting out of the debate, and King Charles V added flame to the fire with a rather weaseling decree that took no stand on the justice of the past but suspended all new expeditions of exploration and conquest until their legitimacy could be established.

When Garcilaso appeared in Spain in 1560, the issue was far from resolved, and the controversy continued. In the Andes, the Viceroy Francisco de Toledo undertook to collect information and prepare a history that would "prove" that the Incas were tyrants and Spain's invasion and conquest of Peru

---

[19] Because Spain was a major power in the sixteenth century, it had a great many enemies, among them France and England. The campaign against Spain made use of the literature generated by Spanish reformers who fought to improve the conditions of the natives, and the propaganda that resulted—much of it translations of the work of Spanish reformers—is known as the "Black Legend."

[20] As noted above, the term "Indies" referred to the Americas until the end of the eighteenth century.

[21] Francisco de Vitoria, "Letter to Miguel de Arcos, OP, Salamanca, 8 November [1534], in *Political* Writings, ed. Anthony Pagden & Jeremy Lawrence (Cambridge: Cambridge University Press, 1991) p. 331.

was legitimate. Garcilaso's outrage toward Toledo is evident in those pages in which he describes the Viceroy—written nearly three decades after the events—and his insistence on demonstrating the rationality, moral excellence, and civilized customs of the Incas was undoubtedly influenced by having personally experienced the attack upon and disparagement of a society of which he considered himself a member. In the face of these events, his proud assumption of his mixed ancestry as part of his name feels like a challenge to any who would disparage the Incas whose identity he made part of his own.

Garcilaso followed the example of the humanists who used the methods of translation and textual exegesis to undermine scholastic intellectual authority under the guise of "correcting" incorrect translations, using his carefully constructed linguistic authority to present his own interpretation of Inca history and culture in contrast to the version sanctioned by the Spanish crown. For the humanists, reason was essential to the existence of true Christianity—a state that lacked good customs and institutions undermined the Christian virtues. In Garcilaso's version of Inca history, the Incas brought civilized customs and practices, informed and guided by natural reason, to the barbaric natives of the Andes, thereby preparing them for the arrival of Christianity with the Spaniards. The first part of his carefully constructed work argues that the Inca state provided the social framework that made it easier to introduce and build Christian virtues. But the second part, in true tragic format, carries the message that the greed and hatreds that divided the Spaniards led to the violence and exploitation that destroyed the social and moral foundation laid by the Incas and made it impossible for Christian virtues to take root. Literary scholars have noted the similarities between Garcilaso's *History* and Thomas Moore's *Utopia*, a classic of Renaissance humanism that enjoyed great popularity among intellectuals in the sixteenth and seventeenth centuries, and Margarita Zamora argues further that Garcilaso not only used the model of the *Utopia* in his presentation of the Incas, but also applied Moore's implicit criticism of European society in his narrative of the Spanish invasion of Peru.[22] For Garcilaso, the Incas fulfilled their holy mission of laying the foundations for the preordained triumph of Christianity that would arrive with the Spaniards, but the Spaniards, by giving in to their greed and mutual rivalries, botched their own mission by destroying the institutions that would have nurtured the True Faith. The two parts of the *History of the Conquest of Peru*, read together, have the grandeur of true tragedy, driven by human flaws that propel events to their inevitable conclusion, and it is hardly surprising that the

---

[22] See Zamora, *Language, Authority, and Indigenous History,* pp. 129–65.

Spanish censors noticed the implications of the link between them and blocked the publication of the second part under the title Garcilaso planned for it, even though they permitted its printing under a new title. But even the truncated first part—*Royal Commentaries*—contained enough of the contrast made obvious by later events as Garcilaso narrated them to become an authority for readers who found in his story of the noble Incas defeated by Spain a rallying-point for their discontent with their own societies and political systems.

The Inca Garcilaso de la Vega is recognized as one of the great figures of the Spanish Golden Age, whose prose is celebrated for its elegance and clarity. His own command of Spanish has been compared to that of Juan Ruíz de Alarcon and the great Mexican author and nun Sor Juana Inés de la Cruz. Within a few years of the publication of *Royal Commentaries,* Garcilaso was regarded as an authority for anyone who tried to write about the Incas and the conquest of Peru, and his work was read and cited in Spain and Peru. One of the first people in Peru to consult *Royal Commentaries* seems to have been the priest Francisco de Ávila, known for his role in initiating and pursuing the campaigns against idolatry that began in 1615 and periodically swept the archbishopric of Lima over the course of the seventeenth century. Ávila, who seems to have read whatever he could find on the nature of Andean society as part of his investigations into native religion, apparently made a summary of *Royal Commentaries* in 1613, only four years after its publication, which argues that it was being read in Peru shortly after completion. Garcilaso's work was read and cited by clerics and laypersons in the Andes as well as in Spain, and by the eighteenth century, Garcilaso was regarded as an authority not only by Peru's intellectual elite, but also throughout Europe.

Both *Royal Commentaries* and *General History* were rapidly translated into other languages, and soon became the principal authority on anything relating to the Incas. *Royal Commentaries* was even credited with fomenting revolt. In the second edition, published in 1723, the editor described a prophecy contained in Sir Walter Raleigh's *Voyage to Guayana,* which predicted that the Inca Empire would be restored by the English. The edition was undoubtedly read not only by Spaniards and Spanish-Americans but by Indian elites, and Thupa Amaru II, the leader of the great Indian rebellion that bloodied the Andes between 1780 and 1783, when interrogated in his trial about his reading habits, told the judge that he was accustomed to reading "books of mysticism and of history, among them *Commentaries of the Incas* by Garcilaso."[23] The bishop

---

[23] Pedro Guibovich, "Lectura y diffusión de la obra del Inca Garcilaso," *Revista histórica,* tomo XXXVII (1992), p. 112.

of Cusco, in a letter to the inspector José Antonio de Areche, insisted that "[I]f the insurgent Josef Gabriel Tupa Amaru had not had *Commentaries* of Garcilaso, with his denunciation of the Spaniards, as his reading and instruction . . . he would not have so boldly set about his detestable revolution."[24] Areche sent Moscoso's letter on to Madrid, and in 1782 King Charles III banned the circulation of *Royal Commentaries* in Peru, but the ban was ineffective and the book continued to circulate in Peru.

Garcilaso's impact on the popular imagination spread far beyond Spain and Spanish-America; Voltaire drew upon *Royal Commentaries* for his portrait of the enlightened society encountered by Candide in the Americas. And in the nineteenth century, the Incas as depicted by Garcilaso further became the focus of a yearly "historical pageant" in Valencienne, France between 1825 and 1840, when republicans adopted the Incas as models of good government and benevolent reason, victims of the "destructive fanaticism" that destroyed a well-managed and prosperous society. Garcilaso was responsible for the image of the Incas in France, for his *Royal Commentaries,* first translated into French in 1633, went through six editions by 1830, and his depiction was popularized by the encyclopedists, from Voltaire to Jean-Francois Marmontel, whose *Les Incas, ou la destruction de l'Empire du Pérou* (1777) went through at least thirty editions, and inspired patterns for wallpaper as well as several stage adaptations by 1850.[25]

Today, Garcilaso remains one of the great literary figures of the Spanish Golden Age, praised for the elegance and clarity of his prose and the evocative power of his descriptions of places, people, and events. As a historian, however, twentieth-century scholars have tended to criticize him as a romantic who distorted the facts of the past in his effort to present his maternal ancestors in the best possible light. He has been accused of distorting the nature of Inca society in order to counter contemporary efforts to justify Spanish rule by depicting them as oppressive tyrants who exploited their subjects.[26] More recently, John H. Rowe asserted that "Gar-

---

[24] Guibovich, Ibid., p. 108.

[25] Stéphane Gerson, *The Pride of Place: Local Memories & Political Culture in Nineteenth-Century France* (Ithaca & London: Cornell University Press, 2003) pp. 193–7.

[26] Philip Ainsworth Means, who wrote one of the early studies of the chroniclers of the Andes, divided writers on the Incas into "Garcilasistas," writers who followed Garcilaso, and "Toledistas," writers who agreed with the position taken by Francisco de Toledo, the fifth viceroy of Peru who sought to present the Incas as tyrants and usurpers, thereby justifying the Spanish presence on the grounds that Spain "freed" the Andeans from Inca "tyranny." See *Biblioteca Andina. Essays on the Lives and Works of the Chroniclers, or the Writers of the Sixteenth and the Seventeenth Centuries who treated of the Pre-hispanic History and Culture of the Andean Countries,* in *Transactions of the Connecticut Academy of Arts and Sciences,* 29 (1928) 271–525.

cilaso's version of Inca history is in fact largely fictitious," calling it "a pious fraud perpetrated by Garcilaso himself,"[27] while John Hemming argues that "as a historian Garcilaso has forfeited my confidence," accusing him of meandering, romanticizing, and blatantly distorting his material.[28]

But while Garcilaso's interpretations of Inca society—perhaps most obviously, Inca benevolence toward their subjects—can be questioned, I do not agree that he can be dismissed as a historian. *Royal Commentaries* and the *History of Peru* are not literary creations alone; they are works of history that stand up well by contemporary standards, even if some of the author's assumptions and conclusions can be questioned. Garcilaso does not pepper his text with footnotes, but he does credit his sources, including those with which he disagrees, both the few published histories of the conquest of Peru and the much greater number of unpublished manuscript histories, some of which were not published until well after the end of Spanish rule in the Americas. For centuries, Garcilaso was the only available source for some of those manuscripts, and in one case, that of the mestizo Jesuit Blas Valera, whose historical manuscript was loaned to Garcilaso by his Jesuit friends and colleagues, the manuscript was subsequently lost and our only access to Valera's work is the long selections that Garcilaso copied into his history with full credit given the author. Garcilaso did not begin his history for nearly forty years after he left the Andes, but he approached his subject with care, not only requesting help from his one-time schoolmates, by then adults, but also reading both the published histories available and the manuscripts that were not approved for publication but circulated in Spain, and the marginal comments he made in the books in his extensive library are evidence of his careful, as well as impassioned, research.

Garcilaso did not pretend to "objectivity," in the sense of the positivist historians of the nineteenth and early twentieth centuries who attempted, generally without success, to separate themselves from their work in order to present the "truth," as they saw it. In that sense, we might consider him more modern than the ostensibly "objective" scholars whose judgments leak through the often bland prose in which they are wrapped. The Inca regarded history as a moral lesson for readers who learned from the example of the past, and he did his best to teach that lesson with all of the considerable skill he could muster. He saw the Incas from whom he was descended as people who lived by all of the precepts of the philosopher-kings of the ancient world, governing their subjects wisely and carefully, providing for

---

[27] Rowe, Forward to Father Bernabe Cobo, *History of the Inca Empire,* trans. Roland Hamilton (Austin: University of Texas, 1988), p. x.

[28] Hemming, *Conquest,* p. 18.

their needs and extending their rule solely for the greater benefit of those who accepted the benign rule of the lords of Cusco. Garcilaso was an elitist, whose reverence for his Inca ancestors did not extend to the subjects of the Inca state, whom he regarded as backward and uncivilized inferiors who owed their prosperity to their beneficent leaders. He accepted completely the Inca version of their own benevolence, and while that image was attacked by some among the Spaniards, no one challenged the contempt for the Indian masses that was shared by Inca and Spaniard alike.

Royal Commentaries was carefully plotted as a grand tragedy, in which the Incas built a great society whose only flaw was the absence of Christian salvation. The Spaniards were sent to the Andes in order to bring the Christian faith—the last element necessary to build a perfect society. Despite the bravery and honor of some of the Spaniards, however, the great opportunity to fulfill God's design was destroyed by the greed, jealousy, and pride of others, turning what should have been the fulfillment of God's plan into a tragedy which, instead of bringing salvation to the Andes, brought destruction. The sweep and grandeur of the tragedy was truncated by the posthumous publication of Part II of the history under a separate title by order of the crown, obscuring the moral lesson that Garcilaso intended.

Insofar as possible, I have attempted to present in this abridgement some idea of Garcilaso's original intention for his history of the grandeur—and the defeat—of the Inca state. Part of Garcilaso's genius was his ability to craft vivid descriptions of places and people. In addition, he made use of a literary device, common among the Italian humanists, of creating speeches to be delivered by his characters—a dramatic tool that has led many scholars to dismiss his history as untrustworthy, even though it can be argued that the authorial commentary or asides that Garcilaso presents in that fashion is no less valid than the often less interesting judgments offered by more contemporary historians as scholarly interpretation. While the Inca is revered in Spanish literature as a writer and stylist, I am not primarily concerned with presenting Garcilaso as an important representative of the literature of the Spanish Golden Age; despite the undoubted excellence of Harold Livermore's English translations from which I have selected the text that follows, I feel strongly that great literature should be read in the original when possible. My selections have been based on two criteria: (1) that of giving readers an idea of the image of Inca society and culture that Garcilaso sought to present in the first part of his history, and (2) that of retaining Garcilaso's great tale of adventure and betrayal that dominates the history of the Andes from the entry of the Spaniards to the imposition of royal control some four decades later.

In hopes that this taste of Garcilaso will lead a reader to want more and yet avoid breaking up the flow of his narrative, I have opted to reference the selections to Professor Livermore's complete translation. Each selection begins with the book and chapter number of the Livermore translation, separated by a colon and enclosed in brackets, to make it possible to find the original without difficulty. Also, because the book and chapter numbers are the same in the Spanish original, a reader who wishes to find a particular topic in Garcilaso's language can follow the same procedure. Text that has not been included in this edition is indicated by an ellipsis. The body of the text consists of Professor Livermore's great translation, published in two volumes by University of Texas Press in 1966.

Special thanks are due to a group of people who made my task as editor a pleasure. Tamar Herzog not only offered invaluable suggestions that helped me make my selections and clarify the introduction to this edition; she wins my prize for the fastest reader's response I have ever seen, and I owe her heartfelt thanks for her thoughtful and perceptive comments. Manuel Valladares Quijano, director of the Central Library System of the National University of San Marcos, graciously introduced me to members of his staff who agreed to assist with the project, and not only scanned all of my initial selections so that they could be more easily edited, but presented me with a corrected text that was virtually error-free, in a language that is not their own. Judith Natalie León Morales, Director of Cultural Coordination of the Library System, Carmen Risa Huarino Chura, of the data processing division of the Oficina de Informática of the Central Library System of the National University of San Marcos, and Lorena Teófila León Quispe, together made the process of abridging Garcilaso's history a pleasure. There are no contemporary portraits of Inca Garcilaso; the imagined portrait of the Inca on the cover was painted in oils in 1936 by the Peruvian artist Francisco Gonzalez Gamarra. It is reproduced by permission of Dr. Jorge Puccinelli, Executive Director of the Instituto Raúl Porras Barrenechea, affiliated with the National University of San Marcos.

Finally, my thanks to my editors at Hackett Publishing: Rick Todhunter, who talked me into preparing this edition and kept after me until I finished it, and Carrie Wagner, who saw it into print.

March 2006

Further Reading in English

There is an enormous body of literature on the Inca Garcilaso de la Vega in Spanish, but there is not much that is readily available to a reader who is seeking further information about Garcilaso and his age in English. The available English-language sources are listed below, but for those who want to compare Garcilaso's depiction of the Incas and the Spanish with those of contemporary historians, I have also included a selected number of studies in English that focus on the character of Inca state and society as well as the tumultuous period between the arrival of the Spaniards in 1532 and the consolidation of state power by Francisco de Toledo between 1569 and 1581. For the reader who is able and willing to read Garcilaso in the original Spanish, there are many fine editions, although until recently, most editions have been limited to *Royal Commentaries of the Incas* (Part I of Garcilaso's planned work). Among Garcilaso specialists writing in Spanish, I particularly recommend the work of José Durand, José Antonio Mazzotti, Aurelio Miró Quesada, Enrique Pupo-Walker, and Raúl Porras Barrenechea.

Anadón, José, ed. *Garcilaso Inca de la Vega, an American Humanist: Essays in Honor of Jose Durand.* (Notre Dame University Press, 1988).

Brading, David, "Inca Humanist," chap. 12 of *The First America: The Spanish Monarchy, Creole Patriots, and the Liberal State 1492–1867.* (Cambridge: Cambridge University Press, 1991) pp. 255–72.

———, "The Inca and the Renaissance: The Royal Commentaries of Inca Garcilaso de la Vega," *Journal of Latin American Studies,* 18: 1 (May, 1986): p. 1–23.

Hemming, John, *The Conquest of the Incas.* (New York: Harcourt Brace Jovanovich, 1970). A highly readable narrative of the invasion and conquest of the Andes, written by a historian who has clearly explored the land he writes about.

Hernandez, Max, "A Childhood Memory: Time, Place and Subjective Experience," *MLN,* 105: 2 (March, 1990): pp. 316–30. A psychiatrist who uses his professional training to present a fascinating interpretation of Garcilaso's personal history.

Leonard, Irving, "The Inca Garcilaso de la Vega," in L. Iñigo-Madrigal, ed., *Historia de la literatura hispanoamericana,* II Época colonial. (Madrid: Cátedra, 1982): pp. 135–43.

Livermore, Harold V., trans., *Royal Commentaries of the Incas and General History of Peru.* 2 vols. (Austin: University of Texas Press, 1966). The authoritative English translation of Garcilaso's history, from which the selections in this edition were made.

Pagden, Anthony, *The Fall of Natural Man.* (Cambridge: Cambridge University Press, 1982). A vivid reconstruction of the controversy over the nature of the Indians within an examination of Las Casas' role in the shift from authority to eyewitness testimony as the basis of intellectual truth.

Spalding, Karen, "The Crises and Transformations of Invaded Societies: Andean Area, 1500–1580," chap. 2 of Frank Salomon & Stuart B. Schwartz, eds., *The Cambridge History of the Native Peoples of the Americas,* Vol. 3, "South America," Part I (pp. 927–63). A narrative of the interactions between Andeans and Spaniards from their initial contact to the 1580s.

Stern, Steve J., *Peru's Indian Peoples and the Challenge of Spanish Conquest: Huamanga to 1640,* 2nd ed. (Madison: University of Wisconsin Press, 1993). A fine study of the region that is now Ayacucho, a core region of the Inca state, from the entry of the Spaniards to the early seventeenth century. For those who may want to read more about the conquest of Peru, the prologue of the 2nd edition includes a valuable new introduction that examines the history and historiography of the period.

Varner, John Grier, *El Inca: the Life and Times of Garcilaso de la Vega.* (Austin & London: University of Texas Press, 1968.) The principle English-language biography of Garcilaso.

Zamora, Margarita, *Language, Authority and Indigenous History in the Comentarios reales de los incas.* Cambridge Iberian and Latin American Studies. (Cambridge: Cambridge University Press, 1988). The only work in English that focuses on presenting Garcilaso as a thinker and scholar. Carefully researched and well written.

Part I

Chapter One
The New World and Its Inhabitants

Garcilaso begins by considering the nature of the region and the origins of its people and animals.

[1:8] The four boundaries of the empire of the Incas when the Spaniards arrived were as follows. To the north it stretched to the Ancasmayu River, which runs between the limits of Quitu [Quito] and Pastu [Pasto]. In the general speech of Peru it means "Blue River." It is almost exactly on the equator. To the south the limit was the river called Mauli [Maule], running east and west beyond to the kingdom of Chile, before the land of the Araucanians. It is more than forty degrees south of the equator. Between these two rivers there are just under 1,300 leagues of land. The part called Peru is 750 leagues long north to south by land from the Ancasmayu River to the Chichas, which is the last province of the Charcas. What is called the kingdom of Chile is about 550 leagues from north to south, counting from the province of the Chichas to the river Maule.

To the east [the Inca empire] is bounded by the inaccessible chain of snowy peaks, untrodden by man, animal, or bird, and extending from Santa Marta to the Straits of Magellan. The Indians call it "Ritisuyu," "the land of snows." To the west it is limited by the Southern Sea which extends along the whole length of its coast.[1] The boundary of the empire begins at Cape Passau on the coast and runs beyond the equinoctial line as far as the Maule River, which also flows into the Southern Sea. From east to west the whole kingdom is narrow. At its broadest, crossing from the Muyupampa province over the Chachapoyas to the town of Trujillo on the seacoast, it is 120 leagues wide, and at the narrowest, from the port of Arica to the province called Llaricassa it is 70 leagues long. These are the four boundaries of the realms of the Inca kings, whose history we propose to write, with divine aid. . . .

---

[1] The Southern Sea is the name that the Spanish gave to the Pacific Ocean. It appears on Spanish maps to the end of the eighteenth century.

1

The Origin of the Inca Kings of Peru

[1:15] . . . After having prepared many schemes and taken many ways to begin to give an account of the origin and establishment of the native Inca kings of Peru, it seemed to me that the best scheme and simplest and easiest way was to recount what I often heard as a child from the lips of my mother and her brothers and uncles and other elders about these beginnings. For everything said about them from other sources comes down to the same story as we shall relate, and it will be better to have it as told in the very words of the Incas than in those of foreign authors. My mother dwelt in Cusco, her native place, and was visited there every week by the few relatives, both male and female, who escaped the cruelty and tyranny of Atahuallpa (which we shall describe in our account of his life). On these visits the ordinary subject of conversation was always the origin of the Inca kings, their greatness, the grandeur of their empire, their deeds and conquests, their government in peace and war, and the laws they ordained so greatly to the advantage of their vassals. In short, there was nothing concerning the most flourishing period of their history that they did not bring up in their conversations.

From the greatness and prosperity of the past they turned to the present, mourning their dead kings, their lost empire, and their fallen state, etcetera. These and similar topics were broached by the Incas and Pallas[2] on their visits, and on recalling their departed happiness, they always ended these conversations with tears and mourning, saying: "Our rule is turned to bondage" etcetera. During these talks, I, as a boy, often came in and went out of the place where they were, and I loved to hear them, as boys always do like to hear stories. Days, months, and years went by, until I was sixteen or seventeen. Then it happened that one day when my family was talking in this fashion about their kings and the olden times, I remarked to the senior of them, who usually related these things: "Inca, my uncle, though you have no writings to preserve the memory of past events, what information have you of the origin and beginnings of our kings? For the Spaniards and the other peoples who live on their borders have divine and human histories from which they know when their own kings and their neighbors' kings began to reign and when one empire gave way to another. They even know how many thousand years it is since God created heaven and earth. All this and much more they know through their books. But you, who have no books, what memory have you preserved of your antiquity? Who

---

[2] *Palla,* as Garcilaso explains (p. 10), refers to a noblewoman, as defined in Diego González Holguín, *Vocabulario de la lengua general de todo el Perú llamado Lengua Quechua o del Inca* (Lima: UNMSM, 1952) 18.

was the first of our Incas? What was he called? What was the origin of his line? How did he begin to reign? With what men and arms did he conquer this great empire? How did our heroic deeds begin?"

The Inca was delighted to hear these questions, since it gave him great pleasure to reply to them, and turned to me (who had already often heard him tell the tale, but had never paid as much attention as then) saying:

"Nephew, I will tell you these things with pleasure: indeed, it is right that you should hear them and keep them in your heart (this is their phrase for 'in the memory'). You should know that in olden times the whole of this region before you was covered with brush and heath, and people lived in those times like wild beasts, with no religion or government and no towns or houses, and without tilling or sowing the soil, or clothing or covering their flesh, for they did not know how to weave cotton or wool to make clothes. They lived in twos and threes as chance brought them together in caves and crannies in rocks and underground caverns. Like wild beasts they ate the herbs of the field and roots of trees and fruits growing wild and also human flesh. They covered their bodies with leaves and the bark of trees and animals' skins. Others went naked. In short, they lived like deer or other game, and even in their intercourse with women they behaved like beasts, for they knew nothing of having separate wives."

I must remark, in order to avoid many repetitions of the words "our father the Sun," that the phrase was used by the Incas to express respect whenever they mentioned the sun, for they boasted of descending from it, and none but Incas were allowed to utter the words: it would have been blasphemy and the speaker would have been stoned. The Inca said:

"Our father the Sun, seeing men in the state I have mentioned, took pity and was sorry for them, and sent from heaven to earth a son and a daughter of his to indoctrinate them in the knowledge of our father the Sun that they might worship him and adopt him as their god, and to give them precepts and laws by which they would live as reasonable and civilized men, and dwell in houses and settled towns, and learn to till the soil, and grow plants and crops, and breed flocks, and use the fruits of the earth like rational beings and not like beasts. With this order and mandate our father the Sun set these two children of his in Lake Titicaca, eighty leagues from here, and bade them go where they would, and wherever they stopped to eat or sleep to try to thrust into the ground a golden wand half a yard long and two fingers in thickness which he gave them as a sign and token: when this wand should sink into the ground at a single thrust, there our father the Sun wished them to stop and set up their court.

"Finally he told them: 'When you have reduced these people to our service, you shall maintain them in reason and justice, showing mercy, clemency, and mildness, and always treating them as a merciful father treats his beloved and tender children. Imitate my example in this. I do good to all the world. I give them my light and brightness that they may see and go about their business; I warm them when they are cold; and I grow their pastures and crops, and bring fruit to their trees, and multiply their flocks. I bring rain and calm weather in turn, and I take care to go round the world once a day to observe the wants that exist in the world and to fill and supply them as the sustainer and benefactor of men. I wish you as children of mine to follow this example sent down to earth to teach and benefit those men who live like beasts. And henceforward I establish and nominate you as kings and lords over all the people you may thus instruct with your reason, government, and good works.'

"When our father the Sun had thus made manifest his will to his two children he bade them farewell. They left Titicaca and travelled north-wards, and wherever they stopped on the way they thrust the golden wand into the earth, but it never sank in. Thus they reached a small inn or rest-house seven or eight leagues south of this city [of Cusco]. Today it is called Pacárec Tampu, 'inn or resthouse of the dawn.' The Inca gave it this name because he set out from it about daybreak. It is one of the towns the prince later ordered to be founded, and its inhabitants to this day boast greatly of its name because our first Inca bestowed it. From this place he and his wife, our queen, reached the valley of Cusco, which was then a wilderness."

[1:16] "The first settlement they made in this valley," said the Inca, "was in the hill called Huanacauri, to the south of this city. There they tried to thrust the golden wand into the earth, and it easily sank in at the first blow and they saw it no more. Then our Inca said to his wife: 'Our father the Sun bids us remain in this valley and make it our dwelling place and home in fulfilment of his will. It is therefore right, queen and sister,[3] that each of us should go out and call together these people so as to instruct them and benefit them as our father the Sun has ordained.' Our first rulers set out from the hill of Huanacauri, each in a different direction, to call the peo-ple together, and as that was the first place we know they trod with their feet and because they went out from it to do good to mankind, we made there, as you know, a temple for the worship of our father the Sun, in memory of his merciful beneficence towards the world. The prince went northwards, and the princess south. They spoke to all the men and women they found in that wilderness and said that their father the Sun had sent them from the sky to be teachers and benefactors to the dwellers in all that land, delivering them from the wild lives they led and in obedience to the

---

[3] The Inca ruler married his full sister. Garcilaso presents a rationale for the practice, used only by the monarch, on pp. 20–1 ("The Heir to the Throne Married His Sister").

commands given by the Sun, their father, calling them together and removing them from those heaths and moors, bringing them to dwell in settled valleys and giving them the food of men instead of that of beasts to eat. Our king and queen said these and similar things to the first savages they found in those mountains and heaths, and as the savages beheld two persons clad and adorned with the ornaments our father the Sun had given them—and a very different dress from their own—with their ears pierced and opened in the way we their descendants have, and saw that their words and countenances showed them to be children of the Sun, and that they came to mankind to give them towns to dwell in and food to eat, they wondered at what they saw and were at the same time attracted by the promises that were held out to them. Thus they fully credited all they were told and worshipped and venerated the strangers as children of the Sun and obeyed them as kings. These savages gathered others and repeated the wonders they had seen and heard, and a great number of men and women collected and set out to follow our king and queen wherever they might lead.

"When our princes saw the great crowd that had formed there, they ordered that some should set about supplying open-air meals for them all, so that they should not be driven by hunger to disperse again across the heaths. Others were ordered to work on building huts and houses according to plans made by the Inca. Thus our imperial city began to be settled: it was divided into two halves called Hanan Cusco, which as you know means upper Cusco, and Hurin Cusco, or lower Cusco. The king wished those he had brought to people Hanan Cusco, therefore called the upper, and those the queen had brought to people Hurin Cusco, which was therefore called the lower. The distinction did not imply that the inhabitants of one half should excel those of the other in privileges and exemptions. All were equal like brothers, the children of one father and one mother. The Inca only wished that there should be this division of the people and distinction of name, so that the fact that some had been gathered by the king and others by the queen might have a perpetual memorial. And he ordered that there should be only one difference and acknowledgment of superiority among them, that those of upper Cusco be considered and respected as firstborn and elder brothers, and those of lower Cusco be as younger children. In short they were to be as the right side and the left in any question of precedence of place and office, since those of the upper town had been gathered by the men and those of the lower by the women. In imitation of this, there was later the same division in all the towns, great or small, of our empire, which were divided by wards or by lineages, known as *hanan aillu* and *hurin aillu*, the upper and lower lineage, or *hanan suyu* and *hurin suyu*, the upper and lower district.

"At the same time, in peopling the city, our Inca showed the male Indians which tasks were proper to men: breaking and tilling the land, sowing crops, seeds, and vegetables which he showed to be good to eat and fruitful, and for which purpose he taught them how to make ploughs and other necessary instruments, and bade them and showed them how to draw irrigation channels from the streams that ran through the valley of Cusco, and even showed them how to make the footwear we use. On her side the queen trained the Indian women in all the feminine occupations: spinning and weaving cotton and wool, and making clothes for themselves and their husbands and children. She told them how to do these and other duties of domestic service. In short, there was nothing relating to human life that our princes failed to teach their first vassals, the Inca king acting as master for the men and the *Coya,* queen,[4] mistress of the women." . . .

Garcilaso's Declaration of His Own History

[1:19] . . . I was brought up among these Indians, and as I frequented their society until I was twenty I was able to learn during that time something of all the subjects I am writing about, for in my childhood they used to recount their histories, just as stories are told for children. Later, as I grew up, they talked to me at length about their laws and government, and compared the new rule of the Spaniards with that of the Incas, contrasting especially the crimes and punishments and the severity the latter were dealt with under the two regimes. They told me how their kings acted in peace and war, in what manner they treated their vassals, and how their vassals served them. Moreover, they told me, as if I were their own son, all about their idolatry, their rites, ceremonies, and sacrifices, the greater and lesser festivals, and how they were celebrated. They told me their superstitions and abuses, good and evil auspices, including those they discerned in sacrifices and others. In short, I would say that they told me about everything they had in their state; and if I had written it down at the time, this history would have been more copious. Apart from what the Indians told me, I experienced and saw with my own eyes a great deal of their idolatry, festivals, and superstitions, which had still not altogether disappeared in my own time, when I was twelve or thirteen. I was born eight years after the Spaniards conquered my country, and as I have said, was brought up there till I was twenty: thus I saw many of the things the Indians did in the time of their paganism and shall relate them and say that I saw them.

---

[4] *Coya* means queen or empress, as Garcilaso explains on p. 9.

I have also listened to many accounts of the deeds and conquests of those kings in addition to what my relatives told me and what I myself say, for as soon as I resolved to write this history, I wrote to my old schoolmates at my primary school and grammar school, and urged each of them to help me with accounts they might have of the particular conquests the Incas made in the provinces their mothers came from, for each province has its accounts and knots[5] to record its annals and traditions, and thus preserves its own history much better than that of its neighbors. My schoolfellows earnestly complied with my request, and each reported my intention to his mother and relatives, and they, on hearing that an Indian, a son of their own country, intended to write its history, brought from their archives the records they had of their histories and sent me them. . . .

The Inca's Teachings

[1:21] The Inca Manco Capac[6] settled his vassals in villages and taught them to till the soil, build homes, make irrigation channels, and do all the other things necessary for human life. At the same time he instructed them in the urbane, social, and brotherly conduct they were to use toward one another according to the dictates of reason and natural law, effectively persuading them to do unto one another as they themselves would be done by, so that there should be perpetual peace and concord among them and no ground for the kindling of envy and passion. They were not allowed to have one law for themselves and another for the rest. He enjoined them particularly to respect one another's wives and daughters, because the vice of women had been more rife among them than any other. He applied the death penalty to adulterers, murderers, and robbers. He ordered them not to have more than one wife and to marry within their own family group so as to prevent confusion in the lineages, and to wed after the age of twenty when they would be able to rule their households and work on their estates. He ordered them to round up the tame flocks that wandered ownerless over the countryside and so dressed them in wool, through the industry and skill that the queen Mama Ocllo Huaco[7] had given to the Indian

---

[5] The knots to which Garcilaso refers are *quipus,* the knotted-cord recording device used throughout the Andes. The use of *quipus* considerably predates the Incas; for further information on this device, see Frank Salomon, *The Cord Keepers: Khipus and Cultural Life in a Peruvian Village* (Durham: Duke University Press, 2004), and Gary Urton, *Signs of the Inka Khipu: Binary Coding in the Andean Knotted-String Records* (Austin: University of Texas Press, 2003).

[6] Manco Capac is regarded as the founder of Cusco and the first Inca ruler.

[7] Mama Ocllo Huaco, sister and wife of Manco Capac, was the first queen according to Inca tradition.

women in spinning and weaving. He taught them to make the footwear they now have, called *usuta*. For each town or tribe he subdued he chose a *curaca,* which is the same as *cacique* in the language of Cuba and Santo Domingo and means a lord of vassals. He chose them for their merits among those who had labored most in subjugating the Indians and had shown themselves most affable, gentle, and merciful, and most attached to the common good: these he made masters of the rest, so that they should indoctrinate them as fathers do their children. And he ordered the Indians to obey them as children do their fathers.

He ordered the fruits of the earth gathered in each town to be kept in common so as to supply each with his needs, until it should be feasible to give each Indian land of his own. Together with these precepts and ordinances, he taught them the divine worship of his idolatry. He fixed a site for the building of a temple to the Sun, where they were to make sacrifices to it, having persuaded them that they should regard it as their chief deity, whom they should adore and return thanks to for the natural benefits conferred by its light and heat, since they saw that it made their fields produce and their flocks multiply, together with the other mercies they daily received. And they particularly owed adoration and service to the Sun and the Moon for having sent down their children to them to deliver them from the savage life they had led and bring them the advantages of human existence which they now enjoyed. He ordered them to make a house for women of the Sun, so soon as there should be a sufficient number of women of the blood royal to people it. All this he ordered them to observe and comply with out of gratitude for the indisputable benefits they had received, and he promised them on behalf of his father the Sun many other advantages if they did so, assuring them that he did not say these things on his own account, but because the Sun had revealed them to him and bidden him repeat them to the Indians, and in this and everything else he was guided and taught by the Sun as by a father. The Indians, with the simplicity they have displayed then and ever since down to our own times, believed everything that the Inca told them, especially when be said that he was a child of the Sun. For among them too there are tribes that vaunted a similar fabulous descent, as we shall have cause to mention, though they did not make such a good choice as the Inca, but prided themselves on their origin from animals and other low and earthly objects. When the Indians of these and later times contrasted their descent with that of the Inca and saw that the benefits he had conferred on them bore witness to the fact, they believed most firmly that he was the child of the Sun and promised to observe and comply with what he ordered, and in short they worshipped him as a child of the Sun, confessing that no mortal could have done for them the things he had done, and thus they believed that he was a divine man come down from heaven.

The Royal Names and Their Meanings

[1:26] It will be well that we should say briefly the meanings of the royal titles both for men and women, and to whom and how they were given and how they used them, so as to show the care the Inca took in giving names and titles, which in any case is a matter worthy of remark. To begin with the name *Inca,* it must be realized that it means "king" or "emperor," referring to the royal person; but when applied to those of his lineage it means "a man of royal blood"; and the name *Inca* belonged to all of them with this difference alone, provided that they were descendants in the male line and not merely the female. They called their kings *Çapa Inca,*[8] which is "sole king" or "sole emperor" or "sole lord," for *çapa* means "sole," and they gave this name to no one else of his family, even to the heir until he should have inherited; for as the king was unique, the name could not have been applied to others without making many kings. The kings were also called *Huacchacúyac,* "lover and benefactor of the poor," and this title also is not given to any other but the king, by reason of the special care they all had, from first to last, to benefit their subjects. We have already explained the meaning of *Capac,* "rich in magnanimity and royal qualities toward their followers." This was applied to the king alone and no other, because he was their chief benefactor. They also called him *Intip Churin,* or "child of the Sun," and this name was applied to all males of the blood royal, because according to the fable they descended from the Sun, but not to females. The sons of the king and all those of his parentage by the male line they called *Auqui,* which means "infante," the word used in Spain of younger sons of kings. The name was kept till they married, whereafter they were called *Inca.* These were the names and titles they gave to the king and to men of royal blood, as well as others we shall mention which, as proper names, became family names among their descendants.

Turning to the names and titles of the women of the blood royal, we see that the queen, the legitimate wife of the king, was called *Coya,* meaning "queen" or "empress." She was also called *Mamánchic,* meaning "our mother," because in imitation of her husband, she performed the office of mother to all her relatives and subjects. Her daughters were called *Coya* after her, but not as their own natural title, for the name *Coya* belongs only to the queen. The king's concubines of his own stock and all other women of the blood royal were called *Palla,* meaning "a woman of royal blood." The remaining concubines of the king, who were alien women not of his blood, they called *Mamacuna,* which may be translated "matron," but

---

[8] Çapa, (spelled with a cedilla and also spelled Sapa) is an entirely different word from Capa or Capac [hard 'c'], as Garcilaso explains here.

which really means "a woman who is obliged to perform the office of mother." The princesses who were daughters of the king and all other daughters of the royal stock and blood were called *Ñusta,* or "maiden of the royal blood," but the following distinction was made. Those of legitimate royal blood were called simply *Ñusta,* which implied they were of legitimate royal blood. Those who were not of legitimate royal blood were called after the name of the province where their mother was born, as Colla Ñusta, Huana Ñusta, Yunca Ñusta, Quitu Ñusta, and so from the other provinces. This name of Ñusta they kept till they married, and after marriage they were called Palla.

These names and titles were applied to those descended from the blood royal in the male line. If this was wanting, even though the mother might be related to the king—for the kings often gave female relatives of bastard birth to the great lords as wives—the sons and daughters did not take the names of the blood royal, or call themselves *Incas* or *Pallas,* but merely the names of the fathers, for the Incas set no store by female descent so as not to diminish the nobility attributed to the blood royal. Even in the male line it lost a great deal of its royal character by being mixed with the blood of foreign women of a different lineage, quite apart from the question of the female line. Comparing some names with others, we find that the name *Coya,* or "queen," corresponds to that of *Çapa Inca,* or "sole lord"; and the name *Mamánchic,* or "our mother," to *Huacchacúyac,* "lover and benefactor of the people"; and *Ñusta,* or "princess," to *Auqui;* and *Palla,* "woman of royal blood," to *Inca.* Such were the royal names I saw and heard used by the Incas and Pallas, for it was chiefly with these that I conversed as a child. Neither the *curacas,* however great lords they might be, nor their wives nor children, could take these names, for they belonged solely to the blood royal, transmitted in the male line. Although Don Alonso de Ercilla y Zúñiga,[9] in explaining Indian terms in the elegant verse he writes, gives the explanation of *Palla* as a lady of many vassals and estates, he does so because the names *Inca* and *Palla* were improperly applied to many people at the time this gentleman dwelt in those parts. For illustrious and heroic names are coveted by all people, however low and barbarous, and if there is no one to prevent them they soon usurp the noblest names, as has happened in my country.

---

[9] Alonso de Ercilla y Zúñiga was a Spanish soldier and poet who fought in the centuries-long war in Chile against the Indian natives there and later wrote the epic poem, *La Araucana,* which became famous throughout Spain and is a classic of Spanish literature. The epic looks very favorably on the Indians and their struggle against Spain.

Chapter Two
Inca Culture

They divided the empire into four districts and made a census of their subjects.

[2:11] The Inca kings divided their empire into four parts, which they called *Tahuantinsuyu,* meaning "the four quarters of the world," corresponding to the four cardinal points of heaven: east, west, north, and south. They took as the central point the city of Cusco, which in the private language of the Incas means "the navel of the world." The semblance of the navel is a good one, for all Peru is long and narrow like a human body, and the city is almost in the middle. They called the eastern part *Andesuyu,* from a province called *Anta* in the east, whence they called *Anta* the whole of that great range of snowcapped mountains that runs to the east of Peru, indicating that it is to the east. They called the west part *Condesuyu* from a small province called *Conde.* The northern quarter they called *Chinchaysuyu,* from a great province called *Chincha,* to the north of the city. And the district to the south they called *Collasuyu,* from a very extensive province called *Colla* to the south. By these four provinces they implied all the land in the direction of the four parts, even if many leagues beyond the limits of those provinces. Thus the kingdom of Chile, though more than 600 leagues to the south of the province of Colla, was in Collasuyu, and the kingdom of Quito, though above 400 leagues north of Chincha, was in Chinchaysuyu. The names of these quarters were thus the same as saying eastwards, westwards, etcetera, and the four main highways issuing from the city were also so called because they led to the four parts of the empire.

As the basis and foundation of their government the Incas devised a law which they thought would enable them to prevent and stem all the evils that might arise in their empire. They ordered for this purpose a register of all the towns of the empire, great and small, by decuries[10] of ten, with one

---

[10] Livermore has here translated Garcilaso's Spanish word *decuria* into English as "*decury,*" which means "a division or body of ten men under a *decurion* [officer]." The use of terms referring to ancient Rome reflects Garcilaso's comparison of the Incas with Rome. Garcilaso refers here to the administrative divisions of the Inca state, in which the population was divided into *hunu,* or groups of ten, ten of which became a *pachaka,* or group of 100, and ten of those *waranqa,* or group of 1000. The decimal organization is also described by Guaman Poma de Ayala in his monumental "Letter to the

of the ten, called the *decurion,* being put in charge of the other nine. Five decuries of these rulers of ten had a superior decurion who commanded fifty; two decuries of fifty had a superior decurion who ruled a hundred. Five decuries of a hundred were subject to another captain-decurion who ruled five hundred. Two companies of five hundred acknowledged a general with command over a thousand. The decuries never exceeded a thousand, for they said that a commission to command a thousand men was enough to bring out the best in a leader. There were thus decuries of ten, of fifty, of a hundred, of five hundred, and of a thousand, each with a decurion or group leader, subordinated one to another, greater and less, up to the last and highest decurion, which we have called a general.

[2:12] The decurions of ten were obliged to execute two tasks in relation to the men in their decury or group: first, to act as advocate to assist them with diligence and care in any case of need, taking their case to the governor or any other minister whose duty it might be to succor them, perhaps to ask for grain if they had none to sow or eat, or wool to wear, or the rebuilding of their house if it had collapsed or was burnt, or in any other case of need, great or little. The other duty was to be procurator to report any offence, however slight, which must be referred to the decurion above, whose duty it was to apply a punishment or refer it to the decurion above him. The judges were thus superior to one another and settled cases according to the seriousness of the crime, so that there was never any lack of a judge to deal summarily with a case, and it was not necessary to take each case to higher judges with one or more appeals, and so on to the judges of the supreme court. They held that delay in punishment encouraged crime, and that appeals, proofs, and objections could make civil suits everlasting, and the poor would rather forgo justice and lose their goods than suffer the vexation of delay, which cost them thirty to recover ten. They therefore provided that every town should have a judge with powers to give a final decision in suits between the inhabitants, excepting those between one town and another about grazing rights or boundaries, for which the Incas would send a special judge, as we shall say.

Any of the officers, of lower or higher rank, who neglected the performance of his duties as advocate was punished more or less severely, according to the need he had failed by his negligence to meet. Anyone who did not inform on the transgression of any subject, even though it was only an unjustifiable delay of a day, made the fault his own, and was punished

---

King." See also Catherine J. Julien, "Inca Decimal Administration in the Lake Titicaca Region," in George A. Collier, Renato I. Rosaldo, & John D. Wirth, eds., *The Inca and Aztec States, 1400–1800: Anthropology and History* (New York & London: Academic Press, 1982) 119–51.

on two accounts: for neglecting his own duty and for the other's sin, which he had made his own by not reporting it. And as each officer had a procurator to watch over him, he tried hard to do his duty conscientiously and fulfil his obligation. There were therefore no vagabonds or idlers, and none dared do what he ought not do, for his accuser was near and his punishment severe—generally a sentence of death, however slight the crime, for they said that the punishment was not for the crime done nor for the wrong given but for the breaking of the commandment and word of the Inca whom they respected as a god. And although the aggrieved person desisted from the suit or did not institute it, justice was applied by obligation as part of the ordinary duties of the officers, and they applied the full penalty prescribed by the law in each case according to the degree of the crime, which might be death, whipping, exile, or the like.

A child was punished for the crimes he committed like anyone else, according to the gravity of his offence, even though it was no more than boyish naughtiness. The penalty was increased or lessened according to the age and innocence of the person, and fathers were severely punished for not having instructed and corrected their children from an early age so that they should not grow up naughty or acquire bad habits. The decurion's duty was to accuse both son and father of any crime, so they brought up their children with great care lest they should be guilty of naughty or wanton acts in the streets or fields. Given the docile nature of the Indians, the boys grew up under the instruction of their parents so well trained that there was no difference between them and gentle lambs. . . .

After describing the laws and science of the Incas, Garcilaso turns to the bridges and roads and temples of the Inca state.

The Construction of the Rope Bridges

[3:7] . . .To make one of these bridges, a very great quantity of osier is collected. This is of a different variety from the Spanish, with fine and tough withies.[11] They make three single osiers into a long rope according to the length needed for the bridge. Three ropes each of three osiers are used to

---

[11] *Osier* are tough but flexible branches, usually willow, like those used in wickerwork. *Withies* are slender and flexible branches or twigs. Fibers made of willow and other native trees, grasses, and vines were used to construct the cables for the bridges as Garcilaso describes. For further information on Andean suspension bridges, see John Hyslop, *The Inka Road System* (Orlando, FL: Academic Press, 1984) 324, and Daniel Gade, "Bridge Types in the Central Andes," *Annals of the Association of American Geographers,* vol. 62:1 (Lawrence, KA, 1972) 94–109.

make one of nine osiers, and three of these are used for others twenty-seven osiers thick, and three of these make even thicker ones. In this way they increase and thicken the ropes until they are as thick as a man's body or thicker. They make five ropes of the thickest kind; and to get them across the river they swim or use rafts carrying a thin cord to which is attached a cable as thick as the human arm made of a hemp the Indians call *cháhuar.* To this cable they fasten one of the ropes and a great crowd of Indians heaves at it until they get it over the river. Having got all five over, they mount them on two high supports that have been cut out of the living rock in a convenient place, or if these are not available they make the supports, of masonry, as strong as rock. The Apurimac bridge, which is on the high-way from Cusco to Lima, has one support of living rock and the other of masonry. The supports are hollowed out near the ground, and the sides are strengthened with walls. From side to side of these hollow spaces run five or six beams, as thick as bullocks, placed one above another like the rungs of a ladder. Each of the thick osier ropes is twisted round each of these beams so that the bridge will remain taut and not sag with its own weight, which is very considerable. But however much it is stretched, it always sinks in the middle and assumes a curved shape, so that in crossing one first descends and then mounts the other side; if there is a strong breeze at all it rocks.

Three of the great ropes are used for the floor of the bridge, and the other two as handrails on either side. The floor ropes are overlaid with wood as thick as a man's arm, crossing the full width of the bridge, which is about two *varas,*[12] rather like hurdles. This wood preserves the ropes from wear and is firmly fixed to them. It in turn is strewn with many boughs fixed in rows so as to give a firm footing to beasts of burden which would otherwise slip and fall. Between the lower floor ropes and the hand-rails they string twigs and thin boards securely fixed so as to make a wall the whole length of the bridge. This is now strong enough to carry men and animals.

The Apurimac bridge, which is the longest, may be about two hundred paces long. I have not measured it, but when I discussed it in Spain with many who have crossed it, they said this is about the length—more rather than less. I have seen many Spaniards cross without dismounting, and some on horseback at a gallop to show how little they were afraid: the feat is rather a rash one. The fabric is begun with only three osiers, but the result is the bold and impressive work that I have described, however imperfectly. It is certainly a marvellous piece of work, and would be incred-ible if one could not still see it, for its very necessity has preserved it from

---

[12] A *vara* is a Spanish linear measure, roughly equivalent to a yard.

destruction, or time might have destroyed it like many others which the
Spaniards found on the same highways, some as big or even bigger. In the
Incas' times the bridges were replaced every year. People came from neighboring provinces for the work, and the supply of materials was divided
between them according to their proximity and capabilities. This system is
still followed today. . . .

The Temple of the Sun and Its Great Wealth

[3:20] One of the chief idols of the Inca kings and their subjects was the
imperial city of Cusco which the Indians worshipped as a sacred thing
because of its foundation by the first Inca Manco Capac, the innumerable
victories it had brought in his conquests and its position as the home and
court of the Incas, who were regarded as gods. This veneration was so great
that it was displayed even in very small things: if two Indians of equal rank
met on the road, one going towards Cusco and one coming from it, the latter was saluted and greeted by the other as his superior, simply because he
had been in the city, and the respect was the greater if he were a resident in
it and greater still if he was born there. Likewise seeds, vegetables, or anything else taken from Cusco to other places were preferred, even if not of
better quality, because whatever came from Cusco was deemed superior to
the product of other regions and provinces. It may be deduced to what
extent this distinction was applied in things of greater moment. Such was
the veneration in which the kings held the city that they ennobled it with
splendid houses and palaces, which many of them had built for themselves,
as we shall see in describing some of the buildings. Among these was the
house and temple of the Sun, to which they devoted special attention,
adorning it with incredible riches, to which each Inca added so as to excel
his predecessor. The splendor of the building was so incredible that I would
not dare to describe it, except that all the Spanish historians of Peru had
already done so. But neither what they have said, nor what I shall say, adequately expresses the truth. The building of the temple is attributed to Inca
Yupanqui, the grandfather of Huayna Capac. He was not the founder, for
it existed from the time of the first Inca, but he completed its adornment
and brought it to the state of wealth and majesty in which the Spaniards
found it.

Coming therefore to the plan of the temple, we should say that the
house of the Sun was what is now the church of the divine St. Dominic. I
do not give the exact length and breadth because I have not got them, but
as far as size is concerned it exists today. It is built of smooth masonry, very
level and smooth. The high altar (I use the term to make myself clear,
though the Indians did not, of course, have altars) was at the east end. The

roof was of wood and very lofty so that there would be plenty of air. It was covered with thatch: they had no tiles. All four walls of the temple were covered from top to bottom with plates and slabs of gold. Over what we have called the high altar they had the image of the Sun on a gold plate twice the thickness of the rest of the wall-plates. The image showed him with a round face and beams and flames of fire all in one piece, just as he is usually depicted by painters. It was so large that it stretched over the whole of that side of the temple from wall to wall. The Incas had no other idols of their own or of any other people in the temple with the image of the Sun, for they did not worship any other gods except the Sun, though some say otherwise. . . . On both sides of the image of the Sun were the bodies of the dead kings, in order of antiquity as children of the Sun and embalmed so that they appeared to be alive, though it is not known how this was done. They sat on golden chairs placed on the golden daises they had used. Their faces were toward the people. Only Huayna Capac was distinguished from the rest by being placed before the figure of the Sun which he faced as the most beloved of his children. He had earned this distinction because in his lifetime he was worshipped as a god on account of his virtues and the royal qualities he displayed from boyhood. The bodies were hidden by the Indians with the rest of the treasure, and most of them have never reappeared. In 1559 licentiate Polo[13] discovered five of them: three kings and two queens.

The main gate of the temple faced north as it does today, but there were other lesser gates for the service of the temple. All were lined with plates of gold. Outside the temple, at the top of the walls, a gold cornice consisting of a plate more than a vara wide ran round the whole temple like a crown. [3:21] Beyond the temple there was a cloister with four sides, one of which was the temple wall. All round the upper part of the cloister there ran a cornice of gold plates more than a vara wide, which crowned the cloister. In its place the Spaniards had a white plaster cornice made of the same width as the golden one[14] in order to preserve its memory. I saw it before I left on the walls which were still standing and had not been pulled down. Round the cloister there were five halls or large square rooms each built separately

---

[13] Juan Polo de Ondegardo was a lawyer who also served as *corregidor* (city manager) of Cusco when Garcilaso was a young man. He was very interested in Inca society and ritual, and his writings, which were prepared in response to administrative requests, are among our most important sources on Andean religion and society.

[14] Plates and statues of gold and silver were collected by the Incas in order to ransom Atahuallpa, who was captured by the Spaniards and held for ransom. Atahuallpa was executed by the Spaniards commanded by Francisco Pizarro in 1532 after the ransom was paid.

and not joined to the others, covered in the form of a pyramid, and forming the other three sides of the cloister.

One of these halls was dedicated to the Moon, the wife of the Sun, and was the one nearest the principal chapel of the temple. All of it and its doors were lined with plates of silver, which by their white color showed it to be the hall of the Moon. Her image and portrait was placed like that of the Sun and consisted of a woman's face drawn on a silver plate. They used to enter this hall to visit the Moon and commend themselves to her as the sister and wife of the Sun and mother of the Incas and all their progeny. Thus they called her Mamaquilla, "Mother Moon." They did not offer sacrifices to her as they did to the Sun. On either side of the figure of the Moon were the bodies of the dead queens, arranged in order of antiquity. Mama Ocllo, mother of Huayna Capac, was placed in front of the Moon and face to face with her, being thus distinguished from the rest as the mother of such a son.

Another hall, next to that of the Moon, was dedicated to the planet Venus, the Seven Kids, and all the other stars. The star Venus they called Chasca, meaning "having long curly hair." They honored it saying that it was the Sun's page, standing closest to him and sometimes preceding and sometimes following him. The Seven Kids they respected for their peculiar position and equality in size. They thought the stars were servants of the Moon and therefore gave them a hall next to that of their mistress, so that they would be on hand to serve her. They said that the stars accompanied the Moon in the sky, and not the Sun, because they are to be seen by night and not by day. . . .

[3:22] . . . Of the five halls, I saw the three that were still standing with their ancient walls and roofs. Only the plates of gold and silver were missing. The other two, those of the Moon and stars, had already been pulled down. In the walls of the rooms giving on to the cloister, four tabernacles were hollowed out in each of the outside walls. They were hollowed into the thickness of the walls which, like the rest of the temple, were of masonry. They had moldings round the edges and in the hollows of the tabernacles, and as these moldings were worked in the stone they were inlaid with gold plates not only at the top and sides, but also the floors of the tabernacles. The edges of the moldings were encrusted with fine stones, emeralds, and turquoises, for diamonds and rubies were unknown there. The Inca sat in these tabernacles when there were festivals in honor of the Sun. He sat sometimes in one and sometimes in another, according to the festivity.

In two of these tabernacles in a wall facing east, I remember noticing many holes in the moldings made in the stonework. Those in the edges passed right through while the rest were merely marks on the walls. I heard the Indians and the religious of the temple say that those were the places in which the precious stones were set in pagan times.[15] The tabernacles and all the doors opening onto the cloister, which were twelve excluding those of the hall of the Moon and of the stars, were all plated with leaves and slabs of gold like portals, while the other two were done in silver in accordance with the white color of their owners.

Besides the five great halls already mentioned, the house of the Sun had many other rooms for the priests and servants, who were Incas by privilege. No Indian who was not an Inca, however great a lord he might be, could enter the house. No women could enter, even daughters or wives of the king. Priests served the temple by the week reckoned according to the quarters of the Moon. During this time they abstained from their wives and never left the temple, either by day or by night. . . .

Garcilaso continues the description of the temple, and the temple garden.

[3:24] . . . That garden, which now serves to supply the monastery with vegetables, was in Inca times a garden of gold and silver such as existed in the royal palaces. It contained many herbs and flowers of various kinds, small plants, large trees, animals great and small, tame and wild, and creeping things such as snakes, lizards, and snails, butterflies and birds, each placed in an imitation of its natural surroundings. There was also a great maize field, a patch of the grain they call *quinua*,[16] and other vegetables and fruit trees with their fruit all made of gold and silver in imitation of nature. There were also in the house billets of wood done in gold and silver, which were also to be found in the royal palace. Finally, there were figures of men, women, and children cast in gold and silver, and granaries and barns, which they call *pirua,* to the great majesty and ornamentation of the house of their god, the Sun. Each year, at the great festivals they celebrated, they presented the Sun with much gold and silver which was used to decorate his temple. New devices were continually invented for this purpose, for the silversmith assigned to the service of the Sun did nothing else but make these figures, together with an infinite quantity of plate as well as pots, jars, vases, and vats used in the temple. In short, in the whole of the house there was no implement necessary for any function that was not

---

[15] When Garcilaso refers to "pagan times," or to the "idolatry" of the Incas, he simply follows official Catholic doctrine. *Pagan* means "before the introduction of Christianity," and idolatry refers to any ritual, practice, or belief that is not part of Christian doctrine.

[16] *Quinua* is a highly nutritious and flavorful grain that is grown at high altitudes. It can be purchased in markets—particularly health markets—today in the United States.

made of gold and silver, even the spades and hoes for weeding the gardens. Thus with good reason, they called the temple of the Sun and the whole building *coricancha,* "the golden quarter." . . .

How They Usually Married and Set Up House

[4:8] It will be well to describe the way in which marriages were celebrated throughout all the realms and provinces subject to the Incas. It must be explained that every year or every two years, at a certain season, the king ordered all the marriageable maidens and youths of his lineage[17] to gather together in Cusco. The girls were between eighteen and twenty years old and the youths from twenty-four upwards. They were not allowed to marry earlier, for they said that it was necessary to be old enough and wise enough to rule their houses and estates, and for them to marry earlier would be childish.

The Inca placed himself in the midst of the contracting parties, who were near to one another, and having looked at them, called a youth and a girl, took each by the hand, united them in the bond of matrimony and delivered them to their parents. They then went to the bridegroom's house and solemnized the wedding in the presence of the nearer relatives. The celebrations lasted two, four, or six days, or longer if they wished. These were legitimate wives, and as a mark of greater honor and favor to them they were said in their language to be "given by the Inca's hand." When the king had married those of his own family, the officials appointed for the purpose married on the following day the sons and daughters of the other residents in the city, keeping separate the two divisions called upper Cusco and lower Cusco, which we described at the beginning of our history.

The houses for the dwellings of bridegrooms who were Incas, of whom we are speaking, were made by Indians from the provinces entrusted with the task, according to the division of labor that was set down for everything. The household requirements were provided by the relatives, each bringing a piece. There were no other ceremonies or sacrifices. If the Spanish historians say that other practices existed in their weddings, it is because they have failed to distinguish between the provinces where different usages were found. In this way barbarous customs that existed in many provinces before the Incas took over are commonly attributed to the Incas, who certainly never knew them, but rather stopped them and severely punished the Indians if they practiced them.

The Incas had no other marriage ceremony than that we have described, and orders were given to every governor in his district together with the

---

[17] Only the ruling Inca married his full sister; see pp. 20–1.

provincial *curaca* to marry disposable youths and girls according to the same rite. The *curacas* had to be present at the weddings or perform them themselves as lords and fathers of their people. For the Incas never oppressed them by usurping the jurisdiction of the *curaca,* and the Inca governor was present at the marriages performed by the chief not to take any active part in them, but to approve in the king's name the proceedings of the *curaca* toward his vassals.

For the marriages of the common people the councils of each village were obliged to have houses built for those who were married, and the relatives provided the furniture. It was not lawful for those of different provinces to intermarry, or even those of different towns. All were to marry within their own towns and their own families, like the tribes of Israel, so as not to confuse and mix the lineages and tribes. They were not to marry their sisters. All those of one village regarded themselves as relatives, like the sheep of one fold. Even those of the same province did so, if they were all of one tribe and the same language. It was not permitted for them to go from one province and live in another, or from one town to another, or one quarter to another, so as not to confuse the decuries of the dwellers in each town and quarter. Also the councils had to make the houses and would not make them more than once, and then only in the quarter or parish to which their relatives belonged.

The Heir to the Throne Married His Sister

[4:9] Having spoken of the marriage customs of the Indians in general it is appropriate to describe how the heir to the throne was married. Since the first of the Inca kings, the custom and law among them was that the heir to the kingdom should marry his eldest sister, the legitimate daughter of his father and mother. She was thus his legitimate wife, and was called *coya* which means "queen" or "empress." The firstborn son of brother and sister was the legitimate heir of the kingdom.

This law and custom was observed from the first Inca Manco Capac and his wife Mama Ocllo Huaco, who declared that they were brother and sister, children of the Sun and Moon, and this was believed by the Indians, both those who were their subjects and others. This tradition was lent force by another that in their heathendom they believed, as we have said, namely that the Moon was the sister and wife of the Sun, from whom the Indians boasted of descending. Consequently, in order to imitate the Sun and his children, the first Incas, in every respect, they established the law that the firstborn son of the Inca should follow both traditions and marry his sister by his own father and mother. In default of a legitimate sister, he married his closest female relative in the royal line, his first cousin, niece, or aunt, whichever would inherit the throne if a male heir were lacking according to the practice in Spain.

If the prince had no children by his eldest sister, he married the second and third, until he had children. This strictly observed custom and law was founded on the principles already mentioned. They thought that as the Sun had wedded his sister and begotten by this marriage his two first children, it was proper that the firstborn of the king should imitate his example. They also had in mind the preservation of the purity of the Sun's blood, saying that it was wrong for it to be mingled with human blood (human blood was any other than that of the Incas). They also said that the princes married their sisters so that the heir might inherit the kingdom as much through his mother as through his father. Had it been otherwise, they would have thought the prince a bastard on his mother's side, so seriously did they consider the succession and the right to inherit the throne. As an additional reason, they considered that the majesty of being queen should not be granted to any woman unless she inherited it in her own legitimate right and not as the king's consort; and if she were not capable of reigning in her own right it was not proper that she should be worshipped and served by others who in other respects were better than she.

Apart from their legitimate wives, the kings had many concubines. Some were relatives within and beyond the fourth degree;[18] others were foreign-born. Children by women related to the Inca were held legitimate because they had no taint of other blood. Purity of descent was highly venerated by the Incas, not only among the kings but among all those of royal blood. Children of foreign concubines were considered bastards; and though respected as children of the king, they did not receive the reverence and internal and external worship which was reserved for those who were of legitimate blood. The Inca king thus had three kinds of children—those by his wife who were legally entitled to inherit the throne, those by his relatives who were of legitimate blood, and bastard children by other women. . . .

---

[18] The fourth degree of consanguinity refers to third cousins in European terms.

Chapter Three
The Inca State

*The Incas establish themselves in Cusco and organize their empire. The lives
and deeds of the first seven Incas are presented, and their conquest of the regions
of Collao, Chucuito, and other provinces. The disgraced son of the seventh Inca,
Yáhuar Huácac, has a dream warning him of an imminent rebellion that
threatens Cusco, which the father refuses to believe.*

The Rebellion of the Chancas[19]

[4:23] Three months after the dream of Prince Viracocha Inca—this name
was afterwards given to the prince on account of the apparition he saw—
there came news, albeit unconfirmed, of the rising of the provinces of
Chinchaysuyu from Antahuailla onwards. This is a distance of forty leagues
to the north of Cusco. The news came from no definite source, but as a
confused and sinister rumor, as often happens in such cases. So although
Prince Viracocha had dreamed it and the news corresponded to his dream,
the king took no notice, regarding it as tittle-tattle and the memory of the
past dream which seemed almost forgotten. A few days later the same news
circulated once more, still doubtful and confused, for the enemy had
closed the roads with great care so that their rising should remain unknown
and they could appear at Cusco before their coming was known. The third
rumor then arrived, and it was definite. The tribes called Chanca, Uramarca, Villca, Utunsulla, Hancohuallu, and other of their neighbors had
rebelled and slain the governors and royal officials. They were coming
against the city with an army of more than forty thousand warriors.

These tribes are the ones we have mentioned as having accepted the rule
of Inca Roca[20] rather from fear of his arms than love for his government,
and as we remarked, they preserved a hatred and rancor against the Incas
which they were to reveal when the opportunity offered. Finding the Inca
Yáhuar Huácac so unwarlike, but rather intimidated by the ill omen of his
name[21] and scandalized and bewildered by the cruel disposition of his son,

---

[19] The Chanca Rebellion is considered by modern historians to mark the beginning of
the expansion of the Incas and the rise of the Inca State.

[20] Inca Roca was the sixth Inca ruler.

[21] The name means "he who weeps blood."

22

Prince Inca Viracocha, and having learnt something of the renewed displeasure of the king toward his son, though the cause was not known, and of the great disfavor into which the latter had fallen, they regarded it as the best occasion to show their hostility toward the Inca and the hatred they felt for his rule and dominion. So with the greatest possible speed and secrecy they sent out the summons to war and roused their neighbors. Between them all a powerful army of over thirty thousand warriors was raised and it marched in the direction of the imperial city of Cusco. The instigators of the rising who had stirred up the other lords of vassals were three leading Indians, the *curacas* of three great provinces of the Chanca tribe (many other tribes are included under the same name). The first was Hancohuallu, a youth of twenty-six, the next Túmay Huaraca, and the third Astu Huaraca. These last were brothers and relatives of the first. The ancestors of the three kinglets had been engaged in perpetual war before the time of the Incas against the neighboring tribes, and especially against the people called Quechuas, under which five large provinces are comprised. They had crushed these and other neighbors, and treated them roughly and tyrannically, for which reason the Quechuas were glad to become subjects of the Incas and accepted their rule readily and with affection, as we have said, in order to be rid of the insolence of the Chancas. The latter, on the other hand, regretted that the Incas had put an end to their doughty deeds, and had reduced them from lords of vassals to tributaries. They nursed the ancient hatred inherited from their fathers, and made the present rebellion, thinking that they could easily conquer the Inca because of the suddenness of the attack they had planned, and the state of unpreparedness they imagined they would find him in. They fancied he would be without warriors and that a single victory would make them masters, not only of their ancient enemies but also of all the Inca empire.

With this hope they summoned their neighbors, both those subjected to the Incas and the rest, promising them a great share of the spoils. It was easy to persuade them, both because of the enormous prize that was offered and because of the ancient reputation of the Chancas as valiant warriors. They chose Hancohuallu as captain general. He was a valiant Indian. His two commanders were the two brothers, and the other *curacas* were leaders and captains of the host, which marched at all speed in search of Cusco.

The Inca Abandons the City and the Prince Saves It

[4:24] Inca Yáhuar Huácac was bewildered by the confirmation that his enemies were on their way. He had never believed such a thing could happen. The experience of the Incas had always been that of all the provinces they had conquered and added to their empire none had rebelled from the time of the first Inca Manco Capac till the present. Because of this uncertainty and because of his hatred for the prince, his son, who had foretold the rebellion, he had not wanted to believe it could happen or to take the advice of his kinsmen, since passion had blinded his understanding. Now he found himself submerged and had no time to call men together to go out against the enemy and no garrison in the city to hold them off until help arrived. He therefore decided to give way to the fury of the rebels and withdraw toward Collasuyu, where he knew his life would be safe because his subjects were noble and loyal. With this intent he withdrew with the few Incas who could follow him, and reached the ravine called Muina, which is five leagues south of the city. There he halted to discover what the enemy was doing on the road and how far he had advanced.

The city of Cusco was defenseless in the absence of the king. No captain or leader dared even speak, much less consider defending it, but all sought safety in flight. Those who could scattered in various directions, according to what they thought would be most likely to save their lives. Some of the fugitives came upon Prince Viracocha Inca and told him the news of the rebellion of Chinchaysuyu, and how his father, the Inca, had retreated toward Collasuyu, thinking there was no possibility of resisting the enemy because of the suddenness of their onslaught.

The prince greatly regretted that his father should have withdrawn and left the city unprotected. He ordered his informants and some of the shepherds he had with him to return to the city and tell all the Indians they met on the roads and those still left in the city that everyone who could was to try to follow the Inca their lord, with whatever arms they could find. He would do the same, and they must pass his order on from one to another. Having given this order, Prince Viracocha set out to follow his father by a shortcut, without entering the city. Hastening, he came upon the Inca in the Muina ravine, for he had still not left the place. Covered with sweat and dust, with a spear he had snatched up on the way in his hand, he presented himself before the king and with a grave and sorrowful face said:

"Inca, why do you let news, whether true or false, that a few of your subjects have rebelled cause you to abandon your palace and court, and turn your back on enemies you have not even seen? How can you bear to deliver the house of your father, the Sun, to enemies who will tread in it with shoes on their feet and commit there the abominations your ancestors taught them to abandon, sacrifices of men, women, and children, and such bestialities and sacrileges? What regard have we for the virgins dedicated as brides of the Sun, with the observance of perpetual virginity, if we leave them unprotected for a brutal and bestial enemy to wreak his will upon them? What honor have we gained if we permit these iniquities to save our lives? I do not want to save my life, and therefore I shall return to take my stand before the enemy and lose it before he enters Cusco. I will not live to see the abominations the barbarians will commit in the imperial and sacred city the Sun and his children founded. Those who wish to follow me, come now, and I will show them how to exchange a shameful life for an honorable death."

Having said this with great grief and feeling, he retraced his steps toward the city, without stopping either to eat or drink. The Incas of the royal blood, who had set out with the king, together with their brothers and many nephews and cousins and many other relatives, to the number of over four thousand, all returned with the prince. Only the aged and incapable stayed with his father. On the way they came across many who were fleeing the city. They called on them to return, and encouraged them by telling them the prince Inca Viracocha had returned to defend the city and the house of his father the Sun. With this news the Indians so took heart that all those who were running away returned, especially the stouthearted. These called to others across the fields, passing the word from hand to hand that the prince had come back to hold the city. The news so stirred them that they returned with great relief to die by the prince's side. His courage and energy were such that they infected all his followers.

Thus he entered the city and ordered that the people who had collected should follow him at once. He marched on up the highway to Chinchaysuyu, whence his enemies were coming, so as to take up a position between them and the city. His intention was not to resist them, for he thought his forces were insufficient, but to die fighting before the foe entered the city and trod its streets with their barbarian and victorious feet, without respect for the Sun, which was what touched him most deeply. And as Inca Yáhuar Huácac whose life we are recounting ended his reign here, as we shall see, I thought it right to cut the thread of this story to divide his deeds from those of his son Inca Viracocha. I shall insert information about the government of the empire to vary the story and prevent it from running all on one theme. This done, we will return to the deeds of Prince Viracocha, which were very great.

Chapter Four
Inca Society

Inca Agriculture

[5:1] When the Inca had conquered any kingdom or province and established the form of government in its towns and the way of life of the inhabitants in accordance with their idolatrous religion and their laws, he
ordered that the agricultural land should be extended. This implies, of
course, the area under maize. For this purpose irrigation engineers were
brought: some of these were extremely skilled, as is clearly demonstrated by
their works, of which some survive today and others have been destroyed
leaving only traces behind. These engineers made the necessary irrigation
channels, according to the amount of land that could be turned to account:
the greater part of Peru is poor in grain-bearing land, and the Incas therefore tried as far as possible to extend what there was. Because the country
falls within the torrid zone, irrigation is necessary, and great attention was
paid to this: not a grain of maize was sown unless channelled water was
available. They also dug channels to water their pastures when the autumn
rains were delayed: as they had an infinite quantity of flocks,[22] they had to
give their pastures the same attention as their grainlands. The channels for
the pastures were destroyed when the Spaniards entered Peru, but traces of
them are still to be found.

Having dug the channels, they leveled the fields and squared them so
that the irrigation water could be adequately distributed. They built level
terraces on the mountains and hillsides, wherever the soil was good; and
these are to be seen today in Cusco and in the whole of Peru. In order to
make these terraces they would construct three walls of solid masonry, one
in front and one at each end. These sloped back slightly (like all the Indian
walls) so as to withstand the weight of earth with which they are filled to
the level of the top of the walls. Above the first platform they built another
smaller one, and above that another still smaller. In this way the whole hill
was gradually brought under cultivation, the platforms being flattened out
like stairs in a staircase, and all the cultivable and irrigable land being put
to use. If there were rocky places, the rocks were removed and replaced by
earth brought from elsewhere to form the terraces, so that the space should

---

[22] The Incas (and other groups) raised llamas and alpacas for their wool and meat.

not be wasted. The first platforms were large, according to the configuration of the place: they might be one or two or three hundred measures[23] broad and long. The second were smaller and they diminished progressively as they were higher up, until the last might contain only two or three rows of maize plants. This shows how industrious the Incas were in extending the area which could be planted with maize. A water channel was commonly brought fifteen or twenty leagues to water a few measures of soil, so that it should not be wasted.

Having thus extended the cultivable land, each settlement in each province measured all the land assigned to it and divided it into three parts, one for the Sun, one for the king, and one for the inhabitants. In the division care was taken that the inhabitants should have enough to sow for themselves, and rather too much than too little. When the population of a town or province increased, part of the area assigned to the Sun or the Inca was transferred to their subjects, so that the only lands reserved by the king for himself or for the Sun were those which would otherwise have remained ownerless and untilled. The terraces were usually assigned to the Sun and the Inca, since the latter had been responsible for constructing them. In addition to the irrigated maize fields, other land without a supply of water was divided among them for dry farming and sown with crops of great importance, such as three they call *papa, oca,* and *añus.* This land was also divided in due proportion between the Sun, the Inca, and a third part for their subjects, but as it was waterless and of low productivity, it was sown only for a year or two and then rested while another part was sown. In this way the poor soil was kept under control, and there was always an abundance of it for use.

The maize fields were sown every year, and as they were always supplied with water and manure like gardens, they always bore fruit. With the maize they planted a seed rather like rice which they call *quinua:* it also grows in a cold climate.

The System of Cultivation

[5:2] They also had an established system in cultivating the soil. They first tilled the part assigned to the Sun and then that of the widows and orphans and those who were unable to work owing to age or ill health. The latter were regarded as the poor, and the Inca therefore bade that their land be tilled for them. In each village, or in each quarter, if it were a large village,

---

[23] By "measure," Garcilaso means a *fanegada de sembradura:* usually the ground needed to sow a *fanega* (1.6 bushels).

there were men appointed exclusively to attend to the cultivation of what we shall call the poor. These men were called *llactacamayu,* "aldermen or councillors of a town." When the time came to plough, or sow, or bring in the harvest, it was their duty to go out at night and climb a sort of watchtower or beacon they had for the purpose and sound a trumpet or horn to attract attention, and then announce: "On such and such a day the lands of the disabled are to be tilled: let each attend to the task assigned him." The inhabitants of each quarter knew from traditional practice which land was assigned to them, since it was that of their relatives or nearest neighbors. Each was obliged to take his own food from his home so that the poor should not have the trouble of feeding them. They used to say that the aged, the sick, and widows and orphans had enough troubles of their own, without attending to others. If the poor had no seed, this was supplied from the storehouses, of which we shall speak later. Land belonging to soldiers on campaign was also tilled by the community, like that of the widows, orphans, and poor, for when their husbands were away on military service, wives were reckoned as widows, and received this service as being in need of charity. The children of those killed in war were very carefully brought up until they married.

After the cultivation of the land of the poor, they tilled their own, taking turn and turn about, as the saying is.[24] They then tilled the *curaca's* land, which was always the last to be attended to in each town or province. Once in the time of Huayna Capac, an Indian *regidor*[25] in a village of the Chachapoyas was hanged for having the land belonging to the *curaca,* who was a relative of his, tilled before that of a widow: this was because he had broken the order established by the Inca for tilling the soil, and the gallows were erected on the *curaca's* own land. The Inca ordered that his subjects' land should be given priority over his own, because it was said that prosperity of the subjects redounded to the king's service: if they were poor and needy, they would be of little use in peace or war.

The last land to be cultivated was that assigned to the king. It was tilled communally. All the Indians went out together to the fields of the Inca and of the Sun with great rejoicing and satisfaction. They wore the clothes and adornments they kept for their greatest festivities, covered with gold and silver plates and with feather headdresses. As they ploughed (which was the work that gave them most pleasure) they sang many songs composed in praise of the Incas: their labor thus became a

---

[24] Garcilaso does not explain or include the saying he refers to, but a "turn" of labor in quechua is a *mit'a,* and the custom of labor exchange, which still takes place among community members today, is called *ayni.*

[25] A magistrate or councilman of a community.

matter for festivity and joy because it was performed in the service of their god and their kings

Inside the city of Cusco, on the skirts of the hill where the fortress is, there used to be a large terrace of many *fanegas* of soil: it may still be there today unless it has been built over. It is called Collcampata. The quarter in which it is takes its name from the name of the terrace, which was the special and chief jewel of the Sun, for it was the first to be dedicated by the Incas to him in the whole empire. This terrace was tilled and cared for by those of the royal blood, and none but Incas and Pallas could work in it. The work was done amidst the greatest celebrations, especially at ploughing time, when the Incas came dressed in all their insignia and finery. The songs they recited in praise of the Sun and their kings were all based on the meaning of the word *hailli,* which means triumph over the soil, which they ploughed and disembowelled so that it should give fruit. The songs included elegant phrases by noble lovers and brave soldiers on the subject of their triumph over the earth they were ploughing. The refrain of each verse was the word *"hailli,"* repeated as often as was necessary to mark the beats of a certain rhythm, corresponding to the movements made by the Indians in raising their implements and dropping them, the more easily to break the soil.

As a plough they use a stick two yards long: its front is flat and its back rounded, and it is about four fingers thick. It has a point to pierce the ground and, half a vara above it, a footrest made of two sticks tightly lashed to the main shaft. On this the Indian sets his foot and forcibly drives the plough in up to the footrest. They work in bands of seven or eight, more or less, according to family or neighborhood groups. By all lowering their ploughs at once they can raise clods of earth so large that anyone who has not seen it could hardly credit it. It is remarkable to see them perform such a considerable task with such weak implements, and they work with great speed and ease and never lose the rhythm of the song. The women work opposite the men and help to lift the clods with their hands, turning the grass roots upwards so that they dry and die, and the harrowing requires less effort. They also join with their husbands in the singing, especially in the *hailli* chorus. . . .

The Tribute They Paid to the Incas

[5:5] Having described how the Incas divided the land and benefited their subjects, we must now refer to the tribute that was paid to the kings. The principal tribute was the tilling and fertilizing of the lands assigned to the Sun and the Inca, the harvesting of whatever crops it produced and their storage in bins and the royal granaries that existed in each village for collecting the harvest. One of the principal crops was the *uchu,* which the Spaniards call *ají,* or otherwise, *pimiento.*

The bins are called *pirua.* They are made of trodden clay mixed with plenty of straw. In Inca times they were very skillfully constructed. Their size varied in proportion to the height of the walls of the building in which they were placed. They were narrow, square, and of one piece, and had to be made with molds of different sizes. They were of various capacities, some bigger than others, some of thirty *fanegas,* or fifty, one hundred or two hundred, more or less as they were required. Each size of bin was kept in a special building, which it had been made to fit. They were placed against the four walls and also in the middle of the building. An alley was left between the rows of bins so that they could be emptied and filled in turn. Once erected they were not moved. In order to empty a bin little holes about an *ochava*[26] in size were made in the front of it. They were made so that it was possible to tell how many *fanegas* had been taken out and how many were left without measuring them. In this way it could easily be reckoned from the size of the bins how much maize there was in each barn and each granary, and the small holes showed what had been extracted and what remained in each bin. I have seen some of these bins which survived from Inca times, and they were some of the first, since they were in the house of the chosen virgins, the wives of the Sun, and were made for the use of these women. When I saw them, the house belonged to the children of Pedro del Barco, who were schoolfellows of mine.

The shares of the crop assigned to the Sun and to the Inca were stored separately, though in the same granaries. The seeds for sowing were supplied by the owner of the land, the Sun or the king, and so was the maintenance of the Indians, for when they were cultivating the lands of either the Sun or the Inca they were fed from the revenue of the respective owners. In this way the contribution of the Indians was limited to their personal service. The Indians paid nothing to the Inca from the crops they derived from their own land. . . .

[5:6] In addition to the main tribute which took the form of sowing the soil, cultivating, and harvesting the crops of the Sun and of the Inca, they paid also a second tribute which consisted of clothes, footwear, and weapons for use in time of war and for the poor, that is those who could not work through age or infirmity. In assessing and collecting this second tribute they followed the same system as in all their other affairs. Throughout the mountainous region clothing was made from wool which the Inca

---

[26] An *ochava* is the eighth part of anything; thus an *ochava* of a storage bin would be an opening that was 1/8 of the size of the bin itself.

supplied from the innumerable flocks belonging to him and to the Sun. On the *llanos,* or seacoast, where the climate is hot and wool is not worn, they made cotton cloth from cotton grown on the land of the Sun and of the Inca. All the Indians supplied was their labor. They made three kinds of woolen cloth. The coarsest, called *avasca,* was for the common people. Another finer sort was called *compi,* which was worn by the nobility, such as captains, *curacas,* and other officials: it was made in all colors and patterns with a reed or comb such as is used in making Flanders cloth. It was finished on both sides. Other very fine clothes, also called *compi,* were made for those of the royal blood, such as captains, soldiers, and royal officials in peace or war. The fine cloth was woven in provinces where the natives were most ingenious and expert in its manufacture, and the coarser sort was made elsewhere where the natives were less skilled. All the wool for this cloth was spun by the women, who also wove the coarse cloth called *avasca.* The finer sort was woven by men, for the work is done standing. . . . Weapons were also furnished by districts that had the most abundant supply of the necessary materials. In some they made bows and arrows, in others lances and darts, elsewhere clubs and axes, and in others slings and ropes for transport, or shields and targets. These last were the only weapons of defense they knew. In short, each province and tribe supplied whatever it produced, and never needed to import from outside what it lacked, for it had no other obligation. Finally, they paid their tribute without having to leave their homes, for the universal law throughout the empire was that no Indian should be obliged to leave his own country in search of what he had to furnish as tribute. . . . There were thus four things to be supplied to the Inca—supplies from the royal domains, woolen clothing from the royal flocks, arms, and footwear, according to what was available in each province. These requirements were apportioned with perfect order and system. The provinces that were required to supply cloth on account of their great skill in producing it were discharged from the obligation to supply weapons and footwear, and in the same way any who were required to furnish more of one thing were relieved of demands for others. The same principle was applied in all matters of taxation so that no one could feel any cause for grievance, either as an individual or in common as a province. . . .

The Storing of Supplies and Their Use

[5:8] We must now explain how the tribute was kept and on what it was used. Throughout the whole kingdom there were three sorts of storehouses to hold the harvest and tribute. Every village, whether large or small, had two storehouses: one was used to hold the supplies kept for the use of the people in lean years, and the other was used for the crops of the Sun and of the Inca. There were other storehouses at intervals of three leagues on the royal highway, and these now serve the Spaniards as inns or taverns.

For a distance of fifty leagues round the city of Cusco the crops of the Sun and of the Inca were brought in for the use of the court, so that the Inca might have adequate supplies on hand to entertain the captain and *curacas* who came to see him. A certain proportion of the revenue of the Sun was left in every village within the radius of fifty leagues for the common store of the vassals.

The crops of the other villages, outside the orbit of the capital, were collected in the royal storehouses that existed and thence transferred to the stores on the royal roads where garrisons, arms, clothes, and footwear were kept for the armies that marched along to the four quarters of the world, which they called Tahuantinsuyu. The wayside deposits were well stocked with all these things, and although many companies or regiments of warriors went past, there was always ample for all. Soldiers were not allowed to billet themselves on the villages at the cost of the vassals. . . .

If the expenses of a war were too great to be borne by the royal revenues, the Inca then laid hands on the property of the Sun, whose legitimate son and universal heir he considered himself to be. The supplies that were not consumed in warfare or by the court were kept in the three kinds of storehouses we have mentioned and distributed in years of want among the people, whose well-being was the first care of the Incas.

Throughout the kingdom the estates of the Sun were applied to the maintenance of the priests and ministers of their idolatry while they officiated in the temples, which they did by weekly rotation. But when they were at home they ate at their own expense, for they too were given land to till like the ordinary people. The expenditure from the estates of the Sun was thus small in proportion to the extent of its income, and a great deal was therefore left over to assist the Inca in case of need.

How the Incas Conquered and Civilized New Vassals[27]

[5:12] . . . Before they went to war, they used to warn their enemies one, two, or three times. After a province had been subdued, the first thing the Inca did was to take the chief idol of the region and carry it off as a sort of hostage to Cusco. He would order it to be kept in a temple until the chief and his men were disillusioned about the deceits of their false gods and

---

[27] The following three sections (5:14, 5:15, and 5:16) were copied by Garcilaso from the lost Latin manuscript of the Jesuit father, Padre Blas Valera.

had taken to the idolatry of the Incas who worshipped the Sun. The other gods were not overthrown immediately on the conquest of a new province, out of respect for it; for the natives would be aggrieved by any disrespect of their own gods until they had been indoctrinated in the vain religion of the Incas.

"They also carried off the leading chief and all his children to Cusco, where they were treated with kindness and favor so that by frequenting the court they would learn not only its laws, customs, and correct speech, but also the rites, ceremonies, and superstitions of the Incas.[28] This done, the *curaca* was restored to his former dignity and authority, and the Inca, as king, ordered the vassals to serve and obey him as their natural lord. And so that the victorious and vanquished warriors should be reconciled and live together in permanent peace and concord, and that any hatred and rancor that had been generated in the course of the war should be buried and forgotten, they ordered great banquets to be held with an abundant supply of good things, to which the blind, the lame, the dumb, and other disabled people were invited to share in the royal liberality. At these feasts there were dances by the maidens, games and celebrations for the boys, and military exercises by the grown men. In addition to this they were given many presents of gold, silver, and feathers to enrich their dresses and to serve as decorations for their principal feasts; and other awards consisting of garments and similar prizes which they greatly esteemed were distributed. The Inca bestowed these and similar gifts on newly conquered Indians, so that however brutish and barbarous they had been they were subdued by affection and attached to his service by a bond so strong that no province ever dreamed of rebelling. And in order to remove all occasion for complaint and to prevent dissatisfaction from leading to rebellion, he confirmed and promulgated anew all the former laws, liberties, and statutes so that they might be more esteemed and respected, and he never changed a word of them unless they were contrary to the idolatry and laws of his empire.

"When necessary, he would move the inhabitants of one province to another, furnishing them with land, houses, servants, and flocks in sufficient abundance; and would replace them in their own area with natives of Cusco or other faithful provinces, who would act as a garrison colony

---

[28] Garcilaso has copied the passage in quotations from a lost manuscript of Blas Valera. Valera was the son of an Andean woman and a Spanish man, like Garcilaso, who joined the Jesuit Order and was regarded by his contemporaries as a major authority on Andean history and customs. For additional information on Valera, see Sabine Hyland, *The Jesuit & the Incas: The Extraordinary Life of Padre Blas Valera, S. J.* (Ann Arbor: University of Michigan Press, 2003).

and teach them the laws, rites, ceremonies, and general language of the kingdom.

"The rest of the mild administration of the Inca kings, which was superior to that of any other kings or peoples of the New World, is clearly shown not only from the annual knots[29] and traditions of the Indians, but also from the trustworthy handwritten reports which Viceroy Don Francisco de Toledo ordered his inspectors, judges, and secretaries to write after many lengthy enquiries among the Indians of each province. These papers are now in the public archives and they give a clear picture of how benignly the Inca kings of Peru treated their people. For, as we have said, apart from certain matters affecting the security of the whole empire, all the laws and rights of the vassals were preserved without change. Their estates and patrimony, both common and private, were left free and undivided by order of the Incas without any reduction or diminution. Soldiers were never allowed to rob or sack provinces or kingdoms that were reduced by force of arms to surrender: their natives who surrendered were quickly appointed to peaceable offices or entrusted with military commands, as if the latter had been long and trusted soldiers of the Inca and the former his most faithful servants.

"The burden of the tributes imposed by the kings was so light that what we are about to say may well appear to the reader to have been written in jest. Yet, not content or satisfied with all these things, the Incas distributed all that was needful for clothes and food with abundant liberality and gave away many other gifts not only to lords and nobles but also to taxpayers and the poor. They might therefore more properly be called diligent fathers of families or careful stewards than kings, and this gave rise to the title *Capac Titu* which the Indians applied to them. *Capac* is 'a prince powerful in wealth and greatness' and *titu* means 'a liberal, magnanimous prince, august demi-god.' This is also the reason why the kings of Peru were so beloved by their vassals that even today the Indians, though converted to Christianity, do not forget them, but rather call upon them in turn by their names with weeping and wailing and cries and shouts, whenever they are in trouble or need. We do not read of any ancient king of Asia, Africa, or Europe having shown himself so careful, affable, beneficent, free, and liberal toward his natural subjects as were the Inca kings toward theirs. Those who read the historical facts as we have written and shall continue to write them will be able to understand what were the ancient laws and rights of the Peruvian Indians, their customs, statutes, occupations, and way of life, which was so reasonable that all these things should be recorded and

---

[29] The knotted cord records, or *quipu*.

observed so that they may be reduced to the Christian religion with more ease and mildness."

How They Paid Their Tribute

[5:15] Coming to the subject of the tribute levied and collected by the Inca kings of Peru from their vassals, this was so moderate that when one realizes what it consisted of and how much it was, it can truthfully be affirmed that none of the kings of the ancients, nor the great Caesars who were called Augustus and Pius can be compared with the Inca kings in this respect. For properly speaking it seems that they did not receive taxes and tributes from their subjects, but rather that they paid their subjects or merely imposed taxes for their benefit, such was their liberality toward their vassals. Considered in relation to the general circumstances of those times, the daily pay of laborers, and the value of commodities, and the expenses of the Incas, the tribute was so small in quantity that many Indians barely paid the value of four reals of the current time. Although there could not fail to be some inconvenience attached to the payment of the tribute or the service of the king or the *curacas,* it was borne cheerfully and contentedly owing to the smallness of the tribute, the perquisites the Indians received, and the numerous advantages that arose from the performance of the tasks. The rights of the tribute payer and the laws in his favor were inviolably preserved so that neither the judges, nor the governors, nor the captain generals, nor the Inca himself could pervert them to the disadvantage of the vassals. They were as follows: the first and most important was that no one who was exempt from tribute could be obliged to pay it at any time or for any reason. All those of royal blood were exempt, as were all captain generals and other captains, even the centurions and their children and grandchildren, and all the *curacas* and their kinsmen. Royal officials who were commoners and held minor posts were exempted from paying tribute during their term of office, as were soldiers on active service and youths of under twenty-five since they were required to serve their parents until that age. Old men of fifty and upwards were exempt from tribute, and so were all women, whether married or maidens, spinsters or widows. The sick were exempt until they were completely recovered, and all the disabled, such as the blind, lame, limbless, and others who were deprived of the use of their limbs, though the deaf and dumb were allotted tasks for which they did not need to hear or speak.[30]

---

[30] The material in quotations that follows is copied from the lost mss. of Blas Valera.

"The second law was that all the rest apart from these were obliged to pay tribute unless they were priests or officials in the temples of the Sun or of the chosen virgins. The third law was that no Indian was ever obliged for any reason to pay anything instead of tribute, but only to pay in labor, with his skill or with the time he devoted to the service of the king and the state. To this extent rich and poor were equal, for none paid more or less than others. The word rich was applied to anyone who had children or family to help him in his work and so to finish his share of the tributary labor sooner: anyone who had no children or family, though he might be well off in other respects, was accounted poor. The fourth law was that no one could compel anyone to perform or undertake any craft but his own, unless it was the tilling of the soil or military service, two duties to which all were liable in general. The fifth law was that each should pay his tribute in whatever goods were found in his own province, without being forced to go abroad in search of things that did not occur where he lived: it seemed to the Inca a great injustice to ask his subjects to deliver fruits their own earth did not produce. The sixth law required that each of the craftsmen who worked in the service of the Inca or his chiefs should be supplied with everything necessary for his work: thus the smith was given gold, silver, or copper, the weaver wool or cotton, the painter colors, and all the other requirements of their respective callings. Each craftsman was therefore only obliged to supply labor and the time needed for the work, which was two months, or at most three. This done, he was not obliged to work any more. However, if there was any work left unfinished, and he wished to go on working of his own free will and see it through, what he did was discounted from the tribute he owed for the following year, and the amount was so recorded by means of their knots and beads. The seventh law required that all craftsmen of whatever occupation should be supplied if they fell ill with all they required for food, clothes, comforts, and medicine instead of having to pay tribute: if the Indian concerned was working alone, he alone was helped, but if he had brought his wife and children so as to finish the work sooner, they too were fed.

"In the allocation of such tasks, the question of time was not taken into consideration but only the completion of the job. Thus if a man could take advantage of the help of his family and friends to complete two months' work in a week, he was regarded as having fully satisfied his obligation for the year, and no other tribute could be pressed upon him. This alone is sufficient to refute the contention of those who say that formerly tribute was paid by sons, daughters, and mothers, whoever they were. This is false, for although these all worked, it was not because the obligation to pay tribute was imposed upon them, but because they helped their fathers, husbands, or masters: if the man did not wish his dependents to share in his work, but preferred to work alone, his wife and children remained free to busy themselves about the house, and the judges and decurions were unable to bring any compulsion to bear on them, as long as they were not idle. It was for this reason that in the days of the Incas those who had many children and large families were accounted rich: those who had none were often taken ill owing to the length of time they had to devote to their work until their tribute was settled. In order to remedy this there was a law that those who were rich by reason of their families, and the rest who had finished their tasks, should help them for a day or two. This was agreeable to all the Indians."

[5:16] The eighth law was about the collection of the tribute: this was done as we shall say, for there was order and reason in everything they did. At an appointed time the judges responsible for the collection and accountants or scribes who kept the knots and beads for reckoning the tribute assembled in the chief town of the province: the calculations and divisions were made in the presence of the *curaca* and the Inca governor by means of the knots on the strings and small stones, according to the number of householders in the province. The calculations were so exact that I hardly know whether to praise the more the accountants who made their reckonings without the use of figures and contrived to divide exactly very small quantities, a thing our mathematicians have great difficulty in doing, or the royal governor and officials who followed the process with perfect ease.

"The knots showed how much work each Indian had done, what crafts he had worked at, what journeys he had made on the instructions of his ruler or his superiors, and any other occupation he had busied himself with: all this was deducted from the tribute he was required to produce. The judges and the governor were then shown separately all the goods stored in the royal warehouses, consisting of supplies, peppers, clothes, footwear, arms, and all the other things the Indians supplied as tribute, including the gold, silver, precious stones, and copper, which were provided in separate portions for the king and the Sun. They also inspected the contents of the storehouses in each village. The Inca governor of each province was required by law to keep a copy of the accounts in his possession so that no deception could be practiced by either the Indian tribute payers or the official collectors.

"The ninth law was that any surplus in the amount of tribute after the royal expenses had been paid should be devoted to the general good and placed in the common storehouses against times of need. The king ordered that of precious objects such as gold, silver, and stones, the plumage of certain birds, colors for painting and dyeing, copper, and many other things that were presented to him by the *curacas* either annually or whenever they visited him, part should be set aside to satisfy the needs of his household and service and those of the royal blood, and the surplus given as a reward to the captains and lords of vassals who had brought them, for even though they possessed these objects in their own provinces they were not allowed to use them except by privilege and with the Inca's permission. This shows that the Inca kings reserved for themselves the smaller part of the tribute they imposed and turned the greater part over to the advantage of their subjects.

"The tenth law stated the various occupations the Indians were to engage in, both in the service of the king and in the interest of the villages and the commonwealth as a whole: these occupations were imposed instead of tribute and were to be performed collectively. They were clearing roads and paving them; decorating, repairing, or reconstructing the temples of the Sun and other sanctuaries of their idolatrous faith; and making anything else that was needed for the temples. They were obliged to make public buildings such as granaries and houses for the judges and governors; to repair bridges; to act as messengers, which they call *chasqui;* to plough the earth; to collect the crops; to graze cattle; to watch estates, sown fields, and other public property; to provide lodginghouses to accommodate travelers; and to attend to the needs of guests from the royal stores. In addition, they were obliged to undertake anything else that was to their common advantage, or to that of the *curacas* or the king. But as there was such a vast number of Indians in those days, the amount of labor required of each of them was so small that they hardly felt it, for they all took their turns and were perfectly honest in seeing that none were more burdened than the rest. This law also required them to mend the roads and fortifications once a year, restore the bridges, and clean out the irrigation channels: all this they were required by law to do without payment, for it was to the general advantage of each kingdom and province and of the whole empire.

"Other minor laws we have omitted lest our account become wearisome: those we have mentioned were the principal laws relating to tribute."

Thus far Padre Blas Valera. At this stage I should like to ask one of the historians who says that the Incas imposed oppressive legislation requiring their subjects to pay them great levies and tributes, what was this oppressive legislation? For the laws we have mentioned, and others we shall refer to later were readily confirmed by the kings of Spain of glorious memory, as Padre Blas Valera himself says. . . .

The narrative returns to Pachacuti Inca Yupanqui, who is facing the revolt of the Chancas. Pachacuti receives last-minute reinforcements for his war with the Chancas, as he had been promised by the phantom Inca Viracocha in a dream, and defeats them.

The Victory over the Chancas

[5:19] Seeing their enemies weaken, the Incas all called on the names of their uncle, the phantom Inca Viracocha, as their prince bade them, and attacked with great fury, carrying the Chancas before them. A great many of them were killed, and the few survivors took to their heels and fled for all they were worth. Having given pursuit for a while, the prince called his men back, and ordered the slaughter of the enemy to cease, since they were already vanquished. He personally visited the whole field of battle and had the wounded brought in to be cured and the dead to be buried. He had the captives released and let them return freely to their own countries, telling them that they were all pardoned. The battle, having been bitterly contested for more than eight hours, was extremely bloody: the Indians say that in addition to what was spilt on the field itself, a stream of gore ran down a dry watercourse that passes through the plain, and which was afterwards known as Yáhuarpampa, "field of blood." More than thirty thousand Indians died: eight thousand being Inca Viracocha's men and the rest members of the Chanca, Hancohuallu, Uramarca, Villca, Utunsulla, and other tribes.

The two field commanders and the Hancohuallu general were taken prisoner. The latter was wounded, and the prince ordered him to be treated with great care: all three were kept for the triumph he proposed to celebrate. A few days after the battle one of the Inca's uncles sternly rebuked the captives for having dared to attack the children of the Sun, who he said were invincible, since stones and trees [who] turned into men fought on their side in obedience to the command of their father the Sun, as they themselves had witnessed and would witness again whenever they tried conclusions with the Incas. He told them many other fables to the Incas' advantage, and finished by bidding them render thanks to the Sun who bade his children treat the Indians with mercy and clemency. For this reason the prince would spare their lives and return their possessions to them and deal likewise with the other *curacas* who had rebelled with them, even though they deserved to die a cruel death. Thenceforward they were to be good vassals, if they did not want the Sun to punish them by bidding the earth to swallow them up alive. . . . The *curacas* humbly thanked him for this generosity and promised to be loyal servants. . . .

After the victory, Pachacuti, also called Pachacuti Inca Viracocha, dispossesses his father of the empire, rewards his allies and continues his conquests, expanding the empire north and west to the sea, and east to the region of Charcas, now Bolivia.

The Death of Inca Viracocha

[5:29] Inca Viracocha died at the height of his power and majesty, and was universally mourned throughout all his empire, and worshipped as a god, a child of the Sun to whom they offered many sacrifices. As his heir he left Pachacútec Inca and many other sons and daughters, both legitimate ones of the royal blood and illegitimate. He won eleven provinces, four to the south of Cusco and seven to the north. It is not known for certain how many years he reigned or lived, but it is commonly thought that his reign lasted more than fifty years. This was confirmed by the appearance of his body, which I saw in Cusco at the beginning of 1560. When I was to come to Spain, I visited the house of Licentiate Polo de Ondegardo, a native of Salamanca who was corregidor of the city, to kiss his hand and take leave of him before departing. Among other favors he showed me, he said: "As you are going to Spain, come into this room, and you shall see some of your ancestors whom I have exhumed: that will give you something to talk about when you get there." In the room I found five bodies of Inca rulers, three males and two females. The Indians said that one of them was this Inca Viracocha: it certainly corresponded to his great age and had hair as white as snow. The second was said to be the great Túpac Inca Yupanqui, the great grandson of Viracocha Inca. The third was Huayna Capac, the son of Túpac Inca Yupanqui and great great grandson of Viracocha. The last two bodies could be seen to be of younger men: they had white hairs but fewer than those of Viracocha. One of the women was Queen Mama Runtu, the wife of Inca Viracocha. The other was Coya Mama Ocllo, mother of Huayna Capac, and it seems probable that the Indians buried husband and wife together as they had lived. The bodies were perfectly preserved without the loss of a hair of the head or brow or an eyelash. They were dressed as they had been in life, with *llautus*[31] on their heads but no other ornaments or royal insignia. They were buried in a sitting position, in a posture often assumed by Indian men and women: their hands were crossed across their breast, the left over the right, and their eyes lowered, as if looking at the ground. Padre Acosta, speaking of one of these bodies which he too saw, says in his Book VI, chapter xxi: "The body was so complete and so well preserved with a certain bitumen that it appeared to be alive. Its eyes were made of cloth of gold, and so well fitted that one did not notice the loss of the real ones,"[32] etcetera. I confess my own carelessness in not

---

[31] A tasseled fringe wrapped around the head of the Inca. The *llautu* was the equivalent of a European crown and was worn only by the ruler.

[32] The Jesuit scholar José de Acosta, author of the *Historia natural y moral de las Indias* [1590], multiple editions. An English translation is available; see José de Acosta, *Natural and Moral History of the Indies*, ed. Jane E. Mangan & trans. Frances López-Morillas (Durham: Duke University Press, 2002).

having examined them so closely, for in those days I had not thought of writing about them: if I had, I should have looked carefully at their state to see how and with what materials they were embalmed, for they would not have refused to tell me as a son of the Incas, as they have refused to tell the Spaniards, how it was done. . . . My own opinion is that the main operation in embalming was to take the bodies above the snow line and keep them there until the flesh dried, after which they would cover them with the bitumen Padre Acosta mentions, so as to take the place of the flesh that had dried away and leave the bodies as whole as if they were still alive and in good health, lacking only the power of speech, as the saying runs. I am led to this supposition by observing that the pemmican the Indians make in all the cold countries is produced simply by placing the meat in the open air until it has lost all its moisture. No salt or other preservative is used, and once dried it is kept as long as desired. This was the method for preparing all the Indians' meat supplies for time of war.

I remember having touched one of the fingers of Huayna Capac, which seemed like that of a wooden statue, it was so hard and stiff. The bodies weighed so little that any Indian could carry them in his arms or his back from house to house, wherever gentlemen asked to see them. They were carried wrapped in white sheets, and the Indians knelt in the streets and squares and bowed with tears and groans as they passed. Many Spaniards took off their caps, since they were royal bodies, and the Indians were more grateful than they could express for this attention. . . .

Chapter Five
The Organization and Festivals of the Incas

The Royal Houses

[6:1] The construction and adornment of the royal palaces of the Inca kings of Peru were no less in grandeur, majesty, and splendor than all the other magnificent things they had for their service. In certain points, as the reader will note, their palaces surpassed those of all the kings and emperors that have ever existed, according to our present information. In the first place, the buildings of their palaces, temples, gardens, and baths were extraordinarily even: they were of beautifully cut masonry, and each stone was so perfectly fitted to its neighbors that there was no space for mortar. . . . It is true that mortar was used, and it was made of a red clay which they call in their own language *llancac allpa*, "sticky clay," which was made into a paste. No trace of this mortar remained between the stones, and the Spaniards therefore state that they worked without mortar. Other writers assert that they used lime; but this is an error, for the Peruvian Indians never learnt the manufacture of lime or plaster, or tiles or bricks.

In many of the royal palaces and temples of the Sun they poured in molten lead and silver and gold for mortar. . . . These substances were used to add majesty to the buildings, which was the chief cause of their total destruction: as these metals were found in some of them, they were all pulled down by seekers for gold and silver, though the buildings themselves were so finely constructed of such solid stone that they would have lasted for centuries if they had been left. . . . The temples of the Sun and the royal apartments, wherever they existed, were lined with plates of gold, and many gold and silver figures copied from life—of men and women, birds of the air and waterfowl, and wild animals such as tigers, bears, lions, foxes, hounds, mountain cats, deer, guanacos and vicunas, and domestic sheep— were placed round the walls in spaces and niches which were left for the purpose as the work proceeded. . . .

They imitated herbs and such plants as grow on buildings and placed them on the walls so that they seemed to have grown on the spot. They also scattered over the walls lizards, butterflies, mice, and snakes, large and small, which seemed to be running up and down. The Inca himself usually sat on a seat of solid gold called *tiana*. It was a *tercia* in height and without arms or back, but with the seat rather hollowed out. It was placed on a great square platform of gold. All the vessels for service in the palace, both

42

tableware and dispensary and kitchen utensils, were of gold and silver. Similar pieces were kept in all the storehouses for the king's use when he was traveling: he did not therefore take his plate with him but every house on the road and in the various provinces was stocked with everything necessary for the Inca's use, whether he was accompanying his army or making a progress through the provinces. Therefore in the royal palaces also were baskets and bins, which the Indians call *pirua,* made of gold and silver: they were not intended for the storage of grain but merely to add grandeur and majesty to the house and its owner. . . .

How the Kings Were Buried

[6:5] The obsequies for the Inca kings were extremely solemn and lengthy. The dead body was embalmed, though it is not known how this was done. The corpses remained so fresh that they seemed to be still alive, as we had occasion to mention in the case of the five bodies of Incas which were discovered in 1559. All their insides were buried in the temple they had in the village of Tampu, less than five leagues from the city of Cusco down the river Yucay. . . .

When the Inca or one of the leading chiefs died, his closest servants and favorite wives killed themselves and [or] allowed themselves to be buried alive, saying that they wished to serve their king and master in the other life—as we have already explained, they held in their pagan religion that this life was followed by another similar to it, corporeal and not spiritual.[33] They either offered themselves for slaughter or died by their own hand, moved by their love for their masters. Some historians say that they were killed so as to be interred with their masters or husbands, but this is false: it would have been considered scandalous tyranny and inhumanity if, for the purpose of sending them with their masters, orders had been given to

---

[33] There is a great deal of controversy about the nature of Inca (and Andean) religion. Garcilaso presents the Incas as natural philosophers who were Christian in spirit, while still unaware of what Christians regarded as the ultimate truth of Christianity. Most of his contemporaries, as well as current scholars, do not share his convictions. As Frank Salomon has pointed out in his introduction to *The Huarochirí Manuscript: A Testament of Ancient and Colonial Andean Religion* (Austin: University of Texas Press, 1991), the only records that we have of Andean belief systems date from several decades after the Spanish invasion, which was accompanied by intense efforts to convert the Indians to Christianity, and it is more than likely that native beliefs had already begun to absorb at least some of the elements of the religion of their new overlords. In short, probably the only thing that we can say for certain about the nature of Inca religion is that it will continue to provoke debate for those interested in religion and its importance to human societies.

kill those who were hated by the latter. The truth is that they themselves volunteered to die, and often in such numbers that their superiors had to intervene saying that that was enough for the present and the rest would, as they gradually came to die, have the opportunity of going to serve their masters. . . .

Posts and Relays, and the Messages They Carried

[6:7] *Chasqui* was the name given to the runners placed along the roads for the purpose of carrying the king's orders rapidly and bringing news and reports of importance from his domains and provinces, far and near. For this purpose, they had four or six young and athletic Indians stationed at each quarter of a league in two huts built to shelter them from inclement weather. They took turns to carry messages, first those in one hut, then those in the other. Some watched the road in one direction and others in the opposite direction, so as to see the messenger before he arrived and be ready to take the message without loss of time. For this reason the huts were always built at high points, and in such positions that each was within sight of the next. The distance apart was a quarter of a league, which they said was how far an Indian could run at speed and in breath, without being tired.

They were called *chasqui,* "to exchange," or "to give and take," it is all one. This was because they exchanged, gave, and took from one another the messages they bore. They were not *cacha,* "a messenger," as this name was used for an ambassador or envoy who personally goes from one prince to another or from lord to vassal. The message carried by the *chasquis* was a verbal one, since the Peruvian Indians could not write. The words were few, plain, and succinct, so that they should not be confused or be so numerous as to be forgotten. When the approaching messenger came within view of the hut, he used to shout, so that his relay could prepare to leave, just as a mailpost plays its horn so that the posthorses shall be ready. On coming within earshot, the message was transmitted and repeated three or four times until the relay was sure of it: if he did not understand it, he would wait for the other to come up with him and deliver it to him formally. In this way it was transmitted from one runner to another until it reached its destination.

Other messages were carried not orally, but written down, so to speak, though, as we have said, they had no letters. These were knots in different threads of various colors, which were placed in order, though not always in the same order: sometimes one color came before another, and on other occasions they were reversed. This type of communication was a system of cyphers by which the Inca and his governors agreed on what was to be done, and the knots and colors of the threads implied the number of men, arms, or clothes or supplies or whatever it was that had to be made or sent or prepared. The Indians called these knotted threads *quipu,* "to knot, a knot," used as both verb and noun, and they were used for their accounts. Elsewhere, in a separate chapter,[34] we shall describe what they were like and how they were used. If there was a rush of messages, they added more runners, and would place ten or twelve *chasquis* at each post. They also had another way of sending messages, by passing on smoke signals by day or flames at night. For this purpose the *chasquis* always kept fire and faggots prepared, and kept permanent watch by night and day in turns, so that they were always ready for any contingency. This method of sending messages by fires was reserved for any rising or revolt in any great province or kingdom, so that the Inca would know about it within two or three hours at most, even though it would be five or six hundred leagues away from the capital, and could take the necessary steps even before he received tidings about the exact province where the rising had occurred. Such were the duties of the *chasquis* and the messages they carried.

They Counted by Threads and Knots

[6:7] *Quipu* means "to knot" and "knot" and is also used for reckoning, since the knots were applied to everything. The Indians made threads of various colors, some were of a single hue, others of two, others of three or more, for single or mixed colors all had separate significances. The threads were closely twisted with three or four strands, as thick as an iron spindle and about three quarters of a vara in length. They were threaded in order on a longer string like a fringe. The colors showed what subject the thread was about, such as yellow for gold, white for silver, and red for warriors.

Objects that had no special colors were arranged in order, beginning with the most important and proceeding to the least, each after its kind, as cereals and vegetables. For illustration let us arrange the plants that grow in Spain: first wheat, then barley, then chickpeas, beans, millet, etcetera. Similarly in dealing with arms, they placed first those they considered noblest, such as spears, then darts, bows and arrows, clubs and axes, slings, and the other weapons they possessed. If they referred to their subjects, they recorded first the inhabitants of each village and then those of each province combined: on the first thread they would enumerate the old people of sixty or more, on the second men in their maturity of fifty upwards, the third stood for those of forty, and so on in groups of ten years, down to babes and sucklings. Women were counted similarly by age groups.

---

[34] The following selection [6:7] explains the use of the *quipu.*

Some of these strings had finer threads of the same color attached, serving as offshoots or exceptions from the general rules. For instance the finer thread on the string referring to men or women of a certain age, who were assumed to be married, would mean the number of widows or widowers of that age in a given year, for all their records were annual, and they never referred to more than a single year.

The knots were arranged in order of units, ten, hundreds, thousands, tens of thousands, and seldom if ever passed a hundred thousand, since as each village kept its own records, and each capital the records of its districts, the numbers never in either case went beyond a hundred thousand, though below that figure they made many calculations. If they had had to count hundreds of thousands, they would have done so, since their language has words for all possible numbers known in arithmetic. But as they had no cause to use larger numbers, they did not go beyond tens of thousands. These numbers were reckoned by means of knots in the threads, each number being divided from the next. But the knots representing each number were made in a group together, on a loop, like the knots found in the cord of our blessed patriarch St. Francis: this was not difficult to do, as there were never more than nine, seeing that units, tens, etcetera, never exceed nine.

The greatest number, say tens of thousands, was knotted at the upper end of the threads, the thousands lower down, and so on down to units. The knots for each number on each thread were exactly alike, precisely as a good accountant set his figures to make a long addition. The knots or *quipus* were in the charge of special Indians called *quipucamayu,* meaning "one who has charge of the accounts," and although in those days there was little difference between good and bad among the Indians, since they were so well governed and had so little harm in them that they might all be described as good, nevertheless for these and similar duties they picked the best and such as had given longest proof of their aptitude. Offices were never obtained by favor, for among these Indians appointments were always made by merit and never out of favoritism. Nor were offices sold or leased, for as they had no money they could not lease, or buy, or sell. They did exchange some things, notably foodstuffs, but that was all, and there was no sale of clothing, houses, or land.

Although the *quipucamayus* were as accurate and honest as we have said, their number in each village was in proportion to its population, and however small, it had at least four and so upwards to twenty or thirty. They all kept the same records, and although one accountant or scribe was all that would have been necessary to keep them, the Incas preferred to have plenty in each village and for each sort of calculation, so as to avoid faults that might occur if there were few, saying that if there were a number of them, they would either all be at fault or none of them.

What They Recorded; Their Histories

[6:9] These men recorded on their knots all the tribute brought annually to the Inca, specifying everything by kind, species, and quality. They recorded the number of men who went to the wars, how many died in them, and how many were born and died every year, month by month. In short they may be said to have recorded on their knots everything that could be counted, even mentioning battles and fights, all the embassies that had come to visit the Inca, and all the speeches and arguments the king had uttered. But the purpose of the embassies or the contents of the speeches, or any other descriptive matter could not be recorded on the knots, consisting as it did of continuous spoken or written prose, which cannot be expressed by means of knots, since these can give only numbers and not words. To supply this want they used signs that indicated historical events or facts or the existence of any embassy, speech, or discussion in time of peace or war. Such speeches were preserved by the *quipucamayus* by memory in a summarized form of a few words: they were committed to memory and taught by tradition to their successors and descendants from father to son. This was especially practiced in the villages or provinces where the event in question had occurred: there naturally such traditions were preserved better than elsewhere, because the natives would treasure them. Another method too was used for keeping alive in the memory of the people their deeds and the embassies they sent to the Inca and the replies he gave them. The *amautas* who were their philosophers and sages took the trouble to turn them into stories, no longer than fables, suitable for telling to children, young people, and the rustics of the countryside: they were thus passed from hand to hand and age to age, and preserved in the memories of all. Their stories were also recounted in the form of fables of an allegorical nature, some of which we have mentioned, while others will be referred to later.[35] Similarly the *harauicus,* who were their poets, wrote short, compressed poems, embracing a history, or an embassy, or the king's reply. In short, everything that could not be recorded on the knots was included in these poems, which were sung at their triumphs and on the occasion of their greater festivals, and recited to the young Incas when they were armed knights. Thus they remembered their history. But as experience has shown, all these were perishable expedients, for it is letters that perpetuate the memory of events. But as the Incas had no knowledge of writing, they had to use what devices they could, and treating their knots as

---

[35] The stories and fables mentioned by Garcilaso are not included in this edition; they can be found in Livermore's complete translation. See, for example, Harold Livermore, *Royal Commentaries,* book 1, ch. 18 and book 2, ch. 27.

letters, they chose historians and accountants, called *quipucamayus,* ("those who have charge of the knots") to write down and preserve the tradition of their deeds by means of the knots, strings, and colored threads, using their stories and poems as an aid. This was the method of writing the Incas employed in their republic. . . .

The Principal Feast of the Sun

[6:20] The name *Raimi* corresponds to our greater festivals such as Easter or Christmas. Of the four festivals celebrated by the Inca kings in the city of Cusco, which was their home, the most solemn was that held in honor of the Sun in the month of June and called Intip Raimi, meaning "the solemn feast of the Sun." It was usually simply called *Raimi,* with no difference of meaning, and if the word was applied to other festivals it was by extension from this, to which the name Raimi properly belonged. It took place after the June solstice.

The festival was dedicated to the Sun in recognition of their worship of it as the sole, supreme, and universal god, who created and sustained everything in the earth with his light and virtue. Out of regard for the fact that the Sun was the natural father of the first Inca Manco Capac and of the Coya Mama Ocllo Huaco and of all the kings and their children and descendants sent down to earth for the universal benefit of mankind, the feast was a very solemn one. It was attended by all the military leaders who were retired or not actually engaged on a campaign and by all the *curacas,* the lords of vassals, of the whole empire. They came not because they were obliged to appear, but because they were glad to attend the observation of so great a feast, which, as it included the worship of their god the Sun, and the veneration of their king the Inca, was attended by absolutely everyone. When the *curacas* could not be present because they were prevented by old age, ill health, or serious business in the royal service, or because of the great distance, they used to send their sons and brothers, escorted by the most noble members of their people, so that they might represent them at the festival. The Inca was present in person, provided he was not prevented by some necessary war or visit to his provinces.

The king performed the first rites as high priest: although there was always a high priest of the blood royal (since he must be a brother or uncle of the Inca of legitimate descent on both sides), nevertheless as this festival was dedicated especially to the Sun, the ceremonies were performed by the king himself, as the first-born child of the Sun and therefore primarily and principally obliged to solemnize the occasion.

The chiefs appeared in their best attire and adornments, some wearing plates of silver and gold on their garments and wreaths of the same on their heads, round their headdresses. Others came exactly as Hercules is depicted, clad in a lion's skin, with the Indian's head inside the lion's, since they boasted of their descent from a lion. Still others appeared in the guise in which angels are depicted, with the great wings of a bird called the *cuntur.* These are black and white, and so large that specimens have been killed by the Spaniards with a wingspan of fourteen or fifteen feet. The Indians in question pretended to originate and descend from a *cuntur.*

Others, notably the Yuncas, came in masks devised with the most repulsive figures imaginable. They made their entry into the festivals grimacing and striking attitudes like fools, madmen, or simpletons, and they carried suitable instruments in their hands, such as ill-devised flutes or tambourines and pieces of skin of which they availed themselves for their follies. Other chiefs brought various other devices. Each tribe carried the weapons it used in time of war, some bows and arrows, other lances, darts, bolts, clubs, slings, and short single-handed axes or long double-handed ones. They carried representations of the deeds they had performed in the service of the Sun and of the Incas, carrying great drums and trumpets, and brought a great many performers to play them. In short each tribe came as well attired and attended as possible, each seeking to outshine his neighbors and countrymen, or the whole assembly, if possible.

They generally prepared themselves for the Raimi of the Sun by observing a strict fast, eating nothing for three days but a little raw white maize, a few herbs called *chúcam,* and some plain water. During the whole time they lit no fires in the city and refrained from sleeping with their wives.

After the fast, the night before the feast, the Inca priests appointed to attend to the sacrifice had the sheep and lambs made ready, as well as the other offerings of food and drink that were to be presented to the Sun. When these arrangements were made it was known what people had come to the feast, since all the tribes had to share in the offerings, not only the *curacas* and ambassadors, but also all their kinsmen, vassals, and servants.

That night the women of the Sun busied themselves with the preparation of enormous quantities of a maizen dough called *çancu,* of which they made little round loaves the size of an ordinary apple, and it is to be noted that the Indians never ate their corn kneaded and made into loaves except at this festival and another called Citua: even so they did not eat these loaves during the whole meal, but only a few mouthfuls at the beginning. Their usual meal in place of bread is the *sara* roasted or cooked in the grain.

The flour for this bread, and especially that which was to be eaten by the Inca and the members of the royal family, was ground and kneaded by the chosen virgins, the wives of the Sun, who also prepared the rest of the food for the feast. The banquet seemed indeed rather a gift from the Sun to his children than from the children to the Sun, and for that reason the virgins prepared it, as wives of the Sun.

An infinite number of other women appointed for the purpose kneaded the bread and prepared the meal for the rest of the people. The bread, though it was for the community, was compounded with care and attention that at least the flour should be prepared by damsels; for this bread was regarded as something sacred and not allowed to be eaten during the year, but only at this festivity, which was their feast of feasts.

[6:21] Everything being prepared, the following day, which was that of the festival, the Inca went out at daybreak accompanied by his whole kin. They departed in due order, each according to his age and rank, to the main square of the city called Haucaipata. There they waited for the sun to rise and stood with bare feet, attentively gazing toward the east. When the Sun began to appear, they all squatted (which among the Indians is as though they were to kneel) to worship it. This they did by raising their arms and placing their hands beside their faces, kissing the air, which is the same as kissing one's hand or the garment of a prince as a mark of respect in Spain. They worshipped the Sun with great affection and acknowledgment that he was their god and natural father.

The *curacas* who were not of the royal blood went to another square next to the main one, called Cusipata,[36] where they worshipped the Sun in the same way as the Incas. Then the king stood up, the rest remaining squatting, and he took two great golden vessels which they called *aquilla*, full of the beverage they drink. He performed this rite in the name of his father, the Sun, as his firstborn, and invited him to drink with the vessel in his right hand. This the Sun was supposed to do, and the Inca invited all his kinsmen to drink too. This custom of inviting one another to drink was the greatest and most usual demonstration of condescension on the part of the superior toward his inferior, and of the friendship of friends for one another. After the invitation to drink, the Inca poured the contents of the vessel in his right hand, which was dedicated to the Sun, into a gold basin, and from the basin it flowed along a beautifully made stonework channel which ran from the square to the house of the Sun. It was thus as if the Sun had drunk the liquid. From the vessel in his left hand the Inca swallowed a draught, which was his portion, and then shared what was left among the other Incas, giving each of them a little in a small bowl of silver or gold which was ready to receive it. At intervals the vessel the Inca held was replenished, so that the first liquid which had been sanctified by the hands of the Sun or of the Inca, or both of them, should transmit its virtue to

---

[36] On the maps of Cusco, this square is identified as Cusipata.

each of the recipients. All the members of the royal blood drank a draught of the beverage. The rest of the *curacas* in the other square drank of the same brew prepared by the women of the Sun, but not of the part that was sanctified, which was reserved for the Incas.

After this ceremony, which was a sort of foretaste of what was to be drunk later, they all went in order to the house of the Sun, and two hundred steps before they reached it they removed their shoes, with the exception of the king who only took them off at the very door of the temple. The Inca and members of the blood went in like natural children and worshipped the image of the Sun. The *curacas,* being unworthy of entering the high place, since they were not children of the Sun, stayed outside in a large square which today stands before the temple gate.

The Inca offered the vessels of gold used for the ceremony with his own hands. The remaining Incas gave their vessels to the Inca priests appointed and dedicated to the service of the Sun: those who were not priests, even though they were of the Sun's blood, were seculars and not permitted to perform the functions of priests. After offering up the vessels of the Incas, the priests went outside to collect the *curacas'* vessels. The *curacas* approached in order of seniority according to the period when their people had been incorporated in the empire, and they handed over their vessels and other objects of gold and silver which they had brought from their own provinces to present to the Sun, such as sheep, lambs, lizards, toads, serpents, foxes, tigers, lions, and a great variety of birds. In short they brought natural models in gold and silver of whatever was found most abundantly in their provinces, though each object appeared only in small quantities.

After the offering, they returned in order to their two squares. Then came the Inca priests with a great number of lambs, barren ewes, and rams of all colors, for the Peruvian sheep[37] is found in all colors, like horses in Spain. All the sheep belonged to the Sun. They would take a black lamb, this being the color these Indians preferred above all others for their sacrifices, regarding it as having greater divinity. Their argument was that the black animal was black all over, while the white, though the whole of the rest of its body might be white, always had a black snout, which they held to be a defect, so that the white was always regarded as inferior to black. For this reason the kings usually dressed in black: when in mourning, they wore the natural grey-brown color of the wool.

The first sacrifice of the black lamb was intended to observe the auguries and omens of the festival. For in everything they did of importance, either

---

[37] The Spaniards referred to llamas as "Peruvian sheep," or "sheep of the land."

for peace or war, they almost always sacrificed a lamb so as to inspect its heart and lungs and discover if it was acceptable to the Sun; that is, whether the expedition would be successful or otherwise, or whether the harvest that year would be good or bad. For some purposes they used a lamb for their auguries, for others a sheep, for others a sterile ewe, and whenever we say an ewe we mean a sterile one, for those capable of bearing were never killed and not even used for eating until they were past breeding.

They took the sheep or lamb and placed it with its head facing the east. Its feet were not tied, but it was held by three or four Indians. While still alive, its left side was opened, and by inserting the hand they drew forth the heart, lungs, and entrails, which were plucked forth with the hand and not cut: the whole must come out together from the throat downwards. . . . [6:22] They regarded it as a most happy omen if the lungs came out still quivering, before they had finished dying, as they put it, and if they obtained this good omen, they ignored the rest, even though they might be bad. They said that the excellence of this lucky omen would overcome the ill effects of all bad omens. Taking out the entrails, they inflated them by blowing and held the air by tying up the main gut or nipping it with their fingers: they then inspected the passages whereby the air enters the lungs and the little veins along them to see if they were swollen or contained little air: the more swollen they were, the happier was the augury. . . .

How the Incas Were Armed Knights

[6:24] The word *huaracu* occurs in the general language of Peru and is equivalent to arming a knight in Spanish,[38] for it was applied to the granting of the tokens of manhood to lads of the royal blood, which qualified them to go to war and to set up house. Until they received these insignia of manhood they were not allowed to do either of these things, being, as the books of chivalry would say, mere squires who were not entitled to bear arms. In order to receive these insignia, which we shall describe later,[39] the youths who were candidates underwent a very severe initiation and were tested in all the hardships and emergencies that might occur in war, whether its fortunes were prosperous or adverse. . . .

In order to explain this the better, we had best describe these solemn rites stage by stage: certainly for a barbarous race, these Indians had some

---

[38] Garcilaso refers here to the ceremony in which a young man is made a knight in Europe.

[39] The insignia were thick gold earplugs, woven wool sandals, and a loincloth. The young men about to be formally recognized as warriors also had their heads bedecked with flowers and leaves.

remarkably civilized practices in military matters. The occasion was one of great rejoicing among the common people and of considerable honor and splendor among the Incas, whether old or young, already approved in the ordeal or still untested. For the honor obtained by the novices in passing the test, or the disgrace in failing it, was shared by their whole kin, and as the Incas formed a single family, consisting mainly of those of the royal blood of legitimate descent, the good fortune or misfortune of each of them affected all the rest, though especially those most nearly related.

More or less every year or every other year, according to circumstances, the young Incas (and it must be emphasized that we are referring to them and not to the rest, even to the sons of great lords) underwent the military ordeal. They had to be over sixteen years of age, and were assembled in a building built for the ordeal in the quarter called Collcampata: I myself saw it while it was still standing and witnessed some of the ceremonies, though they could only be described as shadows of the past, as regards splendor and completeness. The old Incas, experienced in affairs of peace and war, who acted as masters of the novices, repaired to the house to examine them in the points we shall mention and others that are now forgotten. The candidates were required to observe a very strict fast for six days, receiving only a handful of raw *sara* (their corn) apiece and a jug of plain water, without anything else, either salt or *uchu* (which in Spain is called Indian peppers), a condiment that flavors and enriches the poorest and meanest meal, even if it is only a dish or herbs: for this reason the novices were deprived of it.

Such a rigorous fast was not usually permitted for more than three days, but this period was doubled for the initiates undergoing their ordeal, in order to show if they were men enough to suffer any hunger or thirst to which they might be exposed in time of war. The fathers, brothers, and other close relatives of the candidate underwent a less rigorous, but none the less strictly observed, fast, praying to their father the Sun to strengthen and encourage the youths so that they might come through the ordeal with honor. Anyone who showed weakness or distress or asked for more food was failed and eliminated from the test. After the fast they were allowed some victuals to restore their strength and then tried for bodily agility. As a test they were made to run from the hill called Huanacauri, which they regard as sacred, to the fortress of the city, which must be a distance of nearly a league and a half. At the fortress a pennant or banner was set up as a finishing post, and whoever reached it first was elected captain over the rest. Those who arrived second, third, fourth, and down to the tenth fastest were also held in great honor, while those who flagged or fainted on the course were disgraced and eliminated. Their parents and relatives exhorted them as they ran, urging upon them the honor of victory and shame of failure, and representing that they would do better to burst than swoon by the wayside.

The next day they were divided into two equal bands. One group was bidden to remain in the fortress, while the other sallied forth, and they were required to fight one against the other, the second group to conquer the fort and the first defending it. After fighting thus for the whole day, they changed sides on the morrow, the defenders becoming the attackers so that they could all display their agility and skill in attacking or defending strongholds. In such struggles the weapons were blunted so that they were less formidable than in real warfare; nevertheless there were severe casualties which were sometimes fatal, for the will to win excited them to the point of killing one another. . . .

[6:26] Each day one of the captains and overseers of these rites made them an address, reminding them of their descent from the Sun; of the deeds done in peace and war by past kings and other famous men of the royal stock; of the courage and spirit they ought to show in wars to extend the empire; of patience and endurance under hardship as a proof of generosity and magnanimity; of clemency, pity, and mildness toward their subjects and the poor; of rectitude in the administration of justice; of the duty to prevent anyone from being wronged; and of liberality and openhandedness toward everyone, as befitted children of the Sun. In short, they were taught all aspects of moral philosophy as they knew it, having regard to their divine origin and descent from heaven. They were required to sleep on the bare ground, eat little and badly, go barefooted, and do everything else likely to make them good soldiers.

The firstborn son of the Inca who was the legitimate heir to the throne was also subjected to this ordeal, when he reached the proper age. It is noteworthy that in all these exercises he was tested with the same strictness as the rest, and was not exempted from any trial on account of his princely rank, except the contest for the pennant awarded to the fleetest of foot in the race for the captaincy: this was granted to him as part of his birthright. In all other exercises, fasting, military discipline, the making of weapons and shoes, sleeping on the ground, eating little, and going barefoot, the prince enjoyed no privileges of any sort, but was treated rather more harshly than they on the ground that, as he was to be king, it was only right that he should rise above the rest in anything he undertook, as he did in the greatness of his rank: if the royal person underwent experiences similar to his subjects', it would be unseemly that he should emerge below them. Both in prosperity and in adversity he must show his superiority, in spirit and in deed, and especially in military matters.

They would say that these excellences constituted his right to rule, much more than the fact that he was his father's eldest son. They would also say that it was highly necessary that kings and princes should experience the toils of war so as to be able to assess the merits of those who served them in the field and to reward them properly. During the whole period of the ordeal, which lasted from one new moon to the next, the prince went about clad in the poorest and vilest dress imaginable, consisting of wretched tatters, in which he appeared in public whenever necessary. It was said that this was so that in the future, when he became a mighty king, he should not scorn the poor, but remember that he had been one of them and had worn their uniform. He would thus be well disposed to them and become charitable, so as to be worthy of the title *Huacchacúyac,* which they conferred on their kings, meaning "the lover and benefactor of the poor." After the examination, the candidates were qualified to wear, and considered worthy of, the insignia of the Incas. On their being declared true Incas and children of the Sun, their mothers and sisters came and shod them with *usutas* of raw *esparto*[40] in witness of the fact that they had passed through the sharp ordeal of the military exercises.

Pachacútec conquers the Yuncas, Pachacámac, Rímac, Cháncay, and Barranca (the central coast) and then turns to consolidating his conquests and organizing the empire, before turning his attention to the large societies of the northern coast and highlands.

They Go to Conquer King Chimu

[6:32] Inca Pachacútec spent six years in the employments we have mentioned. After this, finding his realms prosperous and peaceful, he had an army of thirty thousand warriors made ready to conquer the valleys of the coast, as far as the district of Cajamarca, which constituted the frontier of the empire on the road to the sierra.

When the army was ready, he appointed six of the most experienced Incas as colonels or commanders and advisers to his son, Prince Inca Yupanqui. The latter was made general for the next conquest, for, as a pupil of such a great master and a soldier under so great a captain as his uncle Capac Yupanqui, he had emerged so experienced in the art of war that any undertaking, however great, could be entrusted to him. The Inca's brother, whom he called "my right arm" on account of his great deeds, was to remain at court and rest from his past exertions. In reward for them and in witness of his own royal qualities, the Inca nominated him his lieutenant, second to him in peace and war, with absolute power and authority throughout the empire.

When the army was made ready, the prince Inca Yupanqui marched with the first regiment toward the sierra until he reached the province of

---

[40] *Esparto* is twisted feather grass or hemp.

Yauyu, which is in the neighborhood of the city of Lima. There he awaited the arrival of the whole army, and when it was gathered together he advanced to Rimac, where the speaking oracle was. According to the Indians, this prince Inca Yupanqui had the honor and fame of being the first of the Inca kings to set eyes on the Southern Sea and of being the one who conquered the most provinces on that coast, as we shall see in the account of his life.[41] The *curacas* of Pachacámac, Cuismancu, and of Runahuánac, called Chuquimancu, came out with their warriors to receive the prince and serve under him in the campaign. The prince thanked them for their zeal, and conferred great favors and rewards upon them. From the valley of Rímac he went to visit the temple of Pachacámac, which he entered without prayers or sacrifices other than the mental adoration the Indians accorded Pachacámac, as we have said.[42] He then visited the temple of the Sun, where there were many sacrifices and great offerings of gold and silver. He likewise visited the idol Rímac to please the Yuncas, and in order to comply with the recent treaty, bade the priests offer sacrifices to the idol and consult it about the success of the present campaign. Having heard that it would prosper, he advanced as far as the valley the Indians call Huancu and the Spaniards La Barranca, whence he dispatched the usual messages offering peace or war to a great chief called Chimu, who was lord of the valleys beyond La Barranca, as far as the city called Trujillo. There are five principal [provinces], named Paramunca, Huallmi, Santa, Huanapu, and Chimu (which is where Trujillo now is). All five are very beautiful valleys, very fertile and thickly populated, and the chief *curaca* was called the mighty Chimu, from the name of the province where his capital was. He was treated as a king and feared by all those whose territories marched[43] with his to the east, north, and south, for to the west lies the ocean.

On receiving the Inca's summons, the mighty Chimu replied that he was ready to die, weapons in hand, in defense of his country, laws, and customs, and that he wanted no new gods: let the Inca take good note of this reply, for he would get no other. When he had received this intimation from Chimu, Inca Yupanqui advanced to the valley of Parmunca, where the enemy was awaiting him. The latter appeared with a large company of skirmishers to try the strength of the Incas. The strife continued for a long time, the natives endeavoring to defend the entrance to their valley. But

---

[41] The account of Inca Yupanqui's life is not included in this edition; see the complete Livermore translation of the *Royal Commentaries,* book 7, ch. 13.

[42] Garcilaso's description of proper behavior when visiting the temple of Pachacámac is not included in this edition; see the complete Livermore translation of the *Royal Commentaries,* book 2, ch. 2.

[43] "march," in this usage, means "bordered on."

they could not prevent the Incas from forcing an entry and gaining a foothold, though only at the cost of many dead and wounded on both sides. The prince, on seeing the resistance of the Yuncas, wished to prevent them from taking courage at the smallness of his force, and sent messengers to his father the Inca to report on what had happened and beg him to furnish twenty thousand warriors, not as a relief for his army as on previous campaigns, but to swell his forces and so shorten the war. He did not wish to give so much time to vanquishing this enemy as he had in the case of his former foes, because the Yuncas had shown themselves so arrogant.

Having dispatched these messages, the Inca intensified the war on all sides. The two *curacas* of Pachacámac and Runahuánac proved very hostile to the mighty Chimu, since in the past, in pre-Inca times, they had had bitter conflicts with him about boundaries and grazing rights and the enslavement of members of those tribes, whom he had subjugated. Now with the powerful aid of the Inca, they wanted revenge for past slights and defeats, and Chimu resented this above anything else and did all he could for his own defense.

The war among the Yuncas was very bloody: because of their ancient enmity, those serving the Incas strove more on their behalf than any other tribe, so that the whole valley of Parmunca was gained in a few days and its natives driven out to Huallmi, where also there were battles and skirmishes, but it could not be defended either, and the natives had to fall back on the valley called Santa, which was then the most beautiful on the whole coast, though today it is almost deserted, since the inhabitants have been destroyed, as in all the other valleys.

The people of Santa proved more warlike than those of Huallmi and Parmunca. They came out to defend their land, fought with valor and energy wherever an opportunity offered, resisted the full force of their enemies for many days without yielding them the advantage, and performed deeds of such courage that they won fame and honor from their very enemies. These efforts increased the hopes of their chief, the great Chimu, who was buoyed up by the bravery of his people and by certain ideas he put about, to the effect that the prince was a delicate and luxury-loving man who would soon tire of the hardships of war and be drawn back to the pleasures of his capital by amorous desires, while all his warriors would soon want to return to their homes and children: even if they did not, they would either be driven away by the heat or destroyed by it if they stayed. In these vain hopes the arrogant Chimu obstinately persisted in pursuing the war, without receiving or listening to the messengers the Incas sent him from time to time. On the contrary, in order to make patent his contumaciousness, he called up the inhabitants of the other valleys under his sway, and as they arrived the war grew daily in intensity. There were many dead and wounded on both sides. Each tried to force the victory, and the war was the bitterest so far waged by the Incas.

Nevertheless, the captains and leaders of Chimu, when they considered the state of affairs dispassionately, would have liked their chief to embrace the offers of peace and friendship made by the Inca, whose power they thought must sooner or later prove irresistible. However, in order to meet their lord's wishes, they suffered the toils of war with patience and energy, even witnessing the enslavement of their relatives, children, and wives, but not daring to tell their ruler what they felt.

How the Great Chimu Surrendered

[6:33] While the war was raging so bitterly and fiercely, the twenty thousand reinforcements the prince had requested arrived. With them he reinforced his army and checked the overweening arrogance of Chimu, which was already turning to melancholy and sadness as he saw his fond hopes frustrated. On the one hand, the power of the Incas was seen to be doubled, when it appeared to be faltering; on the other, Chimu sensed the discouragement of his own forces on seeing themselves faced by a new hostile army. For days past they had sustained the war more to comply with their master's obduracy than out of any hopes they might have entertained of resisting the Inca. Now that the latter's forces were strengthened, they at once faltered, and Chimu's leading kinsmen approached him and asked that his obstinacy should not continue until his men were utterly destroyed, but that he should consider that now was the time to accept the Inca's offers, if only to prevent his former rivals and enemies from battening on the spoils they daily took and from carrying off their wives and children as slaves. This state of affairs should be remedied without delay, before the havoc grew any greater, and before the prince shut the doors of his clemency and mercy against their obstinate resistance and visited them with fire and slaughter.

This speech, uttered in tones of reproach and menace rather than in those of good counsel and advice, made the brave Chimu feel that all was lost. He knew not where to seek remedy nor of whom to ask aid, for his neighbors, offended by his past arrogance and pride, had no cause to help him. His own men were dispirited, and the enemy was strong. Thus beset on all sides, he thought that he could accept the first advances of the Inca prince, but he would not ask for terms himself so as not to show lack of spirit or weakness. He therefore concealed his intention from his own people, but replied that he was not without hope and resources of resisting the Inca and, thanks to their courage, coming out of the war with fame and honor. Let them bestir themselves in defense of their country, for whose freedom and salvation they were obliged to die fighting: let them not show cowardice, for it was in the nature of warfare to be victorious one day and defeated the next. If some of their wives were carried off as slaves today, let them remember how many more they themselves had won from their enemies: he hoped he would soon set them free. Let them be of good cheer and show no weakness, for their enemies had shown none in the past and there was no call for them to do so now. Let them go in peace and be satisfied, for he thought more of his people's salvation than of his own.

With these tenuous hopes and feeble comfort, consisting more of words than facts, the great Chimu dismissed his friends. He was much afflicted to see them so despondent, but put on the best face he could muster, and sustained the war until he received the usual messages from the Inca offering forgiveness, peace, and friendship, as he had so many times before. On hearing this message, wishing to make a show of complete firmness, though in fact he had completely softened, he replied that he had no intention of accepting any terms, but that out of consideration for his people's salvation, he would consult them and do as they thought fit. He then summoned his captains and kinsmen and put the Inca's offer before them, bidding them consider well the interests of them all, for he was prepared to obey the Inca for their sakes, even though it was greatly against his will.

The captains were very glad to find their chief somewhat shifted from his former rigid obstinacy, and they therefore plucked up courage to tell him squarely that it was very proper to obey and acknowledge the overlordship of so mild and clement a prince as the Inca, who still offered them his friendship, though he had almost reduced them to surrender.

This resolute opinion, delivered rather with the boldness of free men than with the subservience of vassals, proved to the mighty Chimu that his rebellious resistance was in vain, and to show that it was over, he sent his ambassadors to prince Inca Yupanqui asking [them] to beg the Inca not to withhold the mercy and mildness that the children of the Sun had displayed in all four quarters of the world they had subdued. They had spared all those who, like him, had been blameworthy and contumacious: he acknowledged his fault and begged pardon, confiding in long experience of the clemency of all the ancestors of the Inca, and knowing that the Inca would not refuse it now since he so greatly prized his reputation as the lover and benefactor of the poor and sought the same forgiveness for all his friends, who were less guilty than he, since they had resisted the Inca because of the *curaca's* obstinacy rather than of their own free will.

The prince was greatly pleased with this embassy, which put an end to the conquest and avoided the bloodshed he had feared. He received the ambassadors very affably, had them rewarded, and told them to return to their chief and then bring him to hear the Inca's pardon from his own mouth, as well as receiving honors from the royal hands to his greater satisfaction.

The brave Chimu, his arrogance and pride now tamed, appeared before the prince with as much submission and humility, and groveled on the ground before him, worshipping him and repeating the same request as he had made through his ambassadors. The prince received him affectionately in order to relieve the grief he was evincing. He bade two of the captains raise him from the ground, and after hearing him, told him that all that was past was forgiven, and much more would have been forgiven too. The Inca had not come to deprive him of his estates and authority, but to improve his idolatrous religion, his laws, and customs. In confirmation of this, if Chimu feared to have lost his estates, he would award them to him as an honor and favor to be possessed in all security, provided that the idols representing fish and animals were cast down, and they worshipped the Sun and served his father the Inca.

Chimu, cheered by the courtesy and kindness shown him by the prince in this encouraging speech, worshipped him anew and replied saying that his greatest grief was in not having obeyed the words of such a lord as soon as he had heard them. He himself would deplore all his life the misdeeds for which the Inca had forgiven him: for the rest, he would carry out with great love and goodwill the Inca's commands touching both religion and customs.

Hereupon peace was established and Chimu did homage, while the Inca offered presents of garments to him and his nobles. The prince visited the valleys of the new domain and ordered them to be improved and adorned with royal buildings and great new channels for irrigating and extending the cultivable fields far beyond their previous limits; storehouses were built for the revenues of the Sun and of the Inca as well as for the use of the natives in years of want, all of which the Incas used to have made by ancient custom. In the valley of Parmunca in particular, the prince had a fort built as a trophy in memory of the victory he had won over King Chimu, a victory he greatly prized because the war had been so bitterly fought on both sides. The fort was built in this valley, because the war had begun there. It was a strong building of admirable construction, handsomely adorned with pictures and other royal curiosities. But the newcomers[44] have not respected any of this, or spared it from destruction. A few pieces still remain as survivors of the ignorance that caused them to be razed and as proof of their former greatness. . . .

---

[44] The newcomers to whom Garcilaso refers are the Spaniards who came to the Andes seeking wealth after the capture and ransom of Atahuallpa.

Chapter Six
Description of Cusco and the Conquests of Inca Yupanqui

The Heirs of Lords Were Brought up at Court; the Reasons for This

[7:2] The Inca kings also disposed that the heirs of lords of vassals should be brought up at court and reside there until they inherited their estates so that they should be well indoctrinated and accustomed to the mentality and ways of the Incas, holding friendly converse with them so that later, on account of this familiar intercourse, they would love them and serve them with real affection. They were called *mítmac,* "settlers." This was also done to ennoble and dignify the capital with the presence and company of so many heirs of kingdoms and chieftaincies as there were in the empire. This dispensation helped them to learn the general language[45] with greater pleasure and less toil and strain. As their servants and subjects took turns to wait on their masters in the capital, whenever they returned to their own countries they had learned something of the courtly tongue and were very proud to speak it among their friends, since it was the language of people they considered divine. This caused great competition among the rest to try to learn it, and those who knew a little sought to press forward with their study of it, conversing often and familiarly with the governors and officials of the royal treasury and judges who resided in their country. In this way they easily learned to speak the tongue of Cusco without the usual labor with teachers throughout almost the whole of the thirteen hundred leagues won by the Inca kings.

In addition to the purpose of adding luster to their court with the presence of so many princes, the Inca kings had another motive, that of assuring their kingdoms and provinces against risings and rebellions, for as the empire was so far-flung, there were many provinces four, five, or six hundred leagues away from the capital, including the largest and most warlike, such as the kingdoms of Quito and Chile and their neighbors. Because of their remoteness and of the ferocity of their inhabitants it was feared that they might revolt on some occasion and seek to throw off the imperial

---

[45] The "general language" to which Garcilaso refers is Quechua, used by the Incas as a *lingua franca* in their polyglot state, and spread later by the Spanish Catholic Church.

yoke; and although each one separately had not the means, they might concert together in a league of many provinces and attack the kingdom from all sides, gravely menacing the authority of the Incas. In order to assure themselves against all these and other troubles that occur in such vast empires they took the course of bidding all the heirs to reside at court, where they were carefully treated with every favor whether the Inca [was] present or not, each one receiving the attentions his merits, rank, and estate entitled him to. The princes frequently reported these general and special favors to their parents, sending them the garments and jewels the Inca gave them from his own wardrobe, objects which were of incalculable esteem among them. The Inca kings sought thus to oblige their vassals to be loyal to them out of gratitude, or if they should prove so ungrateful that they did not appreciate what was done for them, at least their evil desires might be checked by the knowledge that their sons and heirs were at the capital as hostages and gages of their own fidelity. . . .

A chapter of Blas Valera on the language of the Incas is inserted here by Garcilaso.

The Language of the Court

[7:3] . . . "There are some who think it would be wise to oblige all the Indians to learn the Spanish language, so as to spare the priests the vain labor of learning the Indian language. Anyone who hears this argument will realize that it arises more from weakness of spirit than from dullness of understanding. For if the only solution is for the Indians to learn Spanish, which is so difficult for them, why should they not learn the speech of their own capital which comes easily and is almost natural to them? On the contrary, if the Spaniards, who are sharp-witted and versed in learning, cannot, as they say, learn the general language of Cusco, how can they make the Indians, who are untutored and uninstructed in letters, learn Spanish? The truth is that even though there were a great many teachers ready to teach the Indians Spanish for nothing, the latter, being uninstructed—and especially the common people—would have such difficulty in learning that any priest who tried would learn to speak fluently in ten different Peruvian tongues before the Indians could talk Spanish. There is therefore no reason why we should impose two such heavy penalties on the Indians as to bid them forget their own tongue and learn another so as to save ourselves the small task of learning the speech of their court. It will suffice that they should be taught the Catholic faith in the general language of Cusco, which does not greatly differ from the remaining languages of the empire.

"The viceroys and other governors could easily put an end to the confusion of tongues that has arisen by adding to their duties that of seeing that the children of the language teachers appointed by the Incas should resume the teaching of the general language to the rest of the Indians as they did before. It is easy to learn, so much so that a priest I knew who both was learned in canon law, and piously desired the salvation of the Indians of the *repartimiento*[46] it was his duty to indoctrinate, carefully studied the general language for the purpose of teaching them, and repeatedly begged and importuned his Indians to learn it. To please him they studied so hard that in scarcely more than a year they could talk it as if it were their mother tongue, which indeed it became, and the priest learnt by experience how much more docile and ready to receive Christian doctrine they were in that language than in their own. Now if this good priest succeeded with average pains in attaining his object with the Indians, why should not the bishops and viceroys do as much? Indeed if all the Indians of Peru from Quito to the Chichas are ordered to learn the general language they will be governed and taught with the greatest of ease. And it is worthy of note that the Indians whom the Inca ruled with very few judges can now scarcely be governed by three hundred *corregidores*,[47] and then only ineffectively and with great difficulty. The main reason for this is the confusion of tongues, which prevents intercourse.

"Many who have tried to learn the general language of Peru bear witness to how quickly and easily it can be picked up, and I have known many priests who have become proficient in it with average pains. In Chuquiapu there was a theologian who, as a result of the reports of third persons, hated the general language so much that he would grow angry at the very mention of it, thinking that he could not possibly learn it because of the great difficulty he had heard attributed to it. It happened that before the Jesuit College was founded in that village, a Jesuit father chanced to arrive and stayed there several days to teach the Indians and preach to them in public in the general language. Our priest went to hear the sermon, attracted by the novelty, and seeing many passages of holy scripture explained in the Indian tongue and the Indians marveling and accepting the teaching as they listened, he felt some respect for the language.

"After the sermon he spoke to the Jesuit, saying: 'Is it possible that divine words, so sweet and mysterious, can be explained in so barbarous a tongue?'"

---

[46] A *repartimiento* was an administrative district, usually the area encompassed by an *encomienda*, or grant of authority over Indians awarded by the Spanish Crown for services, including conquest, by the recipient.

[47] A *corregidor* was a Spanish official appointed for a term of three to five years, whose duties included the collection of tribute from, and the administration of justice among, the Indians of a district or *repartimiento*.

"He was told that they could, and that if he would study the general language with care, he might do the same himself within four or five months. The priest, desiring to benefit the souls of the Indians, promised to learn it with all care and diligence, and after receiving some rules and advice from the Jesuit, worked so hard at it that six months later, he could hear the confessions of the Indians and preach to them, to his own immense delight and their great benefit." . . .

The Description of the Imperial City of Cusco

[7:8] Inca Capac was the founder of the city of Cusco, which the Spaniards honored with a longer title, though without removing its proper name. They called it the Great City of Cusco, head of the kingdoms and provinces of Peru. They also called it New Toledo, but this other name was soon forgotten, since it was quite inappropriate: Cusco is not girt by a river like Toledo, and does not resemble it in situation, for its population is centered on the slopes and folds of a high hill and stretches in all directions over a broad and spacious plain. It has long, wide streets and large squares, which is why the Spaniards in general, and royal scribes and notaries in public documents in particular, use the first title. For Cusco in relation to its empire was like Rome to the Roman empire, and the two can be compared with one another, for they resembled one another in their nobler aspects. First, and in chief, both were founded by their first kings. Secondly, they resembled one another in the many different tribes they conquered and added to their empires. Thirdly, they had many excellent laws applied to the good government of the two states. Fourthly, they both bred many famous men and taught them good civil and military doctrine. In this Rome had the advantage over Cusco, not because she reared her sons better, but because she was more fortunate in having attained the art of letters, whereby she perpetuated the fame of her offspring. They became indeed as illustrious in the sciences as they were excellent in the use of arms; and soldiers and writers honored one another, the first performing notable deeds in peace and war, and the latter writing them down to the honor of their country and the perpetual memory of all concerned. I do not know which did most, those who wielded their swords or those who wielded their pens, for the two activities are both heroic and occupy an equal place, as we see in the case of the great Julius Caesar, who exercised both professions with such talent that it is hard to say in which he was the greater. Indeed it may be doubted which of these two groups of illustrious men owed most to the other, whether the warriors to the writers who set down their deeds and immortalized them, or the men of letters to the men of war, who daily provided them with such great deeds as to offer material for their whole lives.

Each group could allege many arguments in its own favor, but we shall not repeat them, for we must return to the misfortune of my own country whose sons, though they were distinguished in warfare and for their great wisdom and understanding, and had great aptitude for learning, yet having no knowledge of letters, left no memory of their great deeds and wise sayings. Thus they all perished with their country. All that has remained of their words and deeds is a feeble tradition passed down by word of mouth from father to son. Even this has been lost with the arrival of a new race, the imposition of a foreign rule and a change of government: this indeed always occurs when empires fall.

I myself, moved by the desire to preserve the few shreds of the ancient traditions of my country that have survived, lest they should completely disappear, have undertaken the excessive labor that this work has occasioned me, as far as I have gone, and that still faces me in continuing the history of the ancient institutions till their end. And so that the city of Cusco, the mother and mistress of the ancient empire, shall not be forgotten, I have resolved to include a short description of it in this chapter, following the traditions that I picked up as a native son of the city and setting down what I saw with my own eyes. I shall give the traditional names of its various wards which were retained until the year 1560, when I left. Later some of these names were changed to correspond with those of the parish churches built in some of the wards.

King Manco Capac, having taken into account the advantages possessed by the valley of Cusco—the flatness of the site, surrounded on all sides by high sierras; the four streams (though none of them very large) to irrigate the whole valley, and in the midst a splendid fountain of briny water for making salt; fertile soil; and healthy air—decided to found his imperial city on that site, in obedience to the will of his father the Sun, who, according to the Indian belief, had bidden him set up his court, which was to become the capital of his empire, at the place indicated by the golden wand.[48] The temperature of the city is cold rather than warm, but not so cold as to oblige the inhabitants to light fires for warmth. They have only to go into a room in which there is no current of air to shake off the cold from the street. If they have a brazier, they keep very warm; if not, they manage well without. Similarly with clothes; summer outdoors dress is sufficient: winter outdoors dress is comfortable. In the same way for bedcovers a single blanket is enough, but three are not oppressive throughout the year, with no distinction between winter and summer. This is true of all the regions of Peru, which are constant throughout the year, whether hot, temperate, or

---

[48] See p. 3–4

cold. In Cusco, which, as we have said, is cold and dry rather than hot and damp, meat does not go bad. A piece of meat hung in a room with the windows open will keep a week, a fortnight, or thirty or a hundred days until it is as dry as a bone. I have seen this done with the flesh of the Peruvian sheep. I do not know if it can be done with the flesh of the sheep introduced from Spain, or whether, as the Spanish sheep is more hot-blooded than the Peruvian sheep, its meat will keep in the same way or not stand such treatment. I did not see this, as in my time Castilian sheep were never killed because few of them were bred. Because of the coldness of the temperature there are no flies in the city, or very few, and such as there are live in the open air and do not enter the houses. Stinging mosquitoes are not found, nor are other noxious creatures: the city is quite free of all of them. The first houses and dwellings in Cusco were built on the slopes and folds of the hill called Sacsahuana, which is now between the east and north of the city. On the top of this hill the successors of the first Inca later built that splendid fortress, which was so little esteemed, but rather abhorred by its conquerors that they pulled it down in a very short time. The city was divided into the two parts we mentioned earlier,[49] Hanan Cusco, which is upper Cusco, and Hurin Cusco, or lower Cusco. They were divided by the Andesuyu road which leads eastwards, the part to the north of the road being Hanan Cusco, and that to the south Hurin Cusco. The first and most important district was called Collcampata. *Cóllcam* must have been a word from the special language of the Incas, whose meaning I do not know.[50] *Pata* is "terrace," and also means a stair: as the cultivation terraces were made in the form of a staircase, this name was applied to them. It also means any kind of bench or seat.

It was on this terrace that Inca Manco Capac founded his royal palace, and it was later occupied by Paullu, the son of Huayna Capac. I saw a large and spacious hall which served as a public place for celebrating the great festivals in rainy weather: when I left Cusco it alone was standing and a number of others like it, to which we shall refer, had all fallen in. Beyond Collcampata, moving toward the east, there lay another ward called Cantutpata, meaning the "terrace of pinks." *Cantut* is the name for a very pretty flower somewhat resembling Spanish pinks, though before the arrival of the Spaniards there were no pinks in Peru. The *cantut* has a stalk, leaf, and horns like those of the Andalusian *cambronera* or boxthorn, and the plant grows in large thickets. The ward received its name from the very large quantity of these plants, which I saw when I was there. Still further round toward the

---

[49] See p. 5

[50] See note on the special language of the Incas, p. xxi.

east lies the ward of Pumacurcu, "the lions' beam," from *puma,* "lion," and *curcu,* "beam," referring to some large beams there were in this ward, to which lions presented to the Inca were fastened until they were tamed and could be moved to their permanent quarters. Then followed another very large ward called Tococachi. The meaning of this compound I do not understand. *Toco* is "window" and *cachi,* "salt for eating," so that according to the rules of the language it ought to mean "window salt": I cannot understand what is intended unless it is a proper noun and has a different meaning which I do not know. In this ward stood the primitive building of the convent of St. Francis. Turning a little to the south, continuing the circle, follows the ward called Munaicenca, or "love-nose," from *muna,* "to love," and *cenca,* "nose." Why this name was given I do not know, but it must have been because of some anecdote or superstition, for names were never applied at random. Further toward the south follows another large ward called Rimacpampa, "the talking square," for it was there that some of the decrees issued for the government of the republic were announced. They were proclaimed from time to time so that the inhabitants might hear them and present themselves to carry out whatever obligations they entailed. As the square was in this ward, its name was given to the ward: from the square the royal highway leads out to Collasuyu. Beyond the ward of Rimacpampa lies another to the south of the city, called Pumapchupan, "lion's tail," for the ward tapers to a point between two streams that unite at a right angle. The name was also given to imply that this ward was the last in the city, and they therefore distinguished it with the name of "the lion's tail." Moreover, lions and other fierce animals were kept in it. At a distance to the west of this ward there was a village of over three hundred inhabitants called Cayaucachi. It stood more than a thousand paces from the last houses in the city. This was in 1560. As I write this, in 1602, I am told that it is already within the limits of Cusco, the population of which has so multiplied that the city has surrounded the village on all sides.

To the west of the city, again a thousand paces away, there was another ward called Chaquillchaca, which again as a compound is a meaningless name, unless it is a proper noun. The royal highway to Condesuyu begins here. Near the road there are two streams of excellent water which are channeled underground. The Indians do not know where the water comes from, for the work is a very ancient one and traditions about these things are being forgotten. The channels are called *collquemachác-huay,* "silver snakes," for the water is as white as silver and the channels wind like snakes through the earth. I am told that the population of the city has also reached Chaquillchaca. Following the same circle and turning now from the west northwards there was another ward called Pichu, which was also outside the city. Beyond it lay another named Quillipata, likewise outside the city. Further on, to the north of the city lies the great ward of Carmenca, a proper name with no special meaning in the general tongue of Peru. The royal highway to Chinchaysuyu begins there. Turning eastwards there follows the ward of Huacapuncu, "gate of the sanctuary," from *huaca,* which has many meanings, as we have explained,[51] including that of "temple" or "sanctuary": *puncu* is "door, gate." The ward gets its name from the stream that runs through the main square of Cusco. Beside the stream runs a long, wide street, and both of them traverse the whole city, meeting the royal highway to Collasuyu about a league and a half beyond it. This entrance is called the "gate of the sanctuary" or "of the temple" because in addition to the wards dedicated to the temple of the Sun and the house of the chosen virgins, which were the chief sanctuaries, they regarded the whole city as sacred, and it was one of their chief idols. For this reason they called this entry of the stream and the street the gate of the sanctuary while the place where the stream left the city was called "the lion's tail," indicating that the city was sacred according to their laws and their vain religion and a lion in their arms and warfare. The ward of Huacapuncu touches the limits of Collcampata, from which we began our tour of the wards of the city: we have thus come full circle.

The City Contained the Description of the Whole Empire

[7:9] The Incas divided the wards according to the four parts of their empire, called Tahuantinsuyu. The division dated back to the first Inca Manco Capac, who ordered that the savages he had subjugated should be settled according to their places of origin, those from the east to the east, those from the west to the west, and so on. The dwellings of the first subjects were thus disposed in a circle within the limits of the town, and those from newly conquered areas settled according to the situation of their provinces. The *curacas* built houses to live in when they came to the capital, each next to one another, but settling on the side nearest his own province. If a chief's province was to the right of his neighbor's, he built his house to the right; if to the left, he built it to the left, and if behind, he built his house behind. The result of this arrangement was that anyone who contemplated the wards and the dwellings of the numerous and varied tribes who had settled in them beheld the whole empire at once, as if in a looking glass or a cosmographic plan. In describing the site of Cusco, Cieza de Léon makes the same observation in his chapter xciii:[52]

---

[51] Garcilaso's discussion of the many meanings of the term *huaca* is not included in this edition; see the complete Livermore translation of the *Royal Commentaries,* book 2, ch. 5.

[52] *Crónica del Perú* [1553], multiple editions, ch. xciii.

"And though the city was full of numbers of strange and remote tribes, such as Indians from Chile and Pasto, Cañaris, Chachapoyas, Huancas, Collas, and other peoples of these provinces, each race dwelt together in the place allotted to it by the governors of the city. The latter preserved the customs of their fathers, followed the usages of their provinces, and would easily have been recognized from the insignia they wore on their heads, even though there were a hundred thousand men gathered together," etcetera.

Thus far from Cieza de Léon.

The insignia they wore on their heads were a sort of headdress which served for identification, each tribe and province differing from the rest. This was not an invention of the Incas, but a custom of the various tribes. The Inca kings ordered it to be preserved to prevent confusion among the tribes and nations from Pasto to Chile. According to the same author (chapter xxxviii) the distance is more than thirteen hundred leagues, so that the great ring of the outer wards was inhabited solely by the vassals of the whole empire and not by the Incas or members of the royal blood. These wards formed the suburbs of the city itself, which we shall now describe street by street from north to south, including the various wards and the houses between the streets: we shall mention the royal palaces and say to whom they fell in the distribution that took place after the Spanish conquest.

From the hill called Sacsahuana there runs a stream containing little water which flows north and south as far as the last suburb, called Pumapchupan. It divides the city from the wards. Further in the city there is a street now called St. Augustine which follows the same route from north to south, beginning from the palaces of the first Inca Manco Capac and going straight down to the square called Rimacpampa. There are three or four more streets that cross the broad space between the street and the stream, from east to west, and it was in this broad space that the Incas of the royal blood lived, divided into their *aillus* or clans, though all of them were of the same blood and stock. Although they all descended from King Manco Capac, yet each claimed descent from the one or other of the kings, saying these descend from this Inca, those from that Inca, and so on for all the rest. This is what the Spanish historians refer to when they say confusedly that such and such an Inca founded one line, and another a different one, suggesting that these were different stocks. But the lineages were in fact all the same, as the Indians show when they apply the common name *Capac Aillu,* "august lineage of the royal blood," to them all. They also apply the word *Inca,* meaning "a man of the royal blood," indiscriminately to all males of this lineage, and call the women *Palla,* "woman of the royal blood." In my day the residents in this street from the upper end downwards were, Rodrigo de Pineda, Juan de Saavedra, Diego Ortiz de Guzmán, Pedro de los Ríos and his brother Diego de los Ríos, Jerónimo Costilla, Gaspar Jara (who owned the houses on the site of what is now the monastery of St. Augustine the Divine), Miguel Sánchez, Juan de Santa Cruz, Alonso de Soto, Gabriel Carrera, Diego de Trujillo (one of the first conquerors and one of the thirteen companions who stood by Don Francisco Pizarro, as we shall relate in due course), Antón Ruiz de Guevara, Juan de Salas, the brother of the archbishop of Seville and inquisitor general, Valdés de Salas, besides others whose names I do not recall. They were all lords of vassals and held allocations of Indians, being among the second conquerors of Peru. Apart from these, many other Spaniards who had no Indians dwelt in the same street. In one of the houses the convent of the divine St. Augustine was founded, though after I left the city. We use the term first conquerors for the 160 Spaniards who were with Don Francisco Pizarro at the arrest of Atahuallpa, and second conquerors for those who were with Don Diego de Almagro and Don Pedro de Alvarado who arrived in Peru almost at once. The aforesaid and no others were called conquerors of Peru: the second looked up to the first as such, despite the fact that some of the first were of lower rank and less estate.

To return to the top of the street of St. Augustine, whence we shall penetrate further into the city, at its upper end stands the convent of Santa Clara on a site that belonged first to Alonso Díaz, a son-in-law of the governor Pedro Arias de Ávila. To the right of the convent there are many houses belonging to Spaniards, including those of Francisco de Barrientos which later belonged to Juan Alvarez Maldonado. To the right of these were the houses of Hernando Bachicao and later of Juan Alonso Palomino. Facing these, to the south, stands the Episcopal palace, which formerly belonged to Juan Balsa and afterwards to Francisco de Villacastín. Next follows the cathedral church, which gives onto the main square. Its site was occupied in Inca times by a fine hall which was used in bad weather as a place of assembly for festivities. It had been the site of the palace of Inca Viracocha, the eighth king, but I only saw this hall. When the Spaniards entered the city, they all lodged in it so as to be together in case of emergency. When I saw it, it was covered with thatch, and later I saw it being tiled. To the north of the cathedral church and across the street from it, there are many houses with gates giving onto the main square: they are used as shops by craftsmen. To the south of the cathedral, and across the street, stand the main shops of the wealthier merchants. Behind the church are the houses that formerly belonged to Juan de Berrio, and others whose owners I do not recall.

Behind the chief shops are the houses that used to belong to Diego Maldonado called the rich, for he was wealthier than anyone else in Peru: he was one of the first conquerors. In Inca times the place was called Hatuncancha, "big ward." It had been the site of the palace of one of the kings called Inca Yupanqui. South of the house of Diego Maldonado and facing it stands the former house of Francisco Hernández Girón. Beyond this to the south are the houses of Antonio Altamirano, one of the first conquerors, Francisco de Frías, Sebastián de Cazalla, and many others on either side and behind. This ward is called Puca Marca, "the red ward," and the houses belonged to King Túpac Inca Yupanqui. Beyond this ward there is another very large ward to the south, the name of which I forget. It contains the houses of Antonio de Loaisa, Martín de Meneses, Juan de Figueroa, Don Pedro Puertocarrero, García de Melo, Francisco Delgado, and many others belonging to lords of vassals whose names escape my memory. Beyond this, still moving southward, is the square called Intipampa. This means "square of the Sun," for it lay before the house and temple of the Sun, and was the place where those who were not Incas, and could not therefore enter the house of the Sun, delivered their offerings. There the priests received them and presented them to the image of the Sun which they worshipped as god. The ward where the temple of the Sun stood was called Coricancha, "ward of gold, silver, and precious stones," since these treasures existed in that ward, as we have already stated.[53] After this came the ward called Pumapchupan, which is already one of the suburbs. . . .

The Fortress of Cusco

[7:27] The Inca kings of Peru made marvelous buildings, fortresses, temples, royal palaces, gardens, storehouses, roads, and other constructions of great excellence, as can be seen even today from their remaining ruins, though the whole building can scarcely be judged from the mere foundations.

The greatest and most splendid building erected to show the power and majesty of the Incas was the fortress of Cusco, the grandeur of which would be incredible to anyone who had not seen it, and even those who have seen it and considered it with attention imagine, and even believe, that it was made by enchantment, the handiwork of demons rather than of men. Indeed the multiplicity of stones, large and small, of which the three circumvallations are composed (and they are more like rocks than stones) makes one wonder how they could have been quarried, for the Indians had neither iron nor steel to work them with. And the question of how they were conveyed to the site is no less difficult a problem, since they had no oxen and could not make wagons, nor would oxen and wagons have sufficed to carry them. They were in fact heaved by main force with the aid of

---

[53] See pp. 15–9.

thick cables. The roads by which they were brought were not flat, but rough mountainsides with steep slopes, up and down which the rocks were dragged by human effort alone. Many of the pieces were brought a distance of ten, twelve, or fifteen leagues, in particular that stone, or rather rock, which the Indians call Saicasa, "the weary," because it never reached the site. This rock is known to have been brought from a place fifteen leagues from the city and through the Yucay River, which is only a little narrower than the Guadalquivir at Córdova. The nearest source of stone was Muina, five leagues from Cusco. And if one went on to wonder how such large stones could be fitted together so that the point of a knife could scarcely be inserted between them, there would be no end to our pondering. Many of them are so closely set that the seam is scarcely visible. To lodge them in this way it would have been necessary to lift each stone and lower it on the one below a great many times, for they had no set-square or even a ruler to help them to put it in place and see if it fitted. Neither did they know how to make cranes or pulleys or any other device to help them raise and lower masonry, though the pieces they handled are terrifyingly large, as Padre José de Acosta says in speaking of this very fortress. I appeal to the authority of this great man since I have no exact measurements of the size of many of the stones, for although I have asked my former schoolfellows for information and they have sent it to me, their account of the dimensions of the biggest stones is not as clear as I would have liked: they sent me the measurements in fathoms, though I wanted them in varas and ochavas. I would also like to have had attested evidence of this, for the most wonderful thing about the fortress is the incredible size of the stones and the extraordinary labor that was necessary to raise and lower them until they were finally adjusted to their present positions:[54] . . .

The immensity and majesty of this monument seems to show that the Incas intended to demonstrate the greatness of their power. It was indeed made to impress rather than for another reason. They also wished to exhibit the skill of their masons and builders, not only in dressing the smooth masonry (which the Spaniards are never tired of praising) but also in rough stonework, which they executed with no less mastery. They sought also to exhibit their knowledge of military science in the plan of the fortress, including everything necessary for its defense against the enemy.

---

[54] Archaeologists have reconstructed the process used to raise and set the enormous stones used in the construction of the fortress of Sacsahuaman. Stones were upended by building mud or soil slopes to gradually raise the stone to the desired position, and then removing the soil. There are small protuberances on the stones that apparently were used by Inca architects to lever the stones to their assigned positions.

The fortress was built on a high hill to the north of Cusco, called Sacsahuana, at the foot of which begin the outskirts of the city that spread around for a great distance in all directions. On the side toward the city the hill is steep, almost sheer, so that the fort is secure from enemy attack from that direction, whether by companies in regular formation or any other system. Nor is there any room to install artillery, though the Indians had never heard of it until the arrival of the Spaniards. Owing to the natural strength on this quarter it was thought that any defense, however slight, would suffice, and so they merely set up a thick freestone wall, carefully wrought on all five sides except what masons call the *extrados*. This wall was more than two hundred fathoms long. Each line of stone was at a different height, and every stone in each line was alike and set in a row and excellently fitted on all four faces so that there was no room for mortar. They did not indeed use mortar made of sand and lime, for they were unacquainted with lime. They did however employ a mortar consisting of a paste of sticky red clay, which was used to fill up the gashes and pits caused in working the stone. This defense was both stout and smooth, for the wall was thick and carefully polished on both sides. . . .

Garcilaso goes on to discuss the skills of the masons who built the fortress, comparing it to the technological wonders of the Ancient World.

Chapter Seven
The Empire before the Arrival of the Spaniards

Maize and What They Call Rice, and Other Seeds

[8:9] The fruits of the earth on which the natives of Peru lived before the Spaniards came were of various kinds, some of which grew above ground and others below it. Of the fruits that grew above ground the most important was the grain the Mexicans and the inhabitants of the Windward Islands call maize and the Peruvians *sara,* for it is their bread. It is of two kinds, one hard kind called *murchu,* the other soft and very tasty, called *capia.* They eat it instead of bread, roasted or boiled in plain water. The seed of the hard maize is the kind that has been introduced into Spain: the soft sort has not been brought here. In some provinces it is softer and tenderer than in others, especially in the province called Rucana. For their solemn sacrifices, they used, as we have mentioned, a maize loaf called *çancu,* and they made the same bread to eat as an occasional delicacy; they called it *huminta.* The two names were applied, not because the bread was any different, but because one kind was used for sacrifices and the other simply for eating. The flour was ground by the women on broad flat stones. They laid the grain on one of these and applied to it another stone, shaped like a rather elongated half moon, though not rounded. It would be about three fingers broad, and the women held it by the two points of the half moon and moved it to and fro on the maize. In this clumsy way they ground their corn and anything else they needed to grind: because of the difficulty of the process they did not eat bread regularly.

They did not grind with pestle and mortar, though they had these implements. Grinding in a mortar is done by the force of blows, but the moon-shaped stone grinds whatever comes under it by its own weight and the Indian women can easily handle it because of its shape, rocking it to and fro and occasionally heaping the grounds in the middle of the flat stone with one hand so as to grind them over again, while the other hand is left free to hold the grindstone, which we might reasonably describe as a *batán*[55] from the strokes given alternately by the two hands. This method of grinding is still in use. They also made porridge, which they call *api,* and ate it with great relish, because it was only consumed on rare occasions. To

---

[55] A *batán* is a grinder or fulling mill for cloth.

complete our account, the flour was separated from the bran by pouring it onto a clean cotton cloth and smoothing it over with the hand. The pure flour is so fine that it sticks to the cloth while the bran, being coarser, remains detached and is easily removed. The fine flour is collected in the middle of the cloth and poured out; then more is put on the cloth until the necessary quantity has been sifted. The sifting of flour was intended for the bread consumed by the Spaniards rather than for Indian use, since the latter were not so particular as to turn up their noses at bran, and the bran is not so rough, especially that from soft maize, as to need to be removed. The sifting was done in the fashion we have described for want of sieves, which only arrived from Spain with the introduction of wheat. I have seen all this with my own eyes, and until I was nine or ten years old I was brought up on *sara* or maize, the bread of which is known by three names—*çancu,* bread for sacrifices; *huminta,* special bread for celebrations; and *tanta* (the first syllable pronounced in the palate), common bread. Roast *sara* is called *camcha,* "toasted maize," a word that includes both the adjective and the noun: the *m* should be pronounced, for if the word were written with *n,* it would mean "ward, suburb," or "large enclosure." Cooked *sara* is called *mutí* (by the Spaniards *mote*): the word includes both the noun maize and the adjective cooked. With maize flour the Spaniards make little biscuits, fritters, and other dainties for invalids and the healthy. As a remedy in all sorts of treatment experienced doctors have rejected wheat flour in favor of maize flour. The same flour is mixed with plain water to brew their beverage, which can be soured in the Indian fashion to make a very good vinegar. An excellent honey is made from the unripe cane, which is very sweet. The dried canes and their leaves are of great value, and cattle are very fond of them. The leaves from the ear of maize and the stalks are used by those who make statues who thus avoid weight. Some Indians, who are more intent on getting drunk than the rest, [steep] the *sara* . . . and keep it there until it begins to sprout. They then grind it and boil it in the same water as other things. Once this is strained it is kept until it ferments. A very strong drink, which intoxicates immediately, is thus produced. It is called *viñapu,* or in another language *sora.* The Incas forbade its use since it at once produces drunkenness, but I am told that it has recently been revived by some vicious people. Thus the advantages I have mentioned are all derived from the various parts of the *sora,* and there are many other medical derivatives, both beverages and plasters, as we shall have occasion to mention later.[56]

---

[56] Inca medicines are not discussed in this edition; see the complete Livermore translation of *Royal Commentaries,* book 2, chs. 24–5.

The second most important of the crops that are grown above ground is that called *quinua,* or in Spanish "millet" or "little rice" which it rather resembles in the color and appearance of the grain. The plant is rather like the wild amaranth in stalk, leaf, and flower: it is the latter that produces the *quinua.* The Indians eat the tender leaves in cooked dishes, for they are very tasty and nourishing. They eat the grain in pottages prepared in many different ways. The Indians also brew a drink from the *quinua,* as they do from maize, but it is only produced in regions where maize does not grow. The Indian inhabitants use flour made of *quinua* in various illnesses. In 1590 I was sent some of the seeds from Peru, but they were dead, and though planted at different times never sprouted.

In addition, the Peruvian Indians have three or four kinds of beans, shaped like broad beans but smaller: they are quite good to eat, and are used in cooked dishes. They are called *purutu.* They have lupines like those in Spain, though rather larger and whiter: they are called *tarui.* Apart from the edible types, there are others not suitable for eating: they are round and look like cut turquoises, though they have many different colors and are about as big as chickpeas. The general word for them is *chuy,* but they are given various names according to the color. Some of these names are comic and others are appropriate, but we shall not include them so as to avoid prolixity. They are used in many different games played by boys and by grown men: I remember taking part in both sorts.

The Vegetables That Grow in the Earth

[8:10] Many other plants grow underground. They are sown by the Indians and afford them sustenance, especially in the provinces that do not produce *sara.* The principal one is called *papa* [potato], which serves as bread. It can be eaten boiled or roasted and is also put in stews. After exposure to the frost and sun for preservation according to the method we have already mentioned,[57] it is known as *chuñu.* Another type is called *oca* which is very tasty: it is as long and thick as the big finger of a man's hand, and is eaten raw, since it is sweet, or cooked in stews. It is placed in the sun to make it keep, and without the addition of honey or sugar becomes like jam, for it possesses a great deal of sweetness. It is then called *caví.* There is another like it in shape, though not in taste: it is rather the opposite, for it borders

---

[57] The process to which Garcilaso refers is freeze-drying, which is done by alternately exposing potatoes or meats to the sun and cold that occurs naturally in the high Andes between night and morning. Foods processed in this way can be stored for long periods of time and dehydrated and cooked as needed. Garcilaso describes the process in the complete Livermore translation of *Royal Commentaries,* book 5, ch. 29.

on bitterness and can only be eaten cooked. It is called *añus;* and the Indians say that it reduces the procreative powers, but in order to prevent it from harming them, those who prided themselves on their gallantry used to hold a little rod or stick in one hand while they ate it, saying that in this way it lost its peculiar property and did them no harm. I heard them give the explanation and often saw them do this, though they implied that it was intended rather as a joke than as a serious acceptance of the foolish tradition of their elders. . . .

Gold and Silver

[8:24] Spain is a good witness to the wealth of gold and silver that is mined in Peru, since for more than twenty-five years past, without counting the previous period, more than twelve or thirteen millions of gold and silver are brought here without counting other articles that are not included: each million is ten times a hundred thousand ducats. Gold is found throughout Peru: it is more abundant in some provinces than others, but in general it occurs throughout the kingdom. It is found on the surface of the earth and in streams and rivers where it is carried down by spates after the rains. It is obtained by washing the earth or sand, as silversmiths in Spain wash the sweepings of their shops. The Spaniards call what is thus recovered "gold dust" because it is like filings; there are a few bigger grains of two or three pesos or more. I have seen grains of more than twenty pesos: they are called *pepitas* or nuggets. Some are flat like the seeds of melons or calabashes, others are round. Some are as big as eggs. All the gold from Peru is 18 to 24 carat, or rather more or less. That which is extracted from the mines of Callavaya or Callahuaya is extremely fine, of 24 carats, and it is even claimed to be finer, according to what I have heard from some goldsmiths in Spain. In 1556 in a corner of one of the mines of Callahuaya there was discovered one of the stones that occur with the metal, as big as a man's head. In color it resembled a lung, and even in shape, for it was riddled with large and small holes that ran right through it. In all of them points of gold could be seen as though molten gold had been poured over it: some of these points projected from the stone, others were level with it, and others were inside it. Those who understood mining said that if it had not been extracted, the whole stone would in the course of time have turned to gold. In Cusco the Spaniards regarded it as a marvelous thing. The Indians called it *huaca,* which, as we have said, has among other meanings that of a remarkable thing, something admirable for its beauty or also something abominably ugly. I saw it with both Indians and Spaniards. Its owner was a rich man who decided to come to Spain, bringing it as it was as a present for King Philip II, for the gem was a strange one and very estimable. From others who came in his fleet I heard when I was in Spain that his ship was lost with a great deal of other treasure.

Silver needs more work to mine than gold, and is more costly to refine and purify. In many parts of Peru silver mines have been, and are still, found, though none like those of Potosí, which were discovered and explored in 1545, fourteen years after the arrival of the Spaniards there. The hill where they are is called Potocsi, such being the name of the place: I do not know if it has a meaning in the special language of that province, for it has none in the general language of Peru. It stands on a plain and is shaped like a sugarloaf: it is a league round at the base and a quarter of a league at the top. The top of the hill is round. It is beautiful to see, for it stands alone, and nature decked it so that it might be as famous in the world as it now is. Some mornings the hill appears covered with snow, for the site is a cold one. The place used to belong to Gonzalo Pizarro's allocation, which later passed to Pedro de Hinojosa. We shall say later how he got it, if we may without odium delve into and reveal the secret deeds that are done in time of war, for historians usually omit many things for fear of the odium they may arouse. Padre Acosta writes in his Book IV at length of the gold, silver, and quicksilver that have been found in the empire of Peru, and more is discovered every day: I shall therefore not describe all this, but merely refer to a few notable facts of those times, and say how the Indians obtained and founded the metal before the Spaniards discovered the use of quicksilver. I should mention that the mines of the hill of Potosí were discovered by certain Indians in Spanish service called in their language *yanacuna,* which means a man obliged to act as a servant. They enjoyed the use of the first vein they found for some days as friends and partners, keeping their discovery secret; but as its wealth was so great that they could not or would not conceal it from their masters, they then revealed it. The first vein was explored and the rest were then discovered. Among the Spaniards present was one called Gonzalo Bernal, who was later steward to Pedro de Hinojosa. Soon after the discovery, speaking in the presence of Diego Centeno, a famous gentleman, and many other noble people, he said: "The mines promise such wealth that when they have been worked for a few years iron will be worth more than silver." I saw this forecast fulfilled in 1554 and 1555 when, during the war of Francisco Hernández Girón,[58] a horseshoe was valued at five pesos, or six ducats, and a mule's at four: two nails for shoeing cost a tomin or fifty-six maravedis. I saw a pair of buskins sell for thirty-six ducats, a quire of paper for four, and

---

[58] Francisco Hernández Girón was the leader of the last rebellion of Spaniards against royal authority in Peru. The revolt is not included in this edition, but it is described in the complete Livermore translation of the *General History of Peru,* book 7.

a vara of fine Valencian scarlet for sixty; fine Segovia cloth, silks, linen, and other Spanish wares were in proportion. The war produced this dearth, for during the two years it lasted no fleets reached Peru bringing goods from Spain. It was due also to the great quantities of silver extracted from the mines, for three or four years before this time a basket of the herb we call coca had reached thirty-five ducats, and maize the same, and a measure of wheat twenty-four and twenty-five. Maize was the same, and clothes and footwear in proportion. The first wine, until it was available in abundance, sold at two hundred ducats and more the jar. And despite the richness of the land and its abundance of gold, silver, and precious stones, as all the world knows, the natives are the poorest and wretchedest people in the universe.

Quicksilver, and How Metal Was
Founded before the Use of Quicksilver

[8:25] . . . .The Inca kings knew of quicksilver and admired its brightness and mobility, but found no use for it. There was nothing indeed in their service to which it could be applied, and they felt that on the other hand it was dangerous to the lives of those who mined it and handled it, since they noticed that it caused them to tremble and lose their senses. For this reason, these kings who paid such attention to the welfare of their subjects and merited the title of lovers of the poor, prohibited the mining of quicksilver by law and ordered it to be forgotten; and the Indians so abhorred it that its very name was obliterated from their memory and from their language. They have indeed no word for quicksilver, unless they have invented it since its discovery by the Spaniards in 1567. As they had no writing, they rapidly forgot any word that was not in current use. The Incas used, and permitted their vassals to use, the scarlet color of incredibly fine quality which is found in powder form in the ore of quicksilver: the Indians call it *ichma* (the word *llimpi* given by Padre Acosta refers to another purple color which is not so fine and which is obtained from other minerals, for these occur in Peru in all colors). As the Indians became so attached to the color *ichma,* which certainly is enough to inspire passionate attachment, that they would go to all lengths to get it, the Incas feared they would come to harm in the caverns, and prohibited its use by the common people, restricting it only to women of the royal blood. It was not used by men, as I myself saw, and only by young and beautiful women, not by the older ones, for it was rather an adornment for the young than an ornament for mature people. Even the girls did not put it on their cheeks as they do rouge here, but applied it with a little stick like henna between the corner of the eyes and the temple. The line they drew was about as broad as a stalk of wheat and looked very well. The *pallas* used no other cosmetics but powdered *ichma,* and that not every day but only occasionally on feast days. They kept their faces clean, as did all the women of the common people. Those who prided themselves on the beauty of their complexions used to apply a white milk which they made of I know not what so as to preserve their coloring. The stuff was left on for nine days, at the end of which time it was removed from the face and had formed a skin, which came off in pieces, leaving the complexion much improved. The color *ichma* was used as sparingly as I have mentioned in order to spare the vassals the danger of mining it. Painting or staining the face with various pigments in wartime or for feasts, which is mentioned by one author, was never practiced by the Incas or the Indians as a whole, except by a few tribes who were regarded as the most savage and primitive.

It remains to describe how silver ore was founded before quicksilver was introduced. Near the hill of Potosí there is another small hill of the same shape as the first. The Indians call it Huayna Potocchi, or Potocchi junior, to distinguish it from the other which, after the discovery of the lesser one, was known as Hatun Potocsi, or Potocchi—it is all one—saying they were father and son. The silver ore is extracted from the larger, as we have said, but it proved at first very difficult to smelt, for instead of running, it burnt and spent itself in smoke. The Indians did not know the cause of this, though they had mastered other metals. But need or covetousness is a great teacher, especially when gold or silver is in question, and they made so many attempts with different remedies that they at length found a solution. In the small hill there was a base ore consisting almost entirely of lead and when this was mixed with the silver ore it made it melt. It was therefore called *surúchec,* "what makes one slip." The two ores were mingled in due proportion, with so many pounds of silver ore to so many ounces of lead ore, the quantities being varied according to the lessons of daily experience, for not all the silver ore is of the same kind. Some has more silver than others, even though it comes from the same vein, and the proportion of silver varies from day to day, so that the *surúchec* has to be added according to the quality and richness of each ore. Thus tempered, the ore is smelted in small portable furnaces, like clay ovens. They did not smelt with bellows or by blowing down copper tubes, which, as we have said elsewhere,[59] they used when they wanted to melt gold and silver for working them: although they often tried this, the ore would not run and they could not find out the cause. They therefore smelted their ore with the aid of the

---

[59] The smelting process for gold and silver is not included in this edition; it is described in the complete Livermore translation of the *Royal Commentaries,* book 2, ch. 28.

wind. But it was also necessary to temper the wind; if it was very strong it wasted the charcoal and cooled the metal; if it were soft, it had not enough force to heat the fire. Consequently the little ovens were taken out at night and set on high or low points on the hillsides, according to the strength of the wind, which was more or less tempered according to whether the site was sheltered or not. It was a pretty sight in those days to see eight, ten, twelve, or fifteen thousand little furnaces blazing away on the hillsides. The first smelting was done in this way. The second and third were carried out indoors with copper pipes to purify the silver and separate the lead; for the Indians had none of the Spanish devices with acids and other substances to separate gold from silver or copper, or silver from copper and lead, and could only refine by repeated smeltings. In this way, the Indians smelted the silver of Potosí before quicksilver was found; they still practice this to some extent, though nothing like on the scale they did.

The mine owners found that this system of open air smelting spread their treasure among many hands and enabled many others to share their wealth; and they sought to remedy this state of affairs and to keep the metal to themselves by making their own foundries and employing the Indians by the day. Previously the Indians had worked on their own account and undertook to deliver to the owner so much silver for each hundredweight of ore that was mined. Stirred thus by avarice, the owners had great bellows made which blew onto the ovens from a distance like the wind. As this proved useless, they built machines and wheels with sails, like windmills, which were driven by horses. However, this also was of no avail, and they therefore gave up these devices and went on following the system invented by the Indians. Twenty-two years went by, until in 1567 by the ingenuity and skill of a Portuguese called Henrique Garcés quicksilver was found. It was discovered in the province of Huanca to which for reasons I do not know is added the epithet -*villca*, "greatness, eminence," unless the reference is to the abundance of quicksilver that is mined. Apart from what is wasted, eight thousand quintals, or thirty-two thousand arrobas, are extracted yearly for his majesty. Despite its discovery in such quantities, no one knew how to turn it to account for this purpose until 1571, when a Spaniard called Pedro Fernández de Velasco arrived in Peru, after having been in Mexico, where he saw the process of extracting silver with quicksilver, as Padre Acosta reports at length in a curious account to which I refer anyone who is interested in acquiring remarkable and important information.[60]

---

[60] José de Acosta, S. J., *Natural and Moral History of the Indies,* ed. Jane Mangan (Durham: Duke University Press, 2002).

Chapter Eight
The Deeds of Huayna Capac and the
Wars of Huascar and Atahuallpa

Returning to Inca history, Huayna Capac continues his conquests, defeats internal revolts, and divides the empire between two of his sons.

Huayna Capac Makes His Son Atahuallpa King of Quito

[9:12] As we have already noted Huayna Capac had his son Atahuallpa by the daughter of the king of Quito, who was to succeed her father in that kingdom. This son displayed a ready intelligence and understanding, and was astute, sagacious, and prudent: his mettle was brave and warlike, his bearing noble and his features handsome, as those of all the Incas and Pallas usually were. Because of these gifts of body and mind his father loved him tenderly and always took him with him. He would have liked to leave his whole empire to the boy, but could not deprive his firstborn, Huascar Inca, of his legitimate rights, and therefore sought, against the custom and constitution of all his ancestors, to deprive the heir of the kingdom of Quito, giving the proceeding the appearance of justice and restitution. To this effect he summoned Prince Huascar Inca who was in Cusco and on his arrival held a great gathering of his sons and many captains and *curacas* who were with him, and addressed his legitimate heir in the presence of all of them in the following terms:

"It is notorious, prince, that according to the ancient custom that our first father Inca Manco Capac bequeathed to us to observe, this kingdom of Quito belongs to your crown, for this is what has been done hitherto, and all the kingdoms and provinces that have been conquered have been annexed and incorporated in your empire and subjected to the jurisdiction and control of our imperial city of Cusco. But because I love your brother Atahuallpa very dearly and I regret to see him in poverty, I should be glad if you would consent that, of all the domains I have won for your crown, the inheritance and succession of the kingdom of Quito—which belonged to his ancestors on his mother's side and would today have been his mother's—should be left to him so that he can live in royal estate as his virtues well merit, for being a good brother as he is, and having resources, he may serve you better in all you require than if he were poor. And in recompense and satisfaction of the little I now ask of you, you yourself will still

find many other broad kingdoms and provinces around your own possessions which you can conquer, wherein your brother will serve you as a soldier and captain, and when the time comes for me to go and rest with our
father the Sun, I shall go happily from this world.

Prince Huascar Inca readily replied that he would be exceedingly glad to
obey his father the Inca in this matter and in anything else he demanded of
him, and if it were his father's pleasure to take away other provinces so as to
give more to Atahuallpa, he would willingly do so to make him happy.
Huayna Capac was very satisfied with this reply. He ordered Huascar to
return to Cusco, and began to place Atahuallpa in possession of his
domains, giving him other provinces in addition to Quito. He also provided him with experienced captains and part of his army to serve and
accompany him. In short he bestowed every possible favor on Atahuallpa,
even to the disadvantage of his heir. He behaved like a father smitten with
passionate love for his son, and wished to spend the rest of his life in Quito
and its district, taking this decision partly to favor and further Atahuallpa's
reign, and partly to subdue and pacify the newly won provinces of the coast
and interior, which had still not settled down under the rule and administration of the Incas, but behaved like warlike, though savage bestial people.
For this reason it was necessary to shift many of these tribes to other provinces and bring in quiet and peaceful races in their stead, the remedy that
those kings usually resorted to secure themselves against rebellion, as we
explained at length in speaking of the emigrants, called *mítmac*.[61]

The Royal Highways

[9:13] It is proper that in recounting the life of Huayna Capac we should
refer to the two royal highways that run from the north to the south of
Peru, since they are attributed to him. One of them passes through the
llanos, that is by the seacoast, while the other goes inland by the sierra.
They are dwelt on at some length by the historians, but they represent an
achievement so great as to defy description, and as I cannot myself describe
them as well as they have done, I shall quote each of the historians word for
word. Agustín de Zárate (Book I, chapter xiii), speaking of the origin of the
Incas, says:

> "By the succession of the Incas power devolved upon one of their
> number called Huayna Capac (which means "Rich Youth") who
> won more lands, extended their sway more widely, and governed
> with greater justice and right than all the rest. He raised Peru to

---

[61] See the complete Livermore translation of the *Royal Commentaries,* book 5, ch. 27.

such a degree of political consciousness that one would have thought it impossible for an uncivilized and illiterate people to be governed with such regularity and order or to display such love and obedience towards its rulers. And in his service they built two roads which are so remarkable that they should certainly not be overlooked, for none of the monuments that ancient writers referred to as the seven wonders of the world was built with such difficulty, labor, and expense as these. When this Huayna Capac marched with his army from the City of Cusco to conquer the province of Quito, a distance of about five hundred leagues, he had great difficulty on the mountain road because of the roughness of the way and the ravines and cliffs he encountered. The Indians therefore thought it fitting to build a new road for his triumphant return once he had reduced the province of Quito, and they made this smooth, broad highway the whole length of the mountain chain, cutting through the rock and leveling it wherever necessary and filling the ravines with rubble. In some places it was necessary to raise the surface fifteen or twenty times the height of a man, and this road runs for a distance of five hundred leagues. And it is said that when finished the road was so smooth that a wagon could have run along it, though since those times, owing to the wars of the Indians and of the Christians, the rubble-work has been broken down in many places in order to hold up the advance of enemy forces. The difficulty of the feat will be appreciated by anyone who watches the labor and expense of leveling two leagues of mountain road in Spain between El Espinar near Segovia and Guadarrama, a task that has never been completely finished in spite of the fact that it is the route continually used by the kings of Castile and their court and household whenever they come or go from Andalusia or from the kingdom of Toledo to this side of the passes.

And not satisfied with executing this noteworthy work, when Huayna Capac again decided to visit the province of Quito, to which he was much attached because he himself had been the conqueror of it, he returned by the coastal plains and the Indians built for him another system of roads no less difficult than the mountain highway; for in every valley when the road came to the fresh river sides with their groves of trees, which, as we have said, normally extend for a distance of a league, they made thick mud walls on either side nearly forty feet apart and four or five bricks deep; and when the road left these valleys it was continued across the sandy deserts, where stakes and rods were driven in so that no one could miss the way or stray to right or left. And this road also runs for five hundred leagues, just like the mountain highway, and though the stakes in the deserts are destroyed in many places, having been used for fuel by the Spaniards in time of war or peace, yet the walls in the valleys are still standing in most places, and they suffice to give an idea of the great scale of the whole work. Thus Huayna Capac went by one road and returned by the other, and wherever he passed the way was always covered and strewn with branches and sweetly-smelling flowers. . . .

Huayna Capac Hears That the Spaniards Are off the Coast

[9:14] While Huayna Capac was thus engaged at the royal palace of Tumi-pampa, one of the most splendid in Peru, he received news that strange people, never before seen in those parts, had arrived in a ship off the coast of the empire and were asking what land they had come to. This news roused in Huayna Capac a new preoccupation, that of ascertaining what people these were and whence they came. Now this ship belonged to Vasco Núñez de Balboa, the discoverer of the Pacific Ocean, and these Spaniards were those who applied the name Peru, as we said at the outset,[62] to the Inca empire. This was in 1515, the discovery of the Pacific having taken place two years before. One historian says that the Spaniards in this ship were Don Francisco Pizarro and his thirteen companions, whom he describes as the first discoverers of Peru. But this is an error and confuses the conquerors with the discoverers. There is also an error in the date, for sixteen or more years elapsed between the discovery and the conquest: the first discovery of Peru and the application of this name date from 1515, while Don Francisco Pizarro and his four brothers and Don Diego de Almagro entered Peru to conquer it in 1531. Huayna Capac had died eight years earlier in 1524, after reigning forty-two years, as the torn and tattered papers in which that great investigator, Fray Blas Valera, wrote the ancient deeds of these kings, testify.

Huayna Capac spent the eight years between the first news of the discoverers and his death peacefully governing his domains. He did not wish to embark on new conquests but preferred to wait and see what might come from over the sea. The news of the arrival of this ship worried him greatly, and he pondered on an ancient oracle the Incas had, to the effect that after a certain number of kings had come and gone, a strange race, never before seen, would deprive them of their kingdom and destroy their race and religion. As we shall see, this prophecy was due to be fulfilled with the present Inca. Moreover, three years before the arrival of this ship off the coast of Peru, an ill omen or portent occurred in Cusco and greatly alarmed Huayna Capac and terrified the whole empire. This was that, during the

---

[62] Garcilaso's discussion of the origin of the name "Peru" is not included in this edition; see the complete Livermore translation of the *Royal Commentaries,* book 1, chs. 3 & 4.

celebration of the solemn festivity dedicated every year to their god the Sun, they saw a royal eagle, which they call *anca,* approach, pursued by five or six kestrels and other little hawks of a variety which is so handsome that many specimens have been brought to Spain where they are called *aletos:* in Peru they are known as *huaman.* These in turn fell on the eagle, brought it down and dealt it mortal blows. The eagle could not defend itself and sought refuge by dropping into the middle of the main square of the city, among the Incas. The latter picked it up and found it stricken and covered with scales, like a scurf, and almost denuded of its under feathers. They fed it and tried to cure it, but to no avail, and within a few days it died, unable to rise from the ground. The Inca and his companions took this as an ill omen, and the soothsayers interpreted the significance of it using many of the explanations they keep for such occasions. All of these however threatened the ruin of the empire and the destruction of the Inca state and religion. There were also great earthquakes and tremors, and though Peru is greatly subject to this scourge, it was noted that the tremors were much worse than usual and that many high hills fell down. They learnt from the coastal Indians, moreover, that the tides of the sea greatly exceeded their normal limits, and they saw that many fearful and horrifying comets appeared in the air. Among these wonders and alarms, they noticed one clear calm night that the moon was surrounded by three large rings, the first the color of blood; the second, further out, greenish-black; and the third smoky-looking. A soothsayer or magician, called by the Indians *lla-ica,* having seen the rings around the moon, came to Huayna Capac and with a sad and tearful countenance, almost unable to speak, declared:

"Sole Lord, know that your mother the Moon is warning you like a loving parent that Pachacámac, the creator and sustainer of the world, threatens your royal blood and your empire with great plagues with which he will visit you and your people. The first ring round your mother the Moon, which is the color of blood, means that after you have gone to rest with your father the Sun there will be cruel war between your descendants and much shedding of your royal blood, so that in a few years all will be finished; and for this reason she would fain burst with weeping. The second black ring threatens us with the destruction of our religion and our state and the loss of your empire in the midst of the wars and the slaughter of your people. Then all will be turned to smoke, as the third and smoky ring indicates."

The Inca was greatly distressed, but said to the magician in order not to show weakness: "Come, you must have dreamed this nonsense last night, and you say these are revelations from my mother."

The magician answered: "In order that you shall believe me, Inca, you may go out and see your mother's tokens with your own eyes, and you shall bid the other soothsayers appear and you shall know what they say of these omens."

The Inca came forth from his apartment, and after seeing the signs, he ordered all the magicians who were in his court to be assembled, and one of them, of the Yauyu tribe, who was regarded as superior by the rest, also contemplated the rings and said the same as the first. In order that his followers should not be discouraged by such sad auguries, even though they only confirmed what was in his own breast, Huayna Capac pretended not to believe them and told his soothsayers: "If Pachacámac himself does not tell me so, I do not propose to give credit to what you say, for it is unthinkable that my father the Sun should so abhor his own blood as to permit the total destruction of his children." Whereupon he dismissed the soothsayers. However, on considering their words, which so closely followed the ancient oracle that had been handed down from his ancestors, and associating them with the strange wonders that the four elements daily revealed, and further with the arrival of the ship bearing unknown people, Huayna Capac lived in fear and anguish. He was always accompanied by a good army of experienced veterans chosen from the garrisons in these provinces. He ordered many sacrifices to be made to the Sun and bade the soothsayers and wizards, each in their own provinces, consult their familiar devils, particularly the great Pachacámac and the devil Rímac who gave out answers to questions. They were to ask whether the new wonders that had been seen on the sea and in the other elements boded well or ill. From Rímac and other places obscure and confused answers were brought, which neither failed to promise some good nor to threaten much ill. Most of the wizards gave bad auguries, so that all the empire feared some great adversity. But as none of the new things feared occurred in the first three or four years, their former confidence was restored and they lived without care for a few years until the death of Huayna Capac.

Our account of these prophecies is derived both from popular tradition general to the whole empire and in particular from two captains of Huayna Capac's guard, each of whom survived to the age of over eighty. Both were baptized: the elder was called Don Juan Pachuta. He took as his surname the name he had before he was baptized, as most of the Indians have done. The other was called Chauca Rimachi: his Christian name has gone from my memory. Whenever they told of these prophecies and the events of those times, these captains dissolved in tears, and it was necessary to change the subject to make them cease to weep. . . .

Garcilaso describes what was brought to Peru from Europe: plants, animals, and people; the description of the latter follows.

New Names for Various Racial Groups

[9:31] We were forgetting the best imports into the Indies, namely the Spaniards, and the Negroes who have since been taken there as slaves, for they were previously unknown in my country. These two races have mingled [with the Indians] in various ways to form others which are distinguished by the use of different names. Although I spoke a little about this in the *History of Florida,* I have decided to repeat it here as being the proper place. Thus any Spanish man or woman who arrives from Spain is called a Spaniard or Castilian, the two words being quite interchangeable in Peru; and I have used them indifferently in this history and in the *Florida.* The children of Spaniards by Spanish women born there are called *criollos* or *criollas,* implying that they were born in the Indies. The name was invented by the Negroes, as its use shows. They use it to mean a Negro born in the Indies, and they devised it to distinguish those who come from this side and were born in Guinea from those born in the New World, since the former are held in greater honor and considered to be of higher rank because they were born in their own country, while their children were born in a strange land. The parents take offense if they are called *criollos.* The Spaniards have copied them by introducing this word to describe those born in the New World, and in this way both Spaniards and Guinea Negroes are called *criollos* if they are born in the New World. The Negro who arrives there from the Old World is called Negro or Guineo. The child of a Negro by an Indian woman or of an Indian and a Negro woman is called *mulato* or *mulata.* Their children are called *cholos,* a word from the Windward Islands: it means a dog, but is not used for a thoroughbred dog, but only for a mongrel cur: the Spaniards use the word in a pejorative and vituperative sense. The children of Spaniards by Indians are called *mestizos,* meaning that we are a mixture of the two races. The word was applied by the first Spaniards who had children by Indian women, and because it was used by our fathers, as well as on account of its meaning, I call myself by it in public and am proud of it, though in the Indies, if a person is told: "You're a mestizo," or "He's a mestizo," it is taken as an insult. This is the reason why they have adopted with such enthusiasm the name *montañés* which some potentate applied to them, among other slights and insults, instead of the word *mestizo.* They do not stop to consider that, although in Spain the word *montañés* is an honorable appellation, on account of the privileges that have been bestowed on the natives of the Asturian and Basque mountains, if it is applied to anyone who is not from these parts, it assumes a pejorative sense derived from its original meaning "something from the mountains." This is brought out by our great master Antonio de Lebrija,[63] to whom all good Latinists in Spain today are indebted, in his vocabulary. In the general language of Peru the word for a mountaineer is *sacharuna,* properly "savage," and whoever applied the word *montañés* was privately calling them savages: those of my own generation, not understanding this malicious implication, took pride in the insulting epithet, when they should rather have avoided and abominated it, using the name our fathers bestowed on us rather than accepting new-fangled indignities.

The children of a Spaniard and a mestizo, or vice versa, are called *cuatralvos,* meaning they have one part of Indian blood and three of Spanish. The children of a mestizo and an Indian, or vice versa, are called *tresalvos,* meaning that they have three parts of Indian blood and one of Spanish. All these names, and others which we omit to avoid tedium, have been devised in Peru to describe the racial groups that have come into existence since the arrival of the Spaniards, and we can therefore say that they were brought in together with the other things not previously found in Peru. With this we return to the Inca kings, the children of the great Huayna Capac, who are calling us to relate great events that occurred in their time.

Garcilaso returns to the story of the origin of the war between Huascar and Atahuallpa.

Huascar Inca Demands That His Brother Atahuallpa Shall Do Homage to Him

[9:32] On the death of Huayna Capac, his two sons reigned for four or five years in peaceful possession of their domains, without engaging in new conquests or even attempting to do so, for King Huascar found his realms barred on the northern side by those of the kingdom of Quito, belonging to his brother. Beyond this there were new conquests still to be made, though on the other three sides everything between the wilderness of the Antis and the sea, from east to west, had already been subdued, and the kingdom of Chile to the south had also been conquered. Inca Atahuallpa also refrained from attempting new conquests because he wished to attend to the welfare of himself and his subjects. But those who are called upon to rule can never tolerate an equal or a rival, and after passing these few years in peace and quiet, Huascar Inca began to imagine that he had done amiss in obeying his father's orders to the effect that the kingdom of Quito should go to his

---

[63] Antonio de Nebrija (or Lebrija) was the author of the first grammar and vocabulary of the Spanish language, published in 1492.

brother Atahuallpa, for in addition to the loss of so great a kingdom to his empire, he realized that its separation blocked the continued progress of his conquests, while his brother was free to expand his own domains to the north, so that in time Atahuallpa's kingdom might come to exceed Huascar's, and he, though he was called to be monarch, as the name Sapa Inca, or sole lord, implies, would in due course come to have another equal or perhaps superior to himself, and as his brother was ambitious and restless, when he had become powerful he might aspire to deprive him of the empire.

These imaginings increased from day to day and caused such turmoil in the breast of Huascar Inca that, when he could stand it no longer, he sent a relative as his messenger to his brother Atahuallpa, saying that, as Atahuallpa knew, by the ancient constitution of the first Inca Manco Capac, which had been observed by all his descendants, the kingdom of Quito and all the other provinces belonged to the imperial crown of Cusco, and that though he, Huascar, had conceded what his father bade him, it had been from enforced obedience to the latter rather than out of a consciousness that it was right and just, for it was on the contrary prejudicial to the crown and the rights of his successors. For this reason his father should not have bidden him accept the division, and he was not obliged to fulfill it. However, as his father had ordered it and he had consented, he would gladly accept the situation under two conditions, first, that Atahuallpa should not add an inch of land to his realms, for all that was still unconquered belonged to the empire, and second, that Atahuallpa should do homage to him and become his vassal.

Atahuallpa received this communication with all the humility and submissiveness he could feign, and three days later, after considering his own interests, he replied with great astuteness and cunning to the effect that he had always had it in his heart to recognize the authority of his lord the Sapa Inca, which he now did, and he would not add anything to the kingdom of Quito, but if his majesty wanted it, he would give it up, abdicate, and live privately at Huascar's capital, like any other of his kinsmen, and serve him in war and peace, and obey him, as he should obey his prince and lord in anything he wished. Atahuallpa's reply was sent to the Inca by the usual runner, as Huascar himself had ordered, so that it would arrive sooner than if the envoy brought it himself, and the latter remained in Atahuallpa's court to await the Inca's instructions.

Huascar received the answer with great satisfaction, and answered saying that he was very glad that his brother should remain in possession of what his father had left him, and that he would confirm him in his position provided that he would come to Cusco within a certain period and offer him obedience and make the usual oath of fidelity and loyalty. Atahuallpa replied that he was delighted to know the Inca's wishes, the better to fulfill them, and that he would appear within the stated time to offer his obedience. Furthermore, so that the oath should be taken with greater solemnity and completeness, he begged his majesty to give permission for the provinces of his estate to accompany him to Cusco to celebrate the obsequies of his father, Inca Huayna Capac, according to the traditional usage in the kingdom of Quito and the other provinces. When this rite had been performed, he and all his vassals would take the oath together. Huascar Inca granted all that his brother requested of him, and bade him make whatever arrangements he wished for their father's obsequies: for his part, he would be satisfied if they should be solemnized in Quito according to the local tradition and that Atahuallpa should come to Cusco at his own convenience. At this both brothers were very content, the first because he was far from imagining the treacherous design that was being prepared to deprive him of his life and empire, and the other, cunningly engaged in the deepest plot to relieve him of both.

Atahuallpa's Devices to Allay His Brother's Suspicions

[9:33] King Atahuallpa ordered it to be publicly announced throughout his kingdom and all the provinces he possessed that all able-bodied men should prepare for the expedition to Cusco, which would depart within so many days to celebrate the obsequies of the great Huayna Capac, his father, according to the traditional usage of each tribe, and to swear the oath of homage to their monarch Huascar Inca. For both purposes they were to take all their accouterment and adornments, since he desired that the celebrations should attain the greatest possible solemnity. At the same time he secretly bade his captains to select the bravest warriors and bid them secretly take their arms, for he needed them not for obsequies but for war. They were to travel in troops of five or six hundred Indians, more or less, and to pretend that they were engaged on civil and not on military duties: each band was to march two or three leagues from the last. The first captains were to reduce the length of the day's march when they came within ten or twelve days of Cusco, so that those behind might close up with them, while the bands in the rear were to double their marches when they came to this region, so as to catch up with the first. In this order King Atahuallpa sent off more than thirty thousand warriors, most of them chosen veterans left him by his father, with famous and experienced captains who had always attended him. The leaders were two generals, one called Challcuchima and the other Quízquiz, and the Inca announced that he would journey with the rearmost.

Huascar Inca confided in his brother's words and more especially in the long experience among the Indians of respect and loyalty towards the Inca, especially on the part of his brothers and the other members of his family, which is described in the following words by Padre Acosta in his Book VI, chapter vi: "The reverence and affection of these people for their Incas was undoubtedly very great, and the latter were never known to have been betrayed by their own people," etcetera. For this reason Huascar Inca not only did not suspect the treachery that was being prepared, but on the contrary very liberally ordered his people to welcome Atahuallpa's vassals and supply them with food, like their own brothers who were coming to his father's obsequies and to take the oath due to him. Such was the conduct of the two sides, Huascar's followers acting with all their natural simplicity and goodness, and Atahuallpa's with all the malice and cunning they had learnt in his school.

Atahuallpa Inca resorted to this cunning and subtle ruse against his brother because he was not strong enough to declare war on him openly. He expected more from deceit than from his own strength for, by taking King Huascar unawares, as in fact he did, he could not fail to win: if he had given his brother a chance to prepare, he would have lost.

Huascar Is Warned and Calls Up His Warriors

[9:34] In this way, the forces from Quito marched nearly four hundred leagues and came to within a hundred leagues of Cusco. Certain old Incas, the governors of the provinces through which they made their way, men who had been captains and had great experience in peace and war, were disturbed by the movement of so many men: to their minds five or six thousand men, or ten at the outside, would have been enough to celebrate the obsequies, while the presence of the common people was not necessary for the purpose of taking the oath, which was done only by the *curacas* or lords of vassals, the governors, and military leaders, and King Atahuallpa, their leader. But no peace or good fellowship was to be expected from his astute, restless, and warlike spirit; and as their suspicions and fears were aroused, they sent secret messages to King Huascar, begging him to beware of his brother Atahuallpa since it did not seem good to them that he should be accompanied by such large forces.

Thus warned, Huascar Inca roused himself from the dream of heedless confidence in which he had been slumbering. He dispatched urgent messengers to all the governors of the provinces of Andesuyu, Collasuyu, and Condesuyu, and bade them repair to Cusco in all haste with whatever warriors they could raise. He sent no messengers to Chinchaysuyu, the largest and most warlike of the provinces, because it was cut off by the invading army now marching across it. Atahuallpa's followers, aware of the unpreparedness of Huascar and his men, increased daily in courage and cunning, and the vanguard reached a point forty leagues from the capital, where they slowed their rate of advance while those behind accelerated, so that in the space of a few days there were more than twenty thousand warriors ready to cross the river Apurimac, which they did without opposition. Beyond this point they advanced like open enemies with banners unfurled and arms and badges revealed: they came on slowly, in two main formations, the vanguard and the battle array, until they were joined by the rear guard consisting of ten thousand more men. Thus they came to the top of the hill of Villacunca, six leagues from the city. Atahuallpa remained on the borders of his own kingdom, and dared not approach, until he saw the result of the first battle, on which he had placed all his hopes, relying on the good faith and unpreparedness of the adversary as well as on the courage and spirit of his captains and veterans.

While the army approached, King Huascar Inca called up his warriors with all possible speed, but his men could not arrive in time to be of use on account of the great extent of the district of Collasuyu, which is more than two hundred leagues long. As to those from Andesuyu, they were few in numbers, for the area is thinly populated on account of its great mountains. Condesuyu, the most settled and thickly populated district, produced thirty thousand men with all their chiefs, but they were ill-practiced in war since they had had no training during the long period of peace. They were raw recruits with no military instinct. Inca Huascar took all his kinsmen and the men who had obeyed the summons, amounting to nearly ten thousand men, and sallied forth to collect his forces to the west of the city. They were approaching from this direction, and he intended to gather them all here and wait for such other troops as would arrive.

The Battle of the Incas; Atahuallpa's Victory and His Cruelties

[9:35] Atahuallpa's captains realized from experience that delay would compromise their chance of victory and that an immediate issue would guarantee it: they therefore went in search of Huascar Inca so as to offer battle before more forces rallied to him. They found him on a wide plain two or three leagues to the west of the city. A fierce engagement took place there, without any preparation or forewarning on either side. The battle was fought with great cruelty, the attackers seeking to seize the Inca Huascar, who was an inestimable prize, and the others not to lose their beloved ruler. The struggle lasted the whole day with great loss of life on both sides, but finally the absence of the Collas and the fact that Huascar's army was new and unskilled in war told in favor of Inca Atahuallpa, whose seasoned soldiers were each worth ten of their adversaries. In the encounter Huascar Inca was captured, this being the main object of his enemies, who would not have considered they had accomplished anything if he had escaped them. He tried to make his escape with about a thousand men who gathered about him, and they all died in his presence, some killed by the enemy and some taking their own lives when they saw that their king had been captured. In addition to his royal person, those taken prisoner included many *curacas,* lords of vassals, many captains, and a great number of nobles who were wandering like sheep without a shepherd, neither seeking flight nor knowing where to betake themselves. Many of them could have escaped, but knowing that their Inca had been taken prisoner, allowed themselves to be arrested with him out of love and loyalty toward him.

Atahuallpa's forces were full of content and joy at so great a victory and so rich a prize as the imperial person of Huascar Inca and all the leaders of his army. They guarded him extremely closely, appointing four captains and the most trustworthy soldiers in their army to take turns on guard, not losing sight of him by day or by night. They then ordered the announcement of his capture to be made throughout the empire, so that if any forces were on the way to join him they would disband on learning that he was already under arrest. They sent the news of the victory and of the arrest of Huascar posthaste to King Atahuallpa.

Such was the sum and substance of the war between these two brothers, the last kings of Peru. Other battles and skirmishes related by the Spanish historians were incidents that took place in different parts of both kingdoms between captains and garrisons, while Atahuallpa's so-called arrest was an invention which he himself caused to be spread about so as to lull the suspicions of Huascar and his supporters. He later put it about that after his arrest his father the Sun had turned him into a snake so that he could escape through a hole in his cell, a tale that was intended to bolster up his authority and make his usurpation popular by causing the common people to believe that their god, the Sun, had favored his cause by freeing him from the power of his enemies. And the people were so simple that they readily believed any fairy story that the Incas put forward concerning the Sun, since these were held to be his children.

Atahuallpa made very cruel use of his victory. He made a false pretense that he intended to restore Huascar and summoned together all the Incas in the empire, both governors and other civil ministers, and generals, captains, and soldiers. They were all to appear within a certain time in Cusco, where he said he wished to draw up with them certain privileges and statutes that should thenceforward be observed by both kings so that they might live in peace and brotherhood. At this news all the Incas of the royal blood assembled: only those who were prevented by sickness or age, and a few who were too far away or who could not or dared not come or did not trust the victorious Atahuallpa, were missing. When they were all assembled, Atahuallpa ordered them all to be killed in various ways so as to make sure that they would never plan any revolt against him. . . .

Some Members of the Royal Blood
Escape Atahuallpa's Cruelties

[9:38] A number escaped this butchery, some because they did not fall into Atahuallpa's power, and others because his own followers were filled with pity to see the extermination of the blood they had considered divine and, weary with the merciless carnage, permitted some of the victims to escape from the ring in which they were kept, and even drove them forth, removing their royal robes and giving them ordinary garb so that they should not be recognized; for, as we have explained,[64] the rank of the wearer was known from the quality of his dress. All those who were spared in this way were boys and girls of ten or eleven years or less. One was my mother and a brother of hers called Don Francisco Huallpa Túpac Inca Yupanqui, whom I knew: he has written to me since I have been in Spain. All that I have written about this disastrous end of the Incas is derived from the account I have many times heard them tell. In addition I know a few others who escaped. I knew two *auquis,* or princes. They were sons of Huayna Capac, one called Paullu, who was already an adult at the time of the catastrophe and is mentioned by the Spanish historians, the other Titu, a legitimate member of the royal blood: he was a boy at the time. I have written elsewhere about their baptism and the Christian names they adopted. Paullu had descendants with Spanish blood, for his son Don Carlos Inca, who was my fellow pupil and studied grammar with me, married a noblewoman born in Spain, the daughter of Spanish parents. They had a son, Don Melchor Carlos Inca, who came to Spain last year, in 1602, partly to see the capital and partly to receive the grants he was supposed to be awarded in Spain in return for his grandfather's services in the conquest and pacification of Peru and against the rebels, as can be seen from the histories of that empire. But he was chiefly entitled to these rewards as the direct descendant of Huayna Capac in the male line, for he is the most famous and distinguished of the few surviving members of the royal family. He is at present in Valladolid, awaiting the grants he is to receive: however great they are he will deserve better.

I have not heard that Titu left issue. Of the *ñustas,* or princesses, the daughters of Huayna Capac known to be legitimate by blood, one was

---

[64] Dress regulations are not included in this edition; see the complete Livermore translation of *Royal Commentaries,* book 5, ch. 9.

called Doña Beatriz Coya: she married Martín de Bustincia, a nobleman who was treasurer or factor of the estates of the emperor Charles V in Peru; they had three sons who were called the Bustincias and another called Juan Serra de Leguiçamo, who was a fellow pupil of mine in the primary and grammar school. The other *ñusta* was Doña Leonor Coya, who married first a Spaniard called Juan Balsa, whom I did not know, for it was when I was a child, and had a son of the same name who was at school with me; and secondly Francisco de Villacastín, one of the first Conquerors of Peru, who had also been a conqueror of Panama and other places. . . .

I knew other Incas and Pallas of the royal blood, of less consequence than the foregoing: there would not be more than two hundred altogether. I have referred particularly to these because they were children of Huayna Capac. My mother was his niece, the daughter of one of his brothers, legitimate on both his father's and his mother's side, called Huallpa Túpac Inca Yupanqui.

I knew a son and two daughters of King Atahuallpa. One of the daughters was called Doña Angelina, by whom the marquis Don Francisco Pizarro had a son called Don Francisco, a great rival of mine as I was of his, for when we were both eight or nine his uncle Gonzalo Pizarro used to make us compete at running and jumping. The marquis also had a daughter called Doña Francisca Pizarro: she turned out a fine lady and married her uncle Hernando Pizarro. Her father the marquis had her by a daughter of Huayna Capac called Doña Inés Huaillas Ñusta, who afterwards married Martín de Ampuero, a *vecino* of Lima. These two, children of the marquis and one of Gonzalo Pizarro called Don Fernando, came to Spain, but the boys died young, to the great sorrow of all who knew them, for they promised to be worthy sons of such parents. I do not remember if the name of Atahuallpa's other daughter was Doña Beatriz or Doña Isabel: she married a gentleman from Extremadura called Blas Gómez and secondly a mestizo gentleman called Sancho de Rojas. The son was called Don Francisco Atahuallpa: he was a handsome boy in body and features, as were all the Incas and Pallas: he died young. . . .

The Surviving Descendants of the Royal Blood of the Incas

[9:40] Many days after finishing this ninth book I received certain information from Peru, from which I have compiled the following chapter, for I thought that this matter belonged to my history and I have therefore added it here. The few Incas of the royal blood who survived the cruelties and tyrannies of Atahuallpa and other later oppressions have more descendants than I had imagined, for at the end of the year 1603 they all wrote to Don Melchor Carlos Inca and to Don Alonso de Mesa, the son of

Alonso de Mesa who was a *vecino* of Cusco, and also to me, to ask us to beg His Majesty in the name of them all to have them exempted from the tribute they are paying and from other vexations that they undergo in common with the rest of the Indians. They sent the three of us powers to act together on their behalf with proofs of their descent, including details of which of them descended from which king, with all their names, and which from which other king, down to the last of their line; and for clearer proof and demonstration they included a genealogical tree showing the royal line from Manco Capac to Huayna Capac painted on a vara and a half of white China silk. The Incas were depicted in their ancient dress, wearing the scarlet fringe on their heads and their ear ornaments in their ears; only their busts were shown. This message was directed to me, and I forwarded it to Don Melchor Carlos Inca and Don Alonso de Mesa who reside at court in Valladolid: for I myself could not undertake their case because of this occupation, though I would be glad to devote my life to it, for it could not be better employed. The letter the Incas sent me is written in a fair hand by one of them, and the turn of language they use partly follows their own tongue and partly the Spanish, for they are all now Castilianized. It is dated April 16, 1603. I do not reproduce it here so as not to cause the reader pain with the miserable account they give of their life. They write with great confidence, which we all entertain, that when His Catholic Majesty knows their plight, he will relieve them and will confer many privileges on them, as befits the descendants of kings. After depicting the figures of the Incas, they have written the list of descendants against each headed: Capac Aillu, "august or royal lineage." This title is used by them all in common and implies that they all descend from the first Inca Manco Capac. Then they put another title in particular for the descent of each king with different names, to show that each comes from a certain king. The descent of Manco Capac is called Chima Panaca and consists of 40 Incas. That of Sinchi Roca is called Rauraua Panaca and embraces 64 Incas. That of Lloque Yupanqui, the third Inca, is called Hahuanina Aillu; it has 63 Incas. Those of Capac Yupanqui are called Apu Maita, and number 56. Those of Maita Capac, the fifth king, are Usca Maita, and number 35. Those of Inca Roca are Uncaquirau: they number 50. Those of Yáhuar Huácac, the seventh king, are called Ailli Panaca, and are 51. Those of Viracocha Inca are called Socso Panaca, and are 69. The descent of Inca Pachacútec and his son, Inca Yupanqui, are put together and called Inca Panaca, and the number of descendants is thus doubled and reaches 99. The descent of Túpac Inca Yupanqui is called Capac Aillu, or imperial descent, confirming what I said above about this title, and numbers only 18. The descent of Huayna Capac is called Tumi Pampa, after a very solemn feast that Huayna Capac dedicated to the Sun at that place, which is in the province of the Cañaris. It had a royal palace, storehouses for the warriors, a house of the chosen women, and a temple of the Sun, all as grand and noble and full of splendor as anywhere in Peru, as Pedro de Cieza relates, with all possible emphasis, in his chapter xliv; and, appearing to think that he has fallen short of the truth, he concludes with the words: "Finally, I cannot say anything that does not fall short of a true description of the great wealth the Incas had in these palaces," etcetera. Huayna Capac wished the memory of this solemn festivity to be preserved in the name of his descendants, and they are therefore called Tumi Pampa: they number only 22; for as the lines of Huayna Capac and his father Túpac Inca Yupanqui were the closest to the royal tree, Atahuallpa did his utmost to extirpate them even more thoroughly than the rest, and very few therefore escaped his inhuman cruelty, as the list shows. The total number of Incas is 567 persons, and it should be noted that this is the descent by the male line, for the female line is, as we have said, ignored by the Incas, unless they are the sons of Spanish *conquistadores* who won Peru, for these too are called Incas, in the belief that they are descendants of their god, the Sun. The letter they wrote to me was signed by eleven Incas, one for each of the eleven lines, each signing for the whole of his line and giving his baptismal name and the names of his ancestors. I do not know the meaning of the names assumed by the other lines, except the two last, for they are names drawn from the special language used by the Incas in talking among one another and are not in the general language spoken in the capital. It remains to speak of Don Melchor Carlos Inca, the grandson of Paullu and great grandson of Huayna Capac, who, as we have said, came to Spain in 1602 to receive grants. At the beginning of the present year of 1604 the result of his request was made known, and he was awarded 7,500 ducats in perpetuity payable from the royal chest of His Majesty in Lima, together with a subsidy to bring his wife and household to Spain, a habit of Santiago,[65] and the promise of a post in the royal household: the Indians he had inherited from his father and grandfather in Cusco were to go to the crown, and he was not to return to the Indies. . . .

---

[65] A habit of Santiago was the habit worn by the members of the knight-order of Saint James who, in his guise of *Santiago Matamoros,* or Saint James the killer of Moors (Muslims), was very popular among the Spanish conquerors, who eagerly petitioned for the right to wear the habit on formal occasions and to be buried in it when they died.

Part II

Chapter One
The Expedition to Peru and the Capture of the Inca

In Panama, Francisco Pizarro and Diego de Almagro, with Hernando de Luque as their chief financial officer, form a company to follow the rumors of rich lands to the south. They begin to explore in 1525, encountering only war-like people who drive them away. On their second voyage, they take refuge on an island called El Gallo, where Pizarro remains with thirteen men while Almagro returns to Panama for reinforcements. After many months, they are finally relieved and explore south to the valley of Túmbez, finding an Inca set-tlement. They return to Panama, and Pizarro goes to Spain in search of the royal approval to conquer the land they discovered. Authority is awarded to Pizarro, without Almagro, which provokes dissension that is eventually papered over. The Spaniards, augmented by additional men recruited by Pizarro in Spain, among them his four brothers, Hernando, Gonzalo, Juan, and Pedro Pizarro, return to Peru, leaving Diego de Almagro to follow with more ships and men. Pizarro's forces reach Túmbez and conquer it. Discovering that there was a civil war between the brothers Huascar and Atahuallpa over control of the Inca state, Pizarro sends two ambassadors to Atahuallpa, who had recently defeated and captured his brother. Atahuallpa receives the two Spaniards in his camp near Cajamarca, together with an Indian interpreter named Felipe. . .by the Spaniards. The Inca agrees to meet the Spaniards the next day in Cajama-rca, and Pizarro and his men prepare for whatever might occur that day. The Indians appear and enter the square unarmed, and the Dominican Fray Vice-nte de Valverde, who is part of the Spanish party, addresses Atahuallpa.

The Discourse Delivered by Fray Vicente de Valverde

[1:22] Padre Blas Valera, that most scholarly student of the events of those days, who studied them with the intention of writing their history, gives the speech or discourse Fray Vicente de Valverde addressed to King Atahuallpa, which he divides into two parts. He says that he saw it in Trujillo when studying Latin: it was written in Fray Vicente's own hand and was owned by one of the conquerors called Diego de Olivares. On his death it passed to a son-in-law of his, who often read it and learnt it by heart. I have therefore thought best to include it as Padre Blas Valera writes it, for he gives it at great length and in more detail than the other historians, owing to his having seen the original. I also include it on my own authority, for it coincides in every way with the reports I have, and differs little or not at all in substance from what the Spanish historians have written. If I set it down in his Paternity's name, I shall relate it in the name of both of us, for I do not wish to appropriate another's version by putting it forward as mine, though this would do me much honor, but to assign everything to its author, and it is honor enough for me to be associated with such great men.

When Fray Vicente approached to address the Inca, the latter was very surprised at the Dominican's appearance, with his beard and shaven crown, as religious have them, his long habit, and his crucifix in his hand, and a book, which was Silvestre's *Summa.* Others say it was his breviary and others the Bible: the reader shall choose which he wishes. In order to know how to receive this man, the king asked one of the leading Indians who had gone to offer the Spaniards everything they needed four days before.

He said: "What is the rank and degree of this Spaniard? Is he by chance higher or lower than the rest, or is he equal?"

The Indian answered: "All I could find out, Inca, was that this is the captain or leader of the word (he meant preacher), and the minister of the supreme god Pachacámac and his messenger: the rest are not like him." Then Fray Vicente came up to them and having shown his respect in the manner customary among religious, and obtaining the king's leave, he made the following speech.[1]

First part of Fray Vicente de Valverde's speech:

"It is proper that you should know, most famous and most powerful king, that it is necessary that Your Highness and all your subjects should not only learn the true Catholic faith, but that you should hear and believe the following: First, that God, three in one, created heaven and earth and all things in the world, and He offers the prize of eternal life to the good, and punishes the wicked with perpetual suffering. In the beginning this God created man of dust, and gave it the breath of life, which we call the spirit, which God made in his own likeness. Wherefore every man consists of body and rational spirit. From this man, whom God called Adam, all the men in the world are descended, and he is the origin and beginning of our nature. This man Adam sinned by breaking the command of his creator, and with him all men hitherto born and to be born till the end of the

---

[1] This speech is the famous "*requerimiento*" or "requirement," a Spanish legal document that informed the people they met of the Spaniards' holy right to conquer them—a right granted them by the Pope in exchange for the imposition of Christianity.

world have sinned. No man or woman is free of this taint, nor will be, with the exception of our Lord Jesus Christ, who, being the Son of the true God, descended from heaven, was born of the Virgin Mary to redeem the whole of mankind and free it from the bondage of sin. He at last died for our salvation on a wooden cross like the one I have in my hands, for which reason we as Christians worship and revere it.

"This Jesus Christ rose by His own virtue from the dead, and after forty days He ascended into heaven and sits on the right hand of God, our Almighty Father. He left on earth His apostles and their successors so that, through words and sermons and other holy means, they might attract men to the knowledge and worship of God and the preservation of His law.

"It was His will also that Saint Peter, His apostle, should be the prince over the other apostles and all their successors and all other Christians, as the vicar of God, and that all the other pontiffs of Rome, the successors of St. Peter, whom Christians call popes, should have the same supreme authority that God gave him. And the popes, then, now, and forever, strive with great saintliness to preach to men and teach them the word of God."

Second part of Fray Vicente de Valverde's speech:

"Therefore the holy pope of Rome who now lives on earth, understanding that all the peoples and tribes of these realms have left the true God, their maker, and have sunk to worship idols and likenesses of the Devil, has conceded the conquest of these parts to Charles V, emperor of the Romans, most powerful king of Spain and monarch of all the earth, so that, having subjected these peoples and their kings and lords, and having expelled the rebels and recalcitrant from their midst, he alone may reign over and rule and govern these peoples, bringing to them the knowledge of God and obedience to His church. Our most powerful king, though greatly occupied and engaged in the government of his vast realms and provinces, accepted the pope's mission, and did not refuse it out of regard for the salvation of these peoples. He therefore sent his captains and soldiers to accomplish it as has already been done in the conquest of great islands and the lands of Mexico nearby. Having conquered them by the power of his arms, he has won them to the true religion of Jesus Christ, for God Himself said that they were to be obliged to accept it.

"Thus the great emperor Charles V has chosen as his lieutenant and ambassador Don Francisco Pizarro, who is now here, so that Your Highness' kingdoms may also receive the same benefit. He will establish a league and alliance of perpetual friendship between His Majesty and Your Highness, so that Your Highness and all your realms will become tributaries; that is to say, you will pay tribute to the emperor, and will become his vassal and deliver your kingdom wholly into his hands, renouncing the administration and government of it, as other kings and lords have done.

This comes first. Secondly, after establishing this peace and friendship and having submitted willingly or by force, you shall give true obedience to the pope, the supreme pontiff, and receive and believe the faith of Jesus Christ, our God, and scorn and utterly repudiate the abominable superstition of your idols: by this act you shall learn how holy is our law and how false your own, invented by the Devil. All this, oh king, if you believe me, you should willingly grant, for it is greatly to the advantage of yourself and your people. If you refuse, know that you will be constrained with war, fire, and the sword, and all your idols shall be overthrown and we shall oblige you by the sword to abandon your false religion and to receive willy-nilly our Catholic faith and pay tribute to our emperor and deliver him your king-dom. If you seek obstinately to resist, you may rest assured that God will suffer that you and all your Indians shall be destroyed by our arms, even as Pharaoh of old and his host perished in the Red Sea. . . ."

Atahuallpa's Reply

[1:24] After hearing the last part of the speech in which he was asked to renounce his realms willingly or by force and become a tributary as the pope required and the emperor desired, and on hearing the threat of war with fire and the sword, with the destruction of himself and his people like that of Pharaoh and his host, Atahuallpa was filled with sadness, supposing that those whom he and his Indians called Viracochas, believing they were gods, had turned into mortal enemies since they made such harsh demands. He gave a groan, using the word *átac*, "woe is me," expressing with this exclamation his great grief at hearing the last part of the dis-course. Then mastering his emotions, he replied:

"It would have caused me great satisfaction, since you deny everything else that I requested of your messengers, that you should at least have granted me one request, that of addressing me through a more skilled and faithful translator. For the urbanity and social life of men is more readily understood through speech than by customs, since even though you may be endowed with great virtues, if you do not manifest them by words, I shall not easily be able to perceive them by observation and experience. And if this is needful among all peoples and nations, it is much more so between those who come from such widely distant regions as we; if we seek to deal and talk through interpreters and messengers who are ignorant of both languages, it will be as though we were conversing through the mouths of beasts of burden. I say this, man of God, because I perceive that the words you have spoken must mean something different from what the dragoman has told me. The occasion requires it; for when we are to discuss peace, friendship, perpetual brotherhood, and even kinship, as the other messengers who came told me, all that this Indian has said signifies the opposite; you threaten us with war and death by fire and the sword, and with the exile and destruction of the Incas and their family, and say that I must renounce my kingdom and become the tributary of another, either willingly or by force. Whence I deduce one of two things: either your prince and you are tyrants who are destroying the world, depriving others of their realms, slaying and robbing those who have done you no harm and owe you nothing, or you are ministers of God, whom we call Pachacámac, who has chosen you to punish and destroy us.

"If this is so, I and my subjects offer ourselves to die or to suffer whatever you wish to do with us, not out of fear of your arms and threats, but to fulfill what my father Huayna Capac left as instructions at the hour of his death, namely that we should serve and honor a bearded people like yourselves, which would come after his times, and of whose presence off the shore of his empire he had heard many years before. He told us that they would be men who had a better religion and better customs and were wiser and braver than we. So in fulfillment of my father's decree and testament, we have called you Viracochas, believing you to be messengers of the great god Viracocha, whose will and righteous indignation, and power and arms, cannot be resisted. But he has pity and mercy too. You should therefore act like divine messengers and ministers and put a stop to the slayings and lootings and acts of cruelty that have taken place in Tumbes and the district round about.

"Moreover your mouthpiece has told me that you have mentioned five great men I should know. The first is God three and one, or four, whom you call the creator of the universe: he is perchance the same as our Pachacámac and Viracocha. The second is he whom you say is the father of all other men on whom they have all heaped their sins. The third you call Jesus Christ, the only one who did not lay his sins on the first man, but he was killed. The fourth you call pope. The fifth is Charles, whom you call most powerful and monarch of the universe and supreme above the rest, without regard for the other four. If this Charles is prince and lord of the whole world, why should he need the pope to give him a new grant and concession to make war on me and usurp these kingdoms? If he has to ask the pope's permission, is not the pope a greater lord than he, and more powerful, and prince of all the world? Also I am surprised that you should say I must pay tribute to Charles and not to the others, for you give no reason for paying the tribute, and I have certainly no obligation whatever to pay it. If there were any right or reason for paying tribute, it seems to me that it should go to the God you say created everyone and the man you say was the father of all men and to Jesus Christ who did not heap sins on him; and finally it should go to the pope who can grant my kingdoms and my person to others. But if you say I owe these nothing, I owe even less to Charles, who was never lord of these regions and has never set eyes on them. If he has any rights over me after making this concession, it is only just and reasonable that you should tell me before you threaten war, fire, blood, and death, so that I may obey the pope's will, for I am not so lacking in good sense as not to obey whoever has the right justly and lawfully to command.

"I wish also to know about the good man called Jesus Christ who never cast his sins on the other and who you say died—if he died of a sickness or at the hands of his enemies; and if he was included among the gods before his death or after it. I also desire to know if you regard these five you have mentioned to me as gods, since you honor them so. For in this case you have more gods than we, who adore only Pachacámac as the Supreme God and the Sun as the lower god, and the Moon as the Sun's wife and sister. I should therefore be very glad if you would explain these things to me through a better interpreter so that I may know them and obey your will."

The Capture of Atahuallpa

[1:25] Because of his experience of the inadequacy of the interpreter the Inca took care to adjust this reply to his abilities in two respects. Firstly, he uttered it in parts, so that the dragoman would understand and transmit it in sections: he first said one section, then the next, and so on till the end. Secondly, he used the language of the Chinchaysuyu, which the interpreter would understand better because it is commoner in those parts than the speech of Cusco; thus Felipe would understand the Inca's meaning better and might explain it, however barbarously. After delivering the reply he ordered the annalists, who have charge of the knots, to take note of it and include it in their tradition.

By now the Spaniards, who were unable to brook the length of the discourse, had left their places and fallen on the Indians, laying hands on them to seize the many gold and silver jewels and precious stones with which the Indians had adorned their persons to solemnize the occasion of hearing the embassy of the monarch of the universe. Other Spaniards had climbed up a small tower to throw down an idol adorned with many plates of gold, silver and precious stones. This alarmed the Indians and caused a great hubbub. Seeing what was happening, the Inca shouted to his followers not to wound or harm the Spaniards even though they should seize or kill the king himself. Here Padre Blas Valera says that our Lord God, as He changed the wrath of King Ahasuerus into mildness with the presence of Queen Esther,[2] so with the presence of the holy cross which the good friar

---

[2] The story of Queen Esther, the Jewish wife of King Ahasuerus, is the subject of the book of Esther in the *Holy Bible*.

held in his hands, He changed the angry and warlike spirit of King Atahua-llpa, not only to gentleness and mildness, but even to the greatest submission and humility, since he ordered his companions not to fight even though he were killed or captured. It is certainly to be believed that this was a manifestation of divine mercy, for with this and similar marvels which we shall often observe at many points of this history, we shall see how God was disposing the spirits of those gentiles to receive the truth of His doctrine and His Holy Gospel.

The historians bear false witness that Fray Vicente de Valverde gave the alarm, asking the Spaniards to execute justice and vengeance for the fact that the king had thrown on the ground the book he is said to have asked the friar to give him. They bear false witness against the king as well as the priest, for he neither threw the book down, nor even took it in his hands. What happened was that Fray Vicente was alarmed by the sudden shouting of the Indians, and feared they would harm him. He therefore rose abruptly from the chair in which he sat talking to the king, and in rising dropped the cross from his hands and the book from his lap. He snatched them from the ground and hurried to his companions, shouting to them not to harm the Indians, for he was much taken by Atahuallpa, realizing his good sense and understanding from his reply and the questions he put. The friar was on the point of satisfying these questions when the uproar began; and because of this the Spaniards did not hear what the priest was saying on behalf of the Indians.

The king did not say the words the historians ascribe to him: "You believe that Christ is God and that he died: I worship the Sun and Moon, which are immortal. And who told you that your God was the maker of the Universe?"

They go on to say that Fray Vicente answered that the book said so, and the king took it, turned over the leaves and put it to his ear, and when he found it did not speak, he threw it on the ground. Then the friar picked it up and ran to his companions saying: "Christians, the Gospels have been dashed down! Justice and vengeance on these Indians! Come on, cut them down: they scorn our religion and spurn our friendship!"

The reply ascribed to the Inca is also fabulous: "I am free and owe tribute to no one; nor do I intend to pay it, for I recognize no superior and own no king. I would gladly be the emperor's friend, since he shows his great power by sending so many armies to such distant lands. Nevertheless when you say I should obey the pope, I disagree; for a man who tries to give his friends other people's property and bids me give up the kingdom I have inherited, though I do not even know him, shows he is out of his mind. And as to the part about changing my religion when I know it is most sacred, it would be cowardly and ignorant on my part to question what pleases me so well and is approved by ancient tradition and by the witness of my ancestors."

All this is fabulous, and may be set down to the false and flattering reports given to the historians. Atahuallpa did not deny the right to ask for tribute, but insisted on being told the grounds for it, and it was at this stage that the Indians raised their outcry. The Spanish general and his captains sent the version given by the historians to the emperor, and took great trouble and pains to prohibit anyone from setting down the truth about what happened, which is what we have said. Apart from the tradition of the knots of the province of Cajamarca, I have heard this version from many conquerors who were present on the expedition, and Padre Blas Valera says that one of these was his father Alonso Valera, whom he often heard tell the story. In short, more than 5,000 Indians died that day. Of these, 3,500 died by the sword, and the rest were old men, women, and children, for great crowds of both sexes and all ages had come to see and celebrate the arrival of those they regarded as gods. More than 1,500 of them perished, trampled down by the crowd of their own people and by the rush of the horses: another great crowd of all ages had collected under the wall which the Indians knocked down with the impetus of their flight, and an incalculable number perished buried alive. The warriors numbered more than 30,000 as has been said. Two days after the rout the cross was found in the place where Fray Vicente had left it, for no one dared to touch it, and the Indians, remembering the affair of Tumbes, worshipped it in the belief that the piece of wood had some great divinity and power from God, and in their ignorance of the mysteries of our Lord Jesus Christ, they begged its pardon for having offended it. They remembered the ancient prophecy and tradition they had received from their Inca Viracocha to the effect that not only their laws, towns, and state were to be changed, but that also their ceremonies and religion were to be ended and extinguished like a fire. Not knowing when this was to be, whether then or later, the king and his subjects were filled with fear and could not bring themselves to do anything in their own defense or against the Spaniards but rather respected them as gods, supposing them to be messengers of the god Viracocha they worshipped, and whose name they applied to the Spaniards for this reason.

The above is drawn from my own information and the pages of Padre Blas Valera, whose history I would like to be able to continue to adorn my own, for he wrote as a religious and as a scholar and sought a true account of each event, satisfying his curiosity by obtaining the versions of both Indians and Spaniards. Where I find he has any relevant material I shall always include it, because of his great authority, and indeed whenever I behold his half-destroyed papers, I weep over them afresh. . . .

The Inca is taken prisoner, and the Indians flee.

Atahuallpa Promises a Ransom in Return for His Liberty

[1:28] . . .On finding himself under arrest and in chains, Inca Atahuallpa sought to escape by ransoming himself, and he promised to cover the floor of the large room in which he was imprisoned with gold and silver plate in return for his liberty: "and as he saw the Spaniards present pull a face, he thought that they did not believe him"—these are López de Gómara's words—"and undertook to give them within a certain time enough plate and other pieces of gold and silver to fill the room as high as he could reach with his hand up the wall. This was settled by the drawing of a red line right round the room. But he made the condition that the jars, pitchers, and vats which he proposed to pile up as high as the line should not be pressed down or broken," etcetera.

Thus López de Gómara in his chapter cxiv.[3] In order not to go into such detail as these historians, to whom I refer the reader for a fuller account, we shall briefly relate the events concerning the life and death of the Inca kings up to the last of them and of their descendants, which was our first intention. Later, if occasion offers, we shall set down the most notable events that occurred during the wars between the Spaniards.

Atahuallpa ordered gold and silver to be brought to pay his ransom, and it seemed impossible to fulfill what he had promised, however much was brought. The Spaniards therefore complained that as the prisoner had not carried out his promise and that the time had expired, the delay would allow the Indians to raise an army and attack and kill them, so as to free the king. These imaginings filled the Spaniards with discontent. Atahuallpa, who was very intelligent, sensed this and asked the reason. When Pizarro told him, he said that the Spaniards' suspicions about the delay arose from the fact that they did not know the distances between the chief places from which the greater part of the ransom had to be brought, Cusco, Pachacámac, Quito, and many other provinces. He told them that the nearest place was Pachacámac, over eighty leagues away, and Cusco was two hundred leagues and Quito three hundred, and suggested that Spaniards should be sent to inspect the treasure in these places and the whole of the rest of the kingdom, so that they could satisfy themselves as to the quantity and collect it themselves.

---

[3] *Historia General de las Indias* [1552], various editions. Garcilaso had a much-annotated copy of the *History* in his personal library. See Jose Durand, "La biblioteca del Inca," *Nueva revista de filología hispánica*, II:3 (1948) 239–64.

Seeing that the Spaniards doubted the safety of those who might volunteer to go to inspect the treasure, Atahuallpa said: "You have nothing to fear, for you have me here in iron chains." Then Hernando de Soto and Pedro del Barco, a native of Lobón, decided to go to Cusco. Atahuallpa regretted that Soto should go, for as he was one of the first two Christians he had seen, he was attached to him and realized that he would be a friend in case of need; but he dared not oppose the idea lest the Spaniards should say that he was going back on what he had asked and they had accepted, thus increasing their suspicions. As well as these two, four other Spaniards went to visit various provinces and see the treasure that was stored there. One went to Quito, and others to Huaillas, Huamachucu, and Sicllapampa. They were instructed to watch carefully if armies were being raised anywhere in the kingdom for the purpose of freeing King Atahuallpa. But he had no idea of doing anything the Spaniards suspected him of, and his one thought was to obtain for them the quantity of gold and silver he had promised in return for his liberty, and so see himself released from the iron chains in which he was kept. He therefore ordered it to be announced throughout the kingdom that the single Spaniards were to be received and lodged with every possible attention and comfort. Because of the Inca's orders and of the marvels that had been told of the Spaniards, that they were gods and messengers of the supreme God, as they themselves had declared, and because they knew about Pedro de Candía's adventure with the lion and tiger in Tumbes,[4] the Spaniards were received in every Indian town and village with the greatest honor and respect. They were presented with gifts of all kinds and even offered sacrifices, for the Indians adored the Spaniards as gods, in their great simplicity and superstition. And although they knew of the slaughter that had taken place at Cajamarca, from those who had escaped and fled to various places, they still held the Spaniards to be gods, though now terrible and cruel gods, and thus offered sacrifices to appease them and prevent them from doing harm, though no longer in the hope that they would do good.

Hernando de Soto, Pedro del Barco, and the other four Spaniards were carried on hammocks on the shoulders of Indians, according to the Inca's instructions, so that they should travel faster and in greater comfort. *Hamaca* is a word from the Indian language of the Windward Islands, where as the climate is very hot those of the better sort sleep in nets made of leaves

---

[4] Garcilaso told a story earlier in the narrative in which the Indians of Tumbes set a lion (puma) and a tiger (probably a leopard) given to them by Huayna Capac on Candía, expecting the animals to kill the Spaniard, but Candía held up his crucifix and the animals lay down at Candía's feet. The story is not included in this edition. See the complete Livermore translation, book 1, chapters 11–12.

of the palm or other trees. The less wealthy sleep in cotton blankets fastened by the opposite corners and slung a yard above the ground: this is cooler than sleeping on mattresses. These beds, which we might call wind-beds, are *hamacas.* In the same way the Peruvian Indians used to tie a blanket to a pole three or four yards long, and the traveler could lie in it, its other corners being knotted over the pole so that the occupant should not fall out: he was carried stretched out like a dead man. Two Indians carried him, and they changed over with others often and with great ease and dexterity. Twenty or thirty Indians would go along to take turns and thus reduce the labor. Each party would be relieved after so many leagues, so that they should not have the strain of carrying the passenger the whole way. Such was the mailpost of the Indians. The instrument was called *huantu,* "stretcher," or *rampa.* The Spaniards call it *hamaca* because it is like the beds. In this way these two brave Spaniards, Hernando de Soto and Pedro del Barco, traveled the two hundred leagues between Cajamarca and Cusco, more safely and better attended than if they had been in their own country; the same was true of the other four, for the Inca's bidding assured their lives and secured them hospitality, with such rejoicings and celebrations that the Spaniards themselves could not find words enough for them when they told the story. . . .

While the ransom is being collected, Almagro follows in another ship. When he reaches Cajamarca, he is told that only those present at the capture of Atahuallpa are entitled to share the ransom. Huascar, Atahuallpa's brother, is killed, and Atahuallpa begins to lose hope of recovering his freedom.

Hernando Pizarro Leaves for Spain

[1:35] While Atahuallpa doubted and feared, Governor Francisco Pizarro was filled with greater hopes and ambitions, as a result of the favor his good fortune had so far shown him. And as he desired to increase his claims in the future, he thought that it would be wise to send His Majesty an account of what had happened so far. He said as much to his companion Don Diego de Almagro and his brothers, and they agreed that Hernando Pizarro should come to Spain with the mission of reporting their achievements so that His Majesty might reward them according to their deserts. Hernando Pizarro took what was necessary for the expenses of the journey from the pile of gold and silver that Atahuallpa had had collected for his ransom, since his negotiations were to be on behalf of all those who had a share in it. For His Majesty he took 100,000 pesos of gold and as many again of silver, to be set against the royal fifth payable to the crown on Atahuallpa's ransom. The gold and silver were the first-fruits of what has since been brought and is still to be brought from my country for His

Majesty. . . . Soon after Hernando Pizarro's departure Hernando de Soto and Pedro del Barco returned from Cusco with news of the incredible riches they had seen there, in the temples of the Sun, in the palaces of the old kings, and in the fortress and other sanctuaries and places where the Devil spoke to the wizards and priests and his other devotees: all such places were adorned with gold and silver since they were considered to be holy places. The other four scouts brought back similar reports, and the Spaniards were delighted at the news, desiring to see and enjoy these great treasures. They therefore hastened to dispatch Atahuallpa so as to relieve themselves of anxiety and remove any obstacle that might prevent or delay their laying hands on the gold and silver in the imperial city and elsewhere. It was therefore decided to kill him as a way to avoid trouble and strife. . . .

Atahuallpa is tried and convicted of killing his brother Huascar, and of conspiring to kill the Spaniards after his arrest. In spite of some opposition, the Inca is convicted and executed, and the ransom collected is distributed among the Spaniards.

The Opinions Expressed by the Spaniards on These Events

[1:39] After the deaths of the two royal brothers and enemies, Huascar and Atahuallpa, the Spaniards remained absolute lords of both their kingdoms, for there was no one to resist them or oppose anything they tried to do thereafter. With the death of the Incas, the Indians of both parties were like sheep without a shepherd, with no one to govern them in peace or war, either for their own good or to the detriment of their foes. On the contrary, the supporters of Huascar still remained at odds with those of Atahuallpa, and each party sought to prevail over the other by trying to serve and ingratiate itself with the Spaniards and thus get the new rulers to side with them against their enemies. Some of Atahuallpa's remaining captains resisted the Spaniards, as we shall see: others disbanded the armies under their control and tried to appoint an Inca of their own choosing, who would be more favorable to them than one appointed by strangers. . . .

On seeing the honor in which the Indians generally held them and how they were adored, the Spaniards frequently conversed among themselves on the subject, especially when the six who had gone out to inspect the riches of the kingdom were present to tell of the marks of veneration and service they had been shown. Many attributed this to their own bravery. They said that the Indians had surrendered out of pure fright on seeing how strong and brave the Spaniards were, and that they could not have done anything else. They set such store by themselves and boasted without any sense of proportion because they were unaware of the superstitions of the Indians or of the prophecy that the great Huayna Capac had uttered about the coming of the Spaniards to Peru, and the destruction of their idolatry and empire.

Other Spaniards were more moderate and regardful of the honor of God and the expansion of the holy Catholic Faith. They saw things differently, and said that the great deeds the others attributed to their own strength and bravery were miracles performed by the Lord on behalf of His Gospel, so that when the faithful and infidels duly pondered them the infidels would be softened and come forward to receive His word with less resistance and greater love, and the faithful would take courage and strive to preach the Gospel with greater fervor and charity toward their neighbors and respect toward God, stirred on by the miracles He had performed through them. They truly asserted that when a single Spaniard or two could travel for two or three hundred leagues through enemy territory, borne on their enemies' shoulders and treated by them with all the honor and respect they displayed toward their gods, when it would have been a simple matter to fling them from a bridge or cast them down from one of the numerous lofty crags—this was not the work of men, but one of God's miracles. They should not therefore attribute these things to themselves, except in so far as they had acted like good Christians and preachers of Jesus Christ.

Others went further in their discussions—which sometimes took place in the presence of the governor—and said that once Atahuallpa had been baptized, it would have been better for the peace of the kingdom and the expansion of the Catholic Faith, not to have killed him, but to have kept him alive, showing him every possible honor and courtesy, and asking him since he was now a Christian, to make another proclamation in favor of the Christian religion, like the one he had made in favor of the Spaniards, and ordering all his vassals to be baptized within a certain time. There is not the slightest doubt that they would all have been baptized, and have competed with one another to obtain baptism, for three or four considerations each would have impelled them in this direction, the more strongly when taken all together. The first was the Inca's bidding, which was regarded as a divine law even in matters of the smallest moment, and therefore much more so in a question of such importance as the adoption of the religion of those they considered to be gods. The second was the natural obedience of the Indians toward their kings. The third was that the king himself had shown them an example in accepting baptism, and they would all have done the same, for the Indians set great store by example. The fourth, and for them the strongest and most compelling consideration, which embraced all the other three reasons, was that Atahuallpa himself should ask them to follow his example in bringing about what his father Huayna Capac had prophesied and willed, namely that they were to obey the new race who came to their country, whose religion would be better than theirs, and who would excel them in all respects. If this step had been taken, the preachers of the Holy Gospel in Peru would have had all this additional assistance. But our Lord God, in His secret wisdom, permitted things to turn out as they did.

The Results of the Discord between the Two Brothers, the Last Inca Kings

[1:40] The war between the two brothers, Huascar and Atahuallpa, brought about the total destruction of their empire, facilitating the entry of the Spaniards and making it possible for them to win Peru with such ease. Otherwise the country could have been defended by a very small force, owing to its rough and rocky character and inaccessibility. But our Lord God took pity on these gentiles and permitted the discord between the two brothers to arise so that the preachers of His Gospel and Catholic Faith might enter the more easily and with less resistance. . . .

Chapter Two
Pizarro and Almagro and the Inca

After Atahuallpa is buried, Pizarro and Almagro go to Cusco, fighting battles with Atahuallpa's commanders along the way. Spanish forces under Sebastián de Belalcázar move north to take Quito; Manco Inca meets Pizarro outside Cusco and allies with the Spaniards.

Manco Inca Asks for the Restoration of His Empire and Is Put Off

[2:12] . . . Two days after his arrival, Prince Manco Inca proposed to the governor that the empire should be restored to him and the terms of the agreement between the Indians and Spaniards under which they might live in peace and brotherhood should be carried out. He asked for priests and ministers to preach the Gospel and teach the Christian religion to the Indians, as the Spaniards themselves had proposed when the agreement was reached; and he undertook to send them out with great reverence and every attention to the chief kingdoms and provinces in his empire to indoctrinate the Indians. The fact that his father Huayna Capac had declared on his death bed that the Christian religion was superior to their own would be sufficient to guarantee that they would be very willingly received. He asked the Viracochas to say in what way they would like to be served and what part of the kingdom they wished to take for themselves: he would duly satisfy their desires and they would find themselves obeyed, for his father had also left instructions in his will that the Spaniards were to be obeyed and served with every mark of love and attention.

The governor replied that His Highness was very welcome in his imperial city, and he hoped he would rest at ease. He was very glad to know the Inca's desire so as to be able to comply with it, and the terms of the agreement were so just that it was only reasonable that they should all be adopted. After this, they spoke of other matters, but the conversation was short for want of interpreters.

The governor consulted his brothers and the other captains about the Inca's requests, about which there were various opposing opinions, but as it was known that the symbol of taking possession of the empire was the wearing of the scarlet fringe, he went next day to the Inca's house, accompanied by his friends, and without more ado, said that he begged Manco

Capac to take possession of his empire forthwith. If he had known before what was involved, he would not have permitted him to be an hour without the imperial crown on his brow. As regards the division of the kingdom, this would be dealt with later when both sides had come to an agreement and settled down, for at present both Indians and Spaniards were in a state of excitement. The services the Indians were to perform for the Spaniards and the conditions of peace between them should be settled by the Inca according to his will and pleasure, and the Spaniards would more willingly obey him. They could not for the moment supply ministers to teach the Indians the Christian religion, for there were so few priests that they had not even enough for themselves: when more came, and they were expected, they would be sent in ample numbers, for the Christians had come to Peru only to undeceive the natives about the errors and barbarities of their heathen faith. The Indians were very satisfied at this, and the Inca assumed his scarlet fringe with the greatest festivities and celebrations, though they could not compare with those of past times, since all the members of the royal blood—who contribute principally to the majesty of all the courts in the world—had disappeared. Moreover many of the lords of vassals who had been swept away by Atahuallpa's cruelties were missing. The older Indians who remembered the days of the great Huayna Capac mourned the decline of the house and court of the Inca: the younger, who had never seen its ancient majesty, were full of rejoicing. . . .

The Foundation of Lima and Trujillo

[2:17] As soon as the governor had dealt with Alvarado,[5] he sent his companion Almagro to Cusco with most of the gentlemen who had come with Alvarado, so as to confer with Prince Manco Inca and the governor's two brothers Juan and Gonzalo Pizarro. He recommended them to serve the Inca and treat the Indians well, so that the natives should not be provoked or the Inca lose his affection for the Spaniards, to whom he had come of his own free will. The governor remained in the valley of Pachacámac, desiring to establish a city on the coast and take advantage of the traffic over the sea. Having consulted his friends, he sent people who were experienced in nautical affairs to explore the coast in both directions to find some good port, which was essential for what he had in mind. He learned from them that

---

[5] Pedro de Alvarado, a lieutenant of Hernán Cortés in the conquest of Mexico, brought a large force to Peru, arriving after the capture of Atahuallpa. In order to avoid conflict, Pizarro bought Alvarado's ships and equipment and allowed the men he brought with him, one of whom was Garcilaso de la Vega, the author's father, to join Pizarro's forces if they chose.

four leagues north of Pachacámac there was a good port at the bottom of the Rímac valley. He went there and inspected the advantages of the port and the valley; and decided to transfer thither the town he had begun to build at Jauja, thirty leagues inland from Rímac. The city was founded on the Day of the Kings, Epiphany 1534.

With regard to the years of these events there is some disparity between the various authors, some of whom place events earlier and others later, while others give the decades, such as 1530, but leave the last number blank, so as to avoid errors. We shall leave opinions aside, and count the years by the most notable occurrences. It is certain, and all authors agree on this, that Pizarro, Almagro, and the schoolmaster Hernando de Luque established their triumvirate in 1525. They spent three years on the discovery before reaching Tumbes for the first time, and took two years more to come to Spain and obtain the right to conquer Peru and to return to Panama and prepare the expedition. They reached the island of Puna and Tumbes in 1531. The capture of Atahuallpa took place in December of the same year, and his death was in March 1532. In October of this year they entered Cusco, where Pizarro remained until April of 1533, when he learned of the coming of Alvarado. In September 1533 he left Cusco to pay Alvarado the sum agreed in their bargain, and he founded Lima on the Day of the Kings at the beginning of 1534. It was for this reason that Lima took as its arms and device the three crowns of the holy Kings and the shining star that appeared to them.

The city was beautifully laid out, with a very large square, unless it be a fault that it is too big. The streets are broad and so straight that the country can be seen in four directions from any of the crossroads. It has a river that runs to the north of the city, from which many irrigation channels are drawn. These water the fields and are brought to all the houses in the city. When seen from a distance, the city is ugly, for it has no tiled roofs. As there is no rain in that region or for many leagues around on the coast, the houses are covered with thatch of excellent local straw. This is covered with two or three fingers' thickness of mud mixed with the straw, which suffices for shade against the sun. The houses are well built inside and out, and are daily improved. It stands two short leagues from the sea, and I am told that the part that has been built in recent years is approaching the sea. Its climate is hot and damp, a little less than Andalusia in summer: if it is less so, it is because the days are not so long and the nights not so short as they are here in July and August. The degree of heat lost by the later rising and earlier setting of the sun and the greater freshness of the night, which begins earlier and lasts longer, explains its greater coolness as compared with Andalusia. But because in Lima the heat is constant throughout the year, the inhabitants grow accustomed to it and take the necessary measures against it. They have cool rooms, wear summer clothes, and use light bed-covering; and take steps so that the flies and mosquitoes (which are numerous on the coast) shall not molest them by day or night. There are day and night mosquitoes in the hot valleys of Peru. The nocturnal ones are like those of Spain, with long legs and of the same color and shape, though they are much bigger. Spaniards emphasize how fiercely they sting by saying they can penetrate a leather boot. They say this because knitted stockings, even if of kersey or worsted, provide no defense, not even when linen is worn underneath. The mosquitoes are more savage in some regions than in others. The day mosquitoes are small and exactly resemble those found in wine cellars in Spain, except that they are as yellow as weld. They are so bloodthirsty that I have been assured that, not content with sating themselves, they have been seen to burst while sucking. In order to test this, I let some of them prick me and take their fill of blood: when sated, they were unable to rise and could only roll away. The sting of these smaller mosquitoes is somewhat poisonous, especially if the flesh is unhealthy, and produces small wounds, though they are not serious.

Owing to the hot damp climate of Lima, meat soon spoils. It has to be bought daily for consumption. This is very different from what we have said of Cusco, for the two cities are quite opposite from one another, one being cold and the other hot. The other Spanish cities and towns on the Peruvian coast all resemble the city of Lima, for the region is the same. The inland cities from Quito to Chuquisaca, over a distance of seven hundred leagues from north to south, are of a very pleasant climate, neither as cold as Cusco nor as hot as Lima, but sharing temperately in the conditions of both, except in the settlement of Potosí, where the silver mines are: this is a very cool region with extremely cold air. The Indians call the region *puna,* meaning that it is uninhabitable on account of the cold; but the love of silver has drawn so many Spaniards and Indians there that it is today one of the largest, best supplied, and most comfortable towns in Peru. Among its other glories, Padre Acosta says in his Book II, chapter vi, it is two leagues in circumference. And this shall suffice for the Spanish towns and cities in Peru: what we have said of them in general makes it unnecessary for us to repeat it of each one in particular.

To return to the city of Lima in particular, we should add that after Pizarro had founded it and divided the land in the city and the fields and estates and Indians among those who were to settle there, he marched up the coast to the valley of Chimu, eighty leagues north of Lima, where he founded the city now called Trujillo. He gave it the name of his native town, which he wished to commemorate in this way. He gave the first conquerors allocations of Indians, assigning by name the province or provinces that each was to receive in payment for the labors he had undergone in the winning of the empire. He did the same in Lima, to the great satisfaction and approbation of them all, for it seemed as though the country was now quiet and becoming settled, and the first comers were now being rewarded according to their various merits; and that all of them would be treated in the same way. In this task, as excellent as all those this famous gentleman performed in the course of his life, we shall leave him, to return to other matters which occurred among the Indians at this time. . . .

Almagro Declares Himself Governor

[2:19] Discord, having achieved a success among the Indians with the death of Quízquiz,[6] now introduced itself among the Spaniards to see if it could do the same, as it well might, had not peace and friendship, its foes, stood in the way and prevented it. A few months after the foregoing events, news reached Peru of Hernando Pizarro's arrival in Spain, of the welcome given to him and his treasure, and of his successful negotiations at court, resulting in the award of the title of marquis to his brother, the governor. Zárate describes this as follows in his Book III, chapter v:[7]

> Among other requests the governor Don Francisco Pizarro made of His Majesty, as a reward for his services in the conquest of Peru, was one that he should receive 20,000 Indians for himself and his descendants in perpetuity in a province called Los Atavillos, with their revenues, tribute, and jurisdiction, and the title of marquis. His Majesty was pleased to grant him the title of marquis of this province: as regards the Indians, information would be sought as to the value of the land and the advantages or disadvantages of awarding them to him, and he would receive such favor as might justifiably be shown him. In this letter he was addressed as marquis, and he gave instructions that he was so to be addressed in future, which was done. We shall call him by this title in future in our *History*.

Thus Zárate. Apart from the title, he was permitted to extend the limits of his jurisdiction a certain number of leagues. This is mentioned by Zárate, though he does not say how many. Hernando Pizarro also obtained for himself a habit of Santiago and other favors, which were said to have included the title of marshal of Peru and the award of a jurisdiction a hundred

---

[6] Quízquiz was a commander of Atahuallpa who continued to fight the Spaniards after his leader's death, and, according to Garcilaso, was killed by his own men.

[7] Agustín de Zárate, *Historia del descubrimiento y conquista del Perú* [1555], various editions. Book III, ch. v.

leagues long from north to south, beyond that of the marquis, for Almagro. This second administrative division was called New Toledo, as the first was New Castile. Almagro received all this news in Cusco (where he was with Prince Manco Inca and the marquis' brothers Juan and Gonzalo) by means of letters from Spain. Without awaiting the arrival of the royal appointment or any other assurance but the first news, he could not help assuming the title of governor straight away; such is the desire of the ambitious for power and command. And as he thought the marquis' jurisdiction extended two hundred leagues from the equator southward, measurable along the coast, or inland, or as the crow flies, and as this did not reach Cusco, he concluded that the city fell within his own administration, and began to award allocations of Indians, as though he had already had the royal letter of appointment. And in order to show that he gave these grants as absolute governor and not by anyone else's authority, he renounced the power he had received from the marquis to govern that city. In this he was advised and incited by many Spaniards, for there was no lack of ministers of discord. These (apart from their own ambition) told him that this was in his own interest and declared themselves his partisans. On the other hand Juan and Gonzalo Pizarro and many other gentlemen from Extremadura who had come with Alvarado objected. They included Gabriel de Rojas, Garcilaso de la Vega, Antonio and Alonso de Altamirano, and the greater part of the army. Passions rose between the two parties: and they often came to blows with dead and wounded on each side. When the marquis heard of this, he hastened alone from Trujillo, where the news reached him, and was carried the two hundred leagues to Cusco on the shoulders of Indians. He dared to trust his person to the Indians and make this long journey alone because he had Prince Manco Inca (whom we call prince and not king, since he never came to reign) in his brother's hands. Out of love for Manco Inca, the Indians outdid one another in offering services and presents to the Spaniards, in the hope of obliging the marquis to restore the empire to them.

The marquis thus arrived in Cusco, and his presence extinguished the flames lit by discord and ambition, for the longstanding and brotherly friendship that had long existed between these two distinguished men soon brought them together in any case of rivalry or unpleasantness, once evil counselors were removed from the scene. Almagro was ashamed of what he had done without seeing the royal letter, though he said that once His Majesty had granted a favor, he had thought it unnecessary to receive papers. The marquis forgave him and restored him to favor, as if there had been no ill-feeling between them. Then they both again swore before the holy Sacrament that they would not break their alliance or oppose one another. And in order to strengthen this pact of peace and concord, they agreed with the common consent of their followers, that Almagro should go and conquer the kingdom of Chile, which was said by the Peruvian Indians to be very rich in gold and had belonged to the Inca empire. In this case they would ask His Majesty to make Almagro governor of it, and if it did not satisfy him, they would divide Peru between them.

They were all very satisfied by this arrangement, though there was no lack of malicious people who said that the Pizarros had forced Almagro out of Peru despite his having been so good a companion and played so great a part in its conquest. It was said they wished to enjoy Peru for themselves and whetted his appetite for a whole great kingdom instead of a hundred leagues of land, so as to get rid of him. This measure was taken also because as a result of the fame of its wealth, many Spaniards had come to Peru from all sides, and what had been conquered was insufficient for the first conquerors, according to what they quite justifiably thought their merits entitled them to expect. It was thus necessary to stimulate new conquests like that Almagro was to make to provide more land and more Indians to go round, and so that the Spaniards engaged in the conquest should not be idle and plot some rebellion, as a result of the envy that was kindled by the sight of the great allocations granted to the first conquerors. It was therefore agreed that Captain Alonso de Alvarado should go to the province of Chachapoyas, which, though a part of the Inca empire, had refused to acknowledge the Spaniards, confiding in the inaccessibility of the country, where horses would be of little use, and presuming on its strength and warlike spirit. Captain Garcilaso de la Vega was given the conquest of the province the Spaniards ironically call Buenaventura. Captain Juan Porcel was sent to the province the Castilians call Bracamoros and the Indians Pacamuru. Help was also sent to Sebastián de Belalcázar who was engaged in conquering the kingdom of Quito.

After the agreement between Almagro and Pizarro and the announcement of the new conquests, each of the captains made preparations and raised men. Alonso de Alvarado raised 300 for his conquest, Garcilaso de la Vega 250 for his, and Porcel as many again. All three then left for their districts, where each underwent great privations owing to the thick forests and great rivers in those provinces, as we shall later say. Sebastián de Belalcázar was sent 150 men as reinforcements. Almagro raised over 550 men, including many of those who already had allocations of Indians, but were glad to leave them, thinking to do better in Chile, according to the fame of its wealth; for in those days any Spaniard, even a poor soldier, thought all Peru together too little for himself alone. Almagro lent his followers more than 30,000 pesos in gold and silver to buy horses and arms, and good equipment: he thus had a very fine expedition. He sent Juan de Saavedra, a native of Seville whom I knew, with 150 men to go ahead as scouts, though the whole country was at peace and quite safe to travel in, since Prince

Manco Inca was with the Spaniards and all the Indians hoped for the restitution of the empire. Almagro left in Cusco Captain Ruy Díaz and his bosom friend Juan de Herrada, who were to raise more men and bring them to his help: he thought this would be necessary owing to the great fame of the kingdom of Chile for difficulty and warlike spirit. . . .

Almagro leaves Cusco for Chile at the beginning of 1535, with Paullu, a brother of Manco Inca, and an Inca priest named Uíllac Umu. Spaniards and Indians alike suffer and die while crossing the mountains and the desert and decide to return to Cusco.

Prince Manco Again Seeks to Restore His Empire

[2:22] . . . As soon as Almagro had left Cusco for Chile and the other captains had gone about their conquests, as we have said, Prince Manco Inca, finding the governor at ease after Almagro's departure, again proposed to him that the conditions agreed between Indians and Spaniards should be carried out. He said that Pizarro had promised to execute them and restore his empire, and begged and urged him to do so, so that the natives might live in peace and realize how they could best serve the Spaniards. The governor and his brothers were at a loss, for they found no sufficient reasons for putting off the Inca's request and expectations. But they told him as best they could, so as not to rouse his suspicions, that they intended to fulfill the conditions which were to the advantage of both sides, Indians and Spaniards alike; but that the past disturbances and present circumstances were inopportune, principally because they hourly expected the reply of their lord the emperor, to whom they had sent a long account of the conditions and the question of the restoration of the empire. They expected the answer would be brought by Hernando Pizarro and that it would satisfy His Highness, for it was not to be expected that so great, so just, and so religious a prince would do less than ratify the conditions; let the Indians await the arrival of Hernando Pizarro, who would remove all their anxieties with the emperor's instructions.

With these vain hopes they held the Inca off for some days. Then came the news of Hernando Pizarro's landing at Tumbes. The marquis saw that this was a good opportunity for him to leave Cusco, as he desired to do, partly to avoid the Inca's demand and partly to return to the new settlement at Lima, which, as he had founded it, he desired to see completed. He therefore spoke to the Inca and told him that, in order to expedite His Majesty the emperor's commands with regard to His Highness the Inca's request, he must go and receive his brother Hernando Pizarro. He begged him to give him leave to undertake this journey: he would soon return and they would then reach the agreement that would be to their mutual advantage. In the meanwhile, it would be best if His Highness for his own tranquility and the comfort and security of the Spaniards, would kindly retire to his royal fortress and remain there until the marquis' return: during this time the marquis' brothers and his other companions would serve His Highness as they were bound.

Pizarro made this request of the Inca because it seemed necessary to him, to his brothers, and to all the rest. They perceived that Manco Inca had a proud and brave spirit, and knew how to dissimulate, as he had done hitherto. They were afraid lest he should begin some disturbance on finding that they delayed restoring the empire to him and fulfilling the conditions, and wanted to have him in a secure place and to be safe from him. The Inca saw that this was not a good augury for the result of his request and the restoration of his kingdom, discreetly disguised his true feelings so as not to alarm the marquis to greater wrongs, and consented to his request or order. He therefore went to the fortress with apparent willingness and climbed the steep slope on foot, refusing to be borne in his litter, so as to make less ceremony. As soon as he was inside, he was shackled, as López de Gómara says in his chapter cxxxiv:

"Manco, the son of Huayna Capac, to whom Francisco Pizarro gave the scarlet fringe at Villcas, was a man of spirit and proved troublesome, for which reason he was put in the fortress of Cusco in iron shackles." These are López de Gómara's words. The Indians greatly resented the imprisonment of their Inca, and the reversal of the promises and hopes that had been held out to them. They wept and lamented bitterly. Prince Manco Inca consoled them saying he wished to obey the Spaniards cheerfully in everything, and they should do the same, since their Inca Huayna Capac had bidden them so in his will; let them not give way till they saw the final outcome of the affair, for he hoped that his arrest would lead to his being treated more liberally and that his release and the restoration of his empire would occur at once, so that the generosity of the Viracochas might resound throughout the world. . . .

The Measures Taken by Prince Manco Inca

[2:23] Prince Manco Inca who was under arrest in the fortress—the fortress built with such splendor and majesty by his ancestors as their grandest trophy, never thinking that it would become the jail of their descendant—tried discreetly to ease his bonds by flattering and serving the Spaniards. He plied them, superiors and inferiors alike, with many presents of fruits, birds, meat, and other delicacies, and with gold, silver, emeralds, and turquoises. His friendly and brotherly intercourse with them, and his lack of resentment for his imprisonment, reassured them all, and they removed his bonds and let him walk freely about the fortress. Meanwhile the Inca had heard that Hernando Pizarro was coming to Cusco to take charge in that city. He then did his best to obtain permission to go down to the city and live in one of his palaces. This was easily gained, for the Spaniards were so attached to him that they readily granted whatever he asked. His anxiety to get out of the fortress was in order that Pizarro should not find him shackled and suspect him, or withhold his confidence from him, or deny what he had asked and the Spaniards had promised. . . .

The Inca asked permission to go to Yucay, which was, as we have said, the garden of the Inca kings, with their cemetery, called Tampu, a league lower down the river: here their intestines were buried after their removal for the embalming of their bodies, and it is probable that the golden statue was kept there as a monument to his father. On reaching the place, the Inca, under pretext of the festivities that were to be celebrated, summoned together some of his father's old captains and some of the chief lords; and addressed them on the disloyalty and obstinacy of the Spaniards in refusing to carry out the terms his brother Titu Atauchi had made with them, and on their arrest of the Inca and his confinement in irons without any justification, and on the fact that the captain general had twice disappeared so as to entertain him with false hopes and to avoid restoring the empire to him. He said that though he had been aware of this faithlessness from the first, he had dissimulated in order to strengthen his case in the sight of God and men: no one could accuse him of disturbing the peace agreed between himself and the Spaniards. But now that he had done all he had been obliged to do on his side, he wished to wait no longer for the fulfillment of vain promises, for it was well known that the Spaniards were dividing the land among themselves in Cusco, Lima, and Tumbes, which was a clear sign that they did not mean to restore the empire. He had no desire to expose his person to the risk of being treated as on the previous occasion, when they had not hesitated to put him in handcuffs and chains, though he had done nothing to annoy them or offered any occasion for such treatment. He therefore enjoined them as loyal servants and faithful vassals to give their prince the benefit of their advice in this important matter, for he proposed to recover his empire by force of arms, being confident that neither Pachacámac nor his father the Sun would allow him so unjustly to be deprived of it. The captains and *curacas* chose one of the oldest of the captains to speak for them all: and he, after showing the deference due to kings, said:

"Sole Lord, it never seemed safe nor yet fitting to the members of your Council that Your Majesty should place his person in the power of these strangers, nor that you should trust them to restore the empire. But we have submitted to your will since we realized how devoted you were to the peace concluded with them by your brother, Titu Atauchi. We now know that there is nothing to be expected of this, since we have seen what they have done to your brother Atahuallpa, whom they killed after they had received the ransom he had promised them in return for his freedom. It has been a great mercy of Pachacámac that they have not done the same with your royal person, since they have had you in their power and under arrest. Nor is the restitution of your empire to be hoped for any longer, for people who have shown such covetousness for the fruit are not likely to think of returning the tree to its owner; it is more to be feared that they will seek his death and that of all his family so that there shall be none who can aspire to the empire. According to what they themselves have taught us, Your Majesty should therefore distrust their promises and give orders for as many warriors as possible to be summoned with all haste and for the necessary supplies to be brought together; let us not lose the opportunity they have offered us by dividing into so many groups, for it will be easier to put them to death than if they were all together. We must attack them all at once so that they cannot succor one another: the roads must be blocked so that they may not have news of one another; and they will thus all perish on the same day, for Your Majesty's men can fall upon them in such multitudes wherever they are that the mountains will be flung down on them if you so order. And if your vassals do not aid them, as they will not, they will undoubtedly die at our hands or from the hunger they will suffer in the siege. The suddenness of the attack is what is most important, for no one can doubt its success, since we have justice on our side."

Here the captains ended, and the rising was decided upon. They very secretly sent messengers the length and breadth of the kingdom to raise what warriors there were, and bid them murder all the newcomers from Castile on a certain day. All the supplies to be found in the royal or communal stores were to be brought forth, and if these had been lost or used in Atahuallpa's wars, more were to be collected from private houses, wherever they might be found; and as soon as their enemies had been killed, any damage or loss suffered by any of the Inca's vassals would be made good. Let them recall that on this deed depended the lives, security, and liberty of them all, great and small, and especially of their Inca. On these instructions from Manco Inca the warriors from Lima to the Chichas, a distance of three hundred leagues and more, rose up in arms. The rest of the kingdom from Lima to Quito could not raise warriors, for they had been killed in those parts in Atahuallpa's wars and with the havoc wrought by the Spaniards when the king was captured and killed.

The Inca also sent disguised messengers to the kingdom of Chile who said in public that they were going to enquire after the health of the infante Paullu and the high priest Uíllac Umu, though they were secretly to warn them of the Inca's decision. They were to give assistance and to execute Almagro and all his companions, which would be necessary for the recovery of their empire, for there was no longer any hope that the Spaniards would return it peacefully. When the rising was launched, the Inca ordered the inland Indians from Antahuailla and the coastal ones from Nanasca in the region of Chinchaysuyu to go to Lima and kill the governor and his companions, while those of Condesuyu, Collasuyu, and Andesuyu went to Cusco to slay Hernando Pizarro and his brothers and the other Spaniards, who numbered two hundred in all. . . .

Prince Manco Inca's Rising

[2:24] The Inca ordered his warriors to make for Cusco and Lima to fight and destroy the Spaniards. He also ordered all those Spaniards who were scattered about the kingdom obtaining gold from the mines to be killed: owing to the peace and the obedience of the Indians, they went about as unconcernedly as if they were in their own country. Many of them were killed in different places. The Indians thus reached Cusco on the appointed day, having traveled with the greatest possible secrecy. On the following night they suddenly attacked the Spaniards with loud war cries and a great hubbub, for there were more than two thousand Indians in the attack. Most of them were armed with bows and arrows, and carried lighted tinder for firebolts. They shot these at all the houses in the city in general without respect for the royal palaces, but only sparing the house and temple of the Sun and all the apartments it contained and the house of the chosen virgins, and the workshops in the four streets inside the house. They did not touch these two houses out of respect for their owners; they had already been stripped of their wealth and largely abandoned by their inhabitants but the Indians still revered them and avoided what they feared would be an act of sacrilege in their vain religion, one being the house of the Sun and the other that of his women. They also spared three great halls that had been used for their festivals on rainy days, wishing still to have places for celebrations when they had butchered the Spaniards. One of these halls was in the upper part of the city, among the houses that had belonged to the first Inca Manco Capac, as we mentioned in our description of the city. The other hall was one of the houses of Pachacútec, called Cassana. The third was among the houses of Huayna Capac, called Amarucancha, which now belongs to the holy Society of Jesus. They also spared a fine round tower standing in front of these. All the rest of the houses were fired, and none was left standing.

The bravest Indians, who had been picked to burn the house of Inca Viracocha where the Spaniards were lodged, attacked it vigorously and set fire to it from a distance with their incendiary arrows: it was burnt down and not a trace of it remains. The great hall inside it, where the cathedral now is, and where the Christians then had a chapel to hear mass, was saved by our Lord from the flames, and though innumerable arrows were shot at it and it began to burn in many places, the flames were put out again, as if there were as many men throwing water on them. This was one of the marvels performed by our Lord in that city to establish His holy Gospel there; and the city has proved this, for it is certainly one of the most religious and charitable in the New World today, among both Spaniards and Indians.

Hernando Pizarro and his two brothers and the two hundred others with them always lodged together because they were so few; and like good and experienced soldiers they did not sleep, but always had sentries carefully stationed round their dwelling and watchmen on the roof. As soon as they heard the noise of the Indians, they armed themselves and harnessed their horses, for they kept thirty of them ready saddled every night in case of any emergency; and thus went out to reconnoiter the enemy. They saw how numerous the Indians were, and as they could not tell what weapons they had against the horses (which were what the Indians most feared), it was agreed to withdraw into the main square, where owing to its great size, they could more easily dominate the enemy than in the streets. This was done, and they drew up there in formation. The infantry, numbering 120, were in the middle, and the 80 horses stationed themselves in twenties on either side and in front of and behind the square, so that they would be able to resist the Indians from whichever direction they launched their attack. When these saw the Spaniards all gathered together, they fell on them with great ferocity, hoping to overrun them at the first onset. The cavalry attacked them and held them up valiantly, and both sides fought with great courage till daybreak when the Indians re-formed. Arrows and stones shot from slings rained on the Spaniards in a remarkable way; but the horses and lances were sufficient to cope with them, and they made no onset without leaving at least 150 or 200 Indians dead on the ground. This was because the Indians had no defensive arms and did not use pikes (though they had them) against the horses, since they had no experience in facing cavalry, but always fought their wars on foot and unprotected. But owing to their weight of numbers they withstood the advantages the Spaniards had in arms and horses, and despite their great losses, bore up in the hope of shortly butchering all the Spaniards.

The Spaniards were held by the Indians in the square of Cusco for seventeen days without being able to leave it, such was the obstinacy of the attack. During all this time, night and day, the Spaniards remained in formation to resist their enemies, and even marched in formation to drink from the stream that runs through the square, or to search the burnt houses to see if there was any maize left to eat, for they felt their horses' need more than their own. They did find some supplies, and though they were much damaged by fire, hunger made them appetizing. Zárate writes of this as follows:

> "Thus the Inca came with all his forces against Cusco and surrounded it for more than eight months, and each full moon there was fighting at many parts. Hernando Pizarro and his brothers defended it valiantly, with many other knights and captains who were within, especially Gabriel de Rojas, Hernán Ponce de León, Don Alonso Enriquez, the treasurer Riquelme, and many more. They did not put down their arms by night or day; for they felt certain the governor and all the other Spaniards had been killed by the Indians, having heard how the latter had rebelled throughout the country. They thus fought and defended themselves like men who had no hope of succor but from God and their own strength, though the Indians daily reduced their number, killing and wounding them."

Zárate thus briefly describes the dangerous plight of the Spaniards in the siege of Cusco, where their strenuous efforts to find food would not have saved them from dying of hunger if their Indian servants had not succored them like true friends. These went over to the hostile Indians by day, giving out that they had forsaken their masters, and even pretending to fight against them, though at night they would return to them bringing all the food they could carry. This is also mentioned by López de Gómara and Zárate, though very briefly. Their account of all the Inca's rising is short, especially with regard to the miracles performed by our Lord Jesus Christ on behalf of the Spaniards in Cusco, where the danger was greatest and the fury of the Indians most fierce. The danger became so acute that after eleven or twelve days the Spaniards and likewise their horses grew very weary from the continuous alarms and daily fighting, and the intolerable hunger they experienced. Thirty Christians were dead, and almost all were wounded, with no means of healing their wounds. They were afraid they would all die in a few days, for they could do nothing themselves and they could hope for no help from anywhere except heaven, whither they directed their groans and prayers, begging God's mercy and the Virgin Mary's intercession and protection.

The Indians had noticed that in the night when they had burnt the whole city they had been unable to set fire to the hall in which the Spaniards were living, and they now went to burn it down, for there was no one to prevent them. They repeatedly set fire to it over a period of many days and at all times of the day and night, but they never succeeded in carrying out their intention, and were astonished because they could not understand the reason. They said that fire had lost its virtue against the house because the Viracochas had lived in it.

Finding themselves in such a plight, the Spaniards decided to perish bravely together in the fray and not to wait until they died of hunger and their wounds, or let their enemies kill them when they could no longer take up their arms. They therefore prepared to sally forth when the Indians attacked, and do what they could until they died. Those who could confessed to the three priests they had, when and as the Indians allowed them; the rest confessed to one another; and they all called on God and the saints of their devotion in order to die like Christians. At dawn on the following day the Indians came forth with their usual ferocity, full of anger and shame that so small a band of Spaniards could ward off such a multitude of enemies for so many days; for there were a thousand Indians for every Spaniard, and they were determined not to give up the struggle until they had slain them all. But the Spaniards attacked the Indians with the same courage and ferocity, calling aloud on the name of the Virgin and on that of their defender the apostle St. James. Both sides fought obstinately with much slaughter among the Indians and many wounds among the Spaniards. After five hours of this the Christians felt weary, and their horses were exhausted from their labors on that and previous days. They expected death and felt it hovering near, while the Indians grew hourly fiercer as they sensed the flagging of the horses, and [became] more determined to slay the Spaniards to avenge the losses they had suffered. Prince Manco Inca watched the battle from a hill and encouraged the Indians by calling on the various tribes and provinces, full of confidence in becoming lord of his empire that day.

In this hour of need our Lord was pleased to favor His faithful with the presence of the blessed apostle St. James, the patron of Spain, who appeared to the Spaniards. Both they and the Indians saw him mounted on a splendid white horse, bearing a shield showing the arms of his military order and carrying in his right hand a sword that seemed like a flash of lightning, so brightly did it shine. The Indians were terrified at the sight of this new knight and asked one another: "Who is the Viracocha with the *illapa* in his hand?" (meaning, lightning, thunder, and thunderbolt). Whenever the saint attacked, the Indians fled as if they were lost, madly trampling one another down as they fled from this wonder. As soon as the Indians attacked the Christians on the opposite side from the saint, they found him among them and fled madly before him. Thus the Spaniards took heart and fought on, killing innumerable Indians who could not defend themselves and lost courage so rapidly they fled helter-skelter and abandoned the fight.

Thus the apostle succored the Christians that day, depriving the infidels of a victory that lay within their hands and granting it to his own people. He did the same the next and each subsequent day when the Indians tried to fight; as soon as they attacked the Christians, they lost their heads and did not know which direction to take, and returned to their posts, where they asked one another: "What is this? How have we become *utic, sampa, llaclla* (fools, cowards, weaklings)?" Nevertheless they did not cease to persist in their quest, as we shall see, and kept up the siege for over eight months. . . .

One hundred seventy Spaniards hold out against an attacking force of 200,000, and retake the fortress, losing Juan Pizarro in the battle. The Indians also besiege Lima, without success.

Prince Manco Inca Abandons His Empire

[2:29] We have said above that Prince Manco Inca sent messengers to Chile to warn his brother Paullu and the priest Uíllac Umu of his determination to kill all the Spaniards in Peru and recover his empire and urging the Chileans to do the same with Almagro and his companions. These messengers reached Chile before Almagro's departure and delivered the prince's warning; but Paullu and his friends, after consulting together, dared not make an attack on the Spaniards, thinking their forces too small for a direct onslaught, since more than ten thousand Indians had perished of suffocation and cold and snow in crossing the mountains. Neither dared they fall on the Spaniards secretly at night, for they saw that the latter were on the watch and vigilant, and there was no hope of a successful surprise attack. They therefore decided to conceal their intentions and serve the Spaniards faithfully until an opportunity should occur to carry out what they desired. When Paullu and Uíllac Umu found themselves in Atacama in Peru and out of the Chilean desert . . . they agreed that the high priest should take flight and that Paullu should remain with the Spaniards in case of emergency, if only to be able to warn his brother the Inca of their hostile intention. And though López de Gómara says they both fled, Zárate mentions only the flight of the priest in his Book III, chapter i; and in chapter iv of the same book, he says the following of Paullu: "Don Diego de Almagro made Paullu Inca, and gave him the imperial fringe because his brother Manco Inca had fled after doing all this with many warriors to some very wild mountains called the Andes."

Such is Zárate's account, and we have already explained that when these authors differ, Zárate is to be followed for preference; for he was in Peru, and the other was not. . . .

Almagro ignored Uíllac Umu's flight since Paullu had remained with him, and advanced toward Cusco, having now been informed of the Inca's rebellion. Hitherto he had had his suspicions but they had not been confirmed, for Paullu and his followers had shown themselves friendly and served him diligently. He went by Collao and was not molested by the Indians; for as the ground is flat, there were no difficult places where they could attack him with advantage as there are between Cusco and Lima. When he reached Cusco Prince Manco Inca had already abandoned the siege, on learning of Almagro's approach to relieve the other Spaniards, though he did not know of Almagro's hostile intentions toward the Pizarros. Almagro tried to see the Inca and speak with him to win him over to his side, for they had known one another of old. The Inca agreed to the interview, hoping to capture Almagro and kill him, if he could; for he thought that if this were done, it might still be possible to kill the rest. They met and talked, but neither had his way, for Almagro, like a prudent soldier, was well escorted by Spaniards on horse and on foot, so that the Inca did not dare to attack, and on the other hand the Inca did not wish to join Almagro's side. After the interview the Inca said that as his object was to recover his empire he did not wish to favor or help either side; and though his friends urged him to accept the suggestion and keep the war going until the Spaniards should have exhausted themselves and killed one another, when it would be much easier to fall on those who remained and finish them off, the prince replied that it was not for Inca kings to go back on their word once it had been given, or to harm those they had received under their favor and protection: he would rather lose his empire than do anything an Inca should not do.

While Almagro had gone to see the Inca, Hernando Pizarro had sent a message to try to persuade Juan de Saavedra, who had remained in charge of Almagro's troops, to hand them over to him, offering great honors and profit. But Juan de Saavedra, who was a gentleman of the very noble family of that name in Seville and himself a man of great goodness and virtue, disregarded the offer, refusing to do anything dishonorable. Thus the three parties remained facing one another without wishing to close in. When the Inca saw that Almagro had come back from Chile and had more than 450 Spaniards, despite the fact that nearly 200 had been lost crossing the mountains and in the conquest of Chile, he realized that as he had not been able to reduce 170 Spaniards in so many months, he had no chance at all of reducing 600. Although they were at the moment divided and at odds with one another, as soon as either party was attacked they would all join together against the Indians. It would therefore only bring death and destruction to continue the war, as experience had shown; for in a little less than a year since the rising had begun they had lost over 40,000 either at the hands of the enemy, or by hunger, or from other hardships that war involves. It was wrong to let them all perish in pursuit of an object that grew daily harder to achieve. He therefore discussed these matters with his few remaining relatives and decided to abandon the war. He then summoned the chief commanders and captains and told them in public:

"Brothers and sons! I have seen the love you have shown in my service since you have so bravely and readily offered your lives and possessions and wives and children to see my empire restored to me; it seems to me that Pachacámac is visibly opposed to this, that he does not wish me to be king, and that we should not go against his will. I believe you all know that if I wished and sought to recover my empire, it was not because of my desire to reign, but so that my realms might enjoy the peace and ease they knew under the gentle sway of my fathers and ancestors; for a good king must study the welfare and prosperity of his vassals, as our Incas did. I fear that the rule of these men we call gods sent from heaven will be very different; but as I can do nothing to remedy this, it would be wrong for me to persist in my quest at so great an expense of life and effort, when what I desire is the opposite. I would rather be deprived and dispossessed of my empire than see my vassals slain, whom I love as my own children. So that I shall give the Viracochas no cause to misuse you by seeing that I am still in one or other of my kingdoms and fearing that you may desire to restore my empire to me, I shall go into exile. They will the lose their suspicions, and treat you better and hold you as friends.

"Now I see the prophecy of my father Huayna Capac fully realized, to the effect that strangers should deprive us of our empire and destroy our commonwealth and our religion. If before we had begun our war against the Viracochas we had pondered on the words of the king my father's will, we should not have rebelled, since he bade us obey and serve these men, saying that their law is better than ours, and their arms more powerful than ours. Both these things have proved true, for as soon as they entered our empire our oracles fell silent, which is proof that they were conquered by theirs! Then their arms overcame our arms: though we at first slew some of them, only 170 of them were able to resist us, and we may even say they defeated us, for we could not execute our plan but were forced to retire. We can in truth say that it was not they who defeated us; nor can they boast that they did so. It was rather the marvels we have all seen—fire lost its force, for it did not burn their houses but did burn ours; then when we had surrounded them there appeared the man with lightning, thunder, and thunderbolts in his hand and destroyed us all; then at night we saw that beautiful princess with the child in her arms,[8] and with the softness of the dew she cast in out eyes, she blinded us and bewildered us so that we could not return to our lodgings, let alone fight against the Viracochas. Moreover

---

[8] Garcilaso here refers to another miracle that ostensibly took place during the siege of Cusco, in which the Virgin Mary appeared with her child in her arms to defend the Spaniards. The story can be found in the complete Livermore translation of the *General History,* Book 2, ch. 25.

we have seen how so few men have defended themselves against such a number of us without food or sleep or an hour's rest, showing themselves braver and stronger when we thought they were dead or exhausted.

"All this clearly shows that it is not the work of men but of Pachacámac, and as he favors them and forsakes us, I am going to betake myself to the Antis, so that their wilderness may defend me and protect me from these men, when all my might has failed to do so. There I shall live quietly, not molesting the strangers lest they should misuse you for my sake. In my solitude and my banishment I shall be relieved and comforted to know that you are prospering under the new rule of the Spaniards. Instead of a testament, I shall accept my father's will, and bid and charge you to obey and serve them as best you can, so that you may be well treated and not abused. Remain in peace, for I would willingly take you all with me so as not to leave you in the power of strangers."

Here the Inca ended his discourse. His friends wept many tears, and groaned and sobbed so that they choked. They did not answer, and did not dare to resist him, for they saw that this was his resolution and will. The warriors and their caciques were soon dismissed and sent to their provinces to obey and serve the Spaniards. The Inca brought together all those of the royal blood he could find, men and women alike, and retired to the wild forest of the Antis to a place called Villcapampa where he lived in exile and solitude as one can imagine a dispossessed and disinherited prince would live, until one day he was slain by a Spaniard whom he had sheltered and protected from enemies who had sought his death: this we shall see in due course[9]. . . .

Almagro claims Cusco as his share of the conquest and is opposed by Hernando Pizarro in Cusco. Almagro takes Hernando and Gonzalo Pizarro prisoners and makes the Cusco city council swear him in as governor of the city and its territory.

Conflict between Francisco Pizarro and Diego de Almagro

[2:34] . . . As to the marquis Don Francisco Pizarro, having sent Alvarado and soon after Gómez de Tordoya to succor his brothers, he stayed in Lima collecting the men who were coming in from all sides in response to his appeal. . . .

When the marquis found himself at the head of such a large and excellent army, consisting, according to Zárate, of over seven hundred Spanish

---

[9] The story of Manco's assassination is not included in this edition; see the complete Livermore translation of the *General History*, Book 3, ch. 8.

horse and foot, he decided to go personally to his brothers' help to relieve the anxiety that is usually caused by waiting for news from a distance. He marched out with his people along the coastal road, and after a few days received Alvarado's message about the retreat of the Inca, Almagro's return, and the arrest of his brothers, and death of the third of them, which greatly grieved the marquis. And to give him more to weep about, he received two days later the second report of the loss of his army and capture of Alvarado, which caused him indescribable sorrow. As the force he had with him was better equipped for fighting against Indians than against Spaniards, he decided to return to Lima, though he had already gone twenty-five leagues, and to equip himself with arms and gear specially for his new undertaking. He also thought he would try the door of peace and concord, for having received two adverse strokes of fortune, he feared a third. When he saw his rival surrounded by many men, with plenty of arms and horses, he began to wish to put out the fire of passion and restore their previous partnership and brotherly association, which they had ratified by so many oaths. And as they had won that great and rich empire as partners and friends, he began to hope that they might enjoy it in the same way and not slay one another on the threshold of their old age.

With this in mind he sent Licentiate Espinosa to Cusco to see if he could make some accommodation between him and Almagro. Among other things the marquis told him to remind Almagro that if His Majesty knew what had happened, and that the governors had failed to agree and were full of passion against one another, he would send another governor in place of both of them, who would thus without stirring a step enjoy what they had won with such hardship and at such cost in blood and treasure. A good peace was better than a bad war, and though the saying was usually the reverse, in their case it sounded better so. Finally the marquis told Espinosa that if he could not obtain anything else, he was to persuade Almagro to release his brothers and to remain himself in Cusco and not advance on Lima, governing that city for the time being until His Majesty knew what had taken place and decided what each of them was to have.

Espinosa went off with this mission and laid the proposals before Almagro and his captains; but they were puffed up with pride and might after their recent victories and would accept no terms. Although Diego de Alvarado, with his usual discretion and good sense, reminded them that the terms offered were what they themselves had been asking for hitherto since they were allowed free enjoyment and possession of Cusco, they turned down his advice and replied that they would have no limits imposed on them and not be told they were not to advance on Lima. In their own jurisdiction and in their situation of strength and good fortune, they would not obey other people's laws or accept conditions, but make them. And although Diego de Alvarado replied that the conditions were so favorable that it seemed almost as if they had set them and not received them, they refused to heed him. It is noteworthy that until then each of the governors had asked the other to relinquish Cusco and to accept the whole area outside the narrow valleys as his jurisdiction, the one to the north and the other to the south. And now that Almagro was offered it, he refused to accept it, thinking that as he already had the city in his possession, the fact that his rival was now willing to offer him it, though he had coveted it so much before, was proof that Pizarro was afraid of losing his whole jurisdiction. And as fortune favored him with flags unfurled, he preferred to follow it as far as it led and see if he might not enjoy the whole empire to himself. Stirred by these insatiable passions of ambition and covetousness, Almagro refused to accept the terms the governor offered him.

This attitude was contributed to by the sudden death of Espinosa, who died at the height of the negotiations before he could conclude them. His judgment, prudence, and good counsel gave promise of a satisfactory result, but death prevented him from seeing the fruit of his efforts and desires, and God too in his mysterious designs denied him it. Espinosa died prophesying the death and destruction of both governors, seeing their reluctance to recognize what was to their own advantage. Almagro left Cusco at the head of his army, as a sign that he rejected the condition the marquis had sent. He left Gabriel de Rojas as his deputy in the city with charge of all the prisoners, who numbered more than 150, including the first group taken with Hernando Pizarro and the second with Alonso de Alvarado, divided between two prisons, as we have said.

Almagro took Hernando Pizarro with him, not daring to leave him with the rest lest he should escape. He went by the coastal road, left the district of Cusco and entered that of Lima reaching the valley of Chincha, a little over twenty leagues from Lima, where he founded a settlement as a sign of possession, indicating and even proving that he claimed both jurisdictions. He remained there with his army to see how the marquis would take this act of defiance, suggesting that if he did not like it, he should take up the challenge, and he, Almagro, would wait for him in the field like a good captain and accept the arbitration of war.

The War between Pizarro and Almagro

[2:35] As soon as the marquis reached Lima, he prepared for the war he was expecting against Almagro. Drums were beaten and messages were sent along the coast with information about what had happened. New troops arrived daily, and as the army increased he appointed captains and officials.

He made Pedro de Valdivia commander and Antonio de Villalva, the son of Colonel Villalva, sergeant major. Pero Ansúrez, Diego de Rojas, and Alonso de Mercadillo were appointed captains of horse, and Diego de Urbina, a native of Orduña and nephew to the commander Juan de Urbina, was made captain of the pikemen. Nuño de Castro and Pedro de Vergara (who had been a soldier in Flanders and brought a great band of harqebuses to the Indies with all the necessary ammunition) were made captains of the harquebusiers. These captains raised eight hundred picked men, six hundred on foot and two hundred horse, with which the marquis left Lima to meet Almagro, announcing that he was going to defend his rights as governor, which Almagro was trying to usurp.

While the affairs of the marquis and Almagro were proceeding in this way, the prisoners in Cusco did not sleep, but sought the precious gift of liberty by all possible means. As everything can be bought in civil wars, especially the most important things, they found some who were ready to sell their loyalty to their captain Almagro and his deputy Gabriel de Rojas. They did not sell it for cash, but for credit, relying on the promises of Gonzalo Pizarro and Alonso de Alvarado, who were with fifty or sixty others in the prison of Cassana. The sellers were forty of the guards who left their own arms in the cells when they went to visit the prisoners, and removed the bolts from their shackles and chains. They also tried to find mounts for them, and as the other soldiers were their friends they were trusted with anything they asked for. When the prisoners and their allies were ready to slip away in the silence of the night, it happened that Gabriel de Rojas came to visit them very late, as he had on many previous nights. On opening the prison, he found that all the prisoners were loose, and he himself was the only captive; for they surrounded him and told him he must go with them or die on the spot. He had no other course but to agree to what they asked, or rather forced on him.

Thus about a hundred men went off to find the marquis. They could take the mountain road quite freely, for Almagro had gone by the coastal plains. There was no lack of malicious people who said that Gabriel de Rojas was in the plot with them; but they were deceived in their malice, for if he had been, he would not have left the others in the fortress in prison; they numbered nearly a hundred more, and included many of the first conquerors, such as Francisco de Villafuerte, Alonso de Mazuela, Mancio Serra de Leguíçamo, Diego de Maldonado, and Juan Julio de Hojeda, Tomás Vázquez, Diego de Trujillo, and Juan de Pancorvo, whom I knew and who had great allocations of Indians in Cusco. In addition, Garcilaso de la Vega, Gómez de Tordoya, and Pero Alvarez Holguín remained in prison. It would have been a great victory if the plotters had carried them all off, but it turned out as I have said. The marquis was full of joy at the arrival of his brother and his friends, for he feared that his enemies might have been stirred by wrath and spite to slay them. He was also glad to see how his men took heart on receiving these excellent reinforcements. He made Gonzalo Pizarro general of the infantry and Alonso de Alvarado general of the cavalry. Many horsemen became foot soldiers, so as to call themselves Gonzalo Pizarro's men, for he was much beloved, even by his opponents.

When Almagro knew the size and quality of the marquis' force, and heard of the freeing of his prisoners and the capture of his deputy, he found anticipated victory snatched from his hands. . . .

The final battle between Pizarro and Almagro takes place near a plain outside Cusco called "Las Salinas." Hernando Pizarro is wounded in the battle.

[2:37] . . . When his friends saw Pizarro fall, they thought he was dead and fell on Almagro's men, and both sides fought bravely with great loss of life; for their passions were kindled more than they thought, and they wounded and killed one another with great fury and desperation, as though they were not all of the same nation and one religion, and forgetful that they had been brothers and companions in arms in the great hardships they had suffered in gaining that empire. The fight lasted much longer than they had thought, without any decision. Though Almagro's men were much weaker in numbers, they were equal in valor and spirit to Pizarro's, and they resisted the might of their foes and the superiority of their harquebuses at the expense of their lives, which they sold dear until they found themselves worn out, or dead or wounded, when those who could turned their backs. Then the fury with which they had fought showed itself more pitiless than ever, for although they surrendered and were seen to be defeated, they were not spared. . . .

The Lamentable Death of Don Diego de Almagro

[2:39] . . . Because of the acts of cruelty committed after the battle the two parties continued full of hatred and enmity, and though Hernando Pizarro did all he could to make friends of the leaders on the other side, he failed to do so: and they daily displayed their hatred and rancor more openly, speaking freely of taking revenge when they could. Moreover his friends also turned against him when they saw their hopes of reward undone, for each of them had promised himself a whole province. And though Hernando Pizarro gave something to many of them, as López de Gómara says, it was impossible to reward them all, and most of his friends were left as dissatisfied as his enemies. And in order to save himself the trouble of rewarding the former and to avoid his fears and suspicions of the latter, he began offering both new conquests, as we shall say in the next chapter.[10] Almagro was condemned to death and his property confiscated for the royal treasury. At first Hernando Pizarro had no intention of killing him, but only of sending him to Spain with the case against him. This was until he saw that Almagro bore his imprisonment badly and openly said that they would have to release him, declaring that Hernando Pizarro was more guilty than he of the charges brought against him, for he had been the chief cause of the discord between the two governors. If Hernando had not incited his brother, the marquis, against Almagro, their passions would never have reached such a pitch; and now he wanted to avenge his own disappointment by executing and robbing of his jurisdiction one who had done more and spent more in conquering Peru than all the Pizarros: all this was intolerable, and the very stones would rise up against them.

When Hernando Pizarro heard this, and knew in particular that one of his officers called Gonzalo de Mesa, who had been a captain of artillery, but had been unrewarded and bore a grudge, as we shall say, was proposing to go out with his friends and release Almagro on the road, he hastily decided to kill Don Diego. He thought by thus getting rid of him all the passions that had been aroused would die down and they would all remain in peace and quiet; but everything turned out very differently, as our history will show. When López de Gómara says that it was never known who Almagro's father was, though enquiries were made, this is true and Zárate confirms it, adding that he was left at the church door. This may well be so, for the church regards such as well-born and admits them to all its dignities and prelacies. But when López de Gómara adds that his father was a priest, this is not to be borne: this must be the tale of some envious slanderers and desperate characters who could not sully his great deeds and sought to condemn him for his birth with poisonous tongues, and without evidence or even the appearance of truth. The sons of unknown fathers should be judged by their deeds and virtues, and when their acts resemble those of the *adelantado*[11] and governor Don Diego de Almagro, one can only say that they are well born, for they are the children of their own virtue and their own right arms. What is the benefit of nobility to the children of noble fathers, if they are unworthy of it and do not confirm it with their

---

[10] Garcilaso's "next chapter" is not included in this edition; see the complete Livermore translation of the *General History,* Book 2, ch. 40.

[11] The word *adelantado* means the governor of a province or region, and is a title conferred on the leader of an expedition. Both Francisco Pizarro and Diego de Almagro had the right to use the title of *adelantado,* although Pizarro was referred to by his superior title of marquis.

own virtues? For nobility was born of these virtues and is sustained by them. We can therefore truthfully say that Don Diego de Almagro was the son of very noble parents: these were his own works, which have magnified and enriched all the princes of the earth, as we have already said and proved at length.

This heroic man was thus garroted in prison, and as if this were not enough, beheaded in the public square, to the great grief and distress of the onlookers, for he was more than seventy-five at the time, and his health was so broken that it was thought that his end was very near, even if it had not been hastened. Slanderers said that he had been killed twice, to show the better the great hatred in which he was held and to take revenge on him. The executioner exercised his rights and claimed his spoils, removing all Almagro's clothes down to his shirt; and he would have taken that if he had not been prevented. His body was left in the square for a great deal of the day, with no one friend or enemy willing to remove it; for his friends were dejected and humbled and could not, and his enemies, though many of them regretted his death, dared do nothing for him in public for fear of angering their friends. This shows how the world rewards those who do it the greatest services. And about nightfall there came a Negro who had been the dead man's slave, bringing a wretched sheet, which was all he had in his poverty or could get as alms, to bury his master in. He wrapped Don Diego in it with the aid of some Indians who had been his servants and carried him to the church of Our Lady of Mercies. The religious charitably and tearfully buried him in a chapel below the high altar. So ended the great Don Diego de Almagro, of whom no memory is left but that of his deeds and his pitiable death, which seems to have been a model and pattern of that suffered by the marquis Don Francisco Pizarro in revenge. For Pizarro's death was very similar, as we shall see; and these two conquerors and governors of the great and rich empire of Peru remained equal partners in everything.

Chapter Three
War among the Spaniards

Francisco Pizarro sends his brother Gonzalo to conquer Collao and Charcas, and attempts to organize Peru.

The Marquis Divides the Province of Los Charcas; Gonzalo Goes to More Conquests

[3:2] After the war was over and the Indians had been pacified, the marquis divided them among the principal Spaniards who had been present at the conquest. He gave a good allocation to his brother Hernando and another to Gonzalo, in whose district the silver mines of Potosí were discovered years later. Hernando Pizarro received a mine as a *vecino*[12] of the city, though he was already in Spain, and it was placed in the hands of his officials so that they could send him the silver that was extracted; it proved so rich that for over eight months it produced fine, pure silver, with no other treatment but melting it. I mention this wealth at this point, because it slipped my memory when discussing the famous hill of Potosí in the first part of these *Commentaries*. The allocation called Tapac-Ri was awarded to my lord Garcilaso de la Vega, and Gabriel de Rojas was given another excellent one, as were many other gentlemen, over an area of more than a hundred leagues which then constituted the jurisdiction of the city: part of this area was later given to the city called La Paz.

The value of these allocations was small at the time when they were awarded, though they had many Indians and their soil was very fertile. It was only with the discovery of the mines of Potosí that their rents increased tenfold, and the allocations that had produced two, three, or four thousand pesos later produced twenty, thirty, and forty thousand. The marquis ordered the foundation of the town called La Plata, now called the city of La Plata, and divided the Indians in its jurisdiction among the Spanish conquerors and settlers, all of which took place in 1538 and 1539. Then having rested less than two years from the past civil wars and conquests, he engaged in new and more arduous enterprises, as we shall say. With the death of Almagro he was left as sole governor of a country extending more

---

[12] A *vecino* is a citizen or property-holder of a city or settlement who is qualified to serve on the town council or *cabildo*.

138

than seven hundred leagues from north to south, from Los Charcas to Quito, where he had much to do in pacifying and arranging the new conquests his captains had made in various directions, and in administering justice and maintaining the peace among the towns and peoples that had already been subdued. But as the desire to command and rule is insatiable, not content with what he had, he sought new discoveries, for his warlike spirit wished to press on with the successes he had thus far had. . . .

Pizarro sends his brother Gonzalo to conquer La Canela in the north, assigning him the government of Quito as his base. Gonzalo and his followers experience great hardships in the expedition. Back in Peru, the followers of Almagro, now led by Almagro's mestizo son, Diego de Almagro the younger, plot revenge.

The Chilean Party (the Followers of Almagro) Plans to Kill the Marquis

[3:5] . . . When the marquis had divided the provinces of the Charcas among the conquerors of the kingdom and repaired some damage caused by the late passions between his own followers and those of Almagro in Cusco, he left all in peace and quiet and went to Lima so as personally to assist in its settlement. In Lima was Don Diego de Almagro the younger, who had been sent there, as we have said, by Hernando Pizarro immediately after the execution of his father. The marquis found that some of the most prominent of the Almagrists now surrounded Almagro's son, who fed them at his table from the proceeds of a good allocation of Indians his father had given him: this he did because all his followers had been deprived of their Indians as traitors for being on his father's side. As the marquis was a man of noble and generous character he tried to satisfy these gentlemen by offering them large subsidies and appointing them to positions in the administration of justice and the royal treasury. But they hoped to see the Pizarros punished for the undeserved death of Almagro and for the cruelties they had committed in the battle of Las Salinas and afterward, and refused any sort of reward, so as to have nothing to thank the marquis for, and no cause to lay down their rancor against the marquis and his friends, for they wished to give no opportunity to anyone to say that they had taken gifts from him and still remained his enemies. They thus went on supporting one another and refusing to receive anything from the Pizarrists, however great their need. When some of the marquis' familiars and advisers saw this and pondered over it, they advised him, like evil counselors, that as the Almagrists would not become his friends by fair means, he should force them to do so, or at least reduce them by hunger and want. The marquis reluctantly complied with his advisers' opinions—

though they were not his own, for he never deliberately harmed anyone, however hostile to him—and took away the younger Almagro's Indians. It was in Almagro's house that the others used to meet for their meals; and it was thought that if they had no food they would go and seek it elsewhere and so leave the city. But this action, instead of reducing the Almagrists to obedience, simply roused them to greater indignation and wrath, which is the usual result of tyrannical rigor, especially if it is undeserved.

So when Almagro's followers saw how harshly they were misused, they wrote letters to many places where they knew there were Spaniards who were well disposed toward them, summoning their friends to Lima to help them press their claims. Among those who came out on their side there were many who had not been with them in the late wars, but who had recently come to Peru: some of these joined one side or the other without any special cause, as always happens when there are divisions. Thus more than two hundred soldiers gathered in Lima, having come three or four hundred leagues. When they found themselves so numerous, they took courage from one another, and began freely to acquire arms; hitherto they had not even dared to mention them, for they were as if under arrest. But because of the mildness which the marquis had assumed toward them, they acted with complete freedom and began to plan to avenge the death of Almagro on the marquis, now that Hernando Pizarro, who was the cause of all their past, present, and future evils, had gone to Spain. Their negotiations were not so secret that they did not come to the ears of the marquis' advisers, and these last importuned him earnestly to punish the rebels by killing the leaders and banishing the rest before they began a rising against him and his followers. The marquis, as Zárate says in his Book IV, chapter vi:

> ". . . was so confident and in such good heart that he said it would be best to leave the poor wretches, who had enough trouble with their poverty and humiliation and defeat. Thus Don Diego and his friends relied on the marquis' patience and equanimity, and gradually treated him with less and less regard, so much so that the leaders on several occasions passed him without removing their caps or showing any sign of respect."

Thus Zárate.

The fact is that their poverty was such that there were groups of seven soldiers with only a single cloak among them, and that not new, but worn out; and each would take his turn to go out and about his business in it, each waiting for the one who was abroad wearing it to come back before he ventured forth. Likewise with their food; they all gave what money they had to Juan de Rada, and also anything they won by gambling, and he acted as treasurer and housekeeper for them all. Their liberty and shamelessness in the face of the marquis' forbearance were in proportion to their poverty. Their most brazen action was to tie three ropes from the gallows in the city square one night; the first was fastened to the house of Antonio Picado, the marquis' secretary, the second to that of Dr. Juan Velázquez, the mayor, and the third to the marquis' own house, a piece of shameless impudence that would have sufficed to hang them all with the same ropes. But the marquis' character was so noble that he not only did not punish or investigate the affair, but even excused its perpetrators in the face of their accusers, saying that they were defeated and broken and did that because they could do no more: leave them alone, for their misfortune was enough. When the Chileans knew this, instead of being appeased they grew more and more shameless and embittered, until they finally killed the marquis, as we shall see.

The Chileans Kill the Marquis

[3:6] For all their impudence and defiance, the supporters of Almagro were still vacillating, not knowing what course to take, for though they had agreed to kill the marquis, they wished to wait for His Imperial Majesty's commands with regard to the punishment of the murder of Don Diego de Almagro, since they knew that Diego de Alvarado, who, as we have said, came to Spain to accuse the Pizarros, had succeeded in getting a judge appointed to try the case, though they had also heard that the judge's jurisdiction was very limited.[13] He was not to punish anyone or to remove the marquis from his post, but merely to obtain information about what had happened and take it to Spain, where His Majesty would decide on the punishment that was to be applied to the guilty. This greatly annoyed the followers of Almagro who wanted a judge with full powers to investigate and cut off as many heads right and left as they thought fit to name, and to confiscate property, and award it to themselves. In this state of doubt they decided to wait until the judge's arrival so as to see how he executed his commission and find how he would proceed and whether his powers would be as limited as they had been told, or wider, as they hoped. Privately they plotted together like conspirators saying that if the judge did not arrest the marquis as soon as he arrived and apply other severe penalties, they would kill them both and raise the standard of revolt, avenging

---

[13] Diego de Alvarado tried to mediate the quarrel between Francisco Pizarro and Diego de Almagro until Almagro's death. Later, in Spain, he brought charges against Hernando Pizarro that led to Hernando's arrest and imprisonment. Diego de Alvarado died suddenly while pursuing his case, leading to rumors that he was poisoned.

themselves for the wrong the marquis had done them and also for the emperor's omission in not punishing a crime so atrocious as they thought the death of Almagro to be. The plan to raise the standard of revolt throughout Peru they later executed, as we shall see.

. . . Thus the good marquis was as heedless of being killed by the Chilean party as they were impatient to kill him. But, as we have said, they awaited the arrival of the judge so as to see how he would handle the case. Their hesitation, however, was turned to rabid indignation and rage by an action of the marquis' secretary, Antonio Picado, at this time.

As the Chileans had fastened ropes from the gibbet and one of them had been directed at him, and as they were full of such brazen imprudence toward the marquis—though they seemed only to threaten to take up arms without actually daring to do so—Picado mocked them for their cowardice by putting in his cap a rich gold metal with a picture of a fig on it and a scroll reading "for the Chileans."[14] The brave soldiers were so insulted and furious at this that they decided to carry out the murder of the marquis without waiting for the judge to arrive. They thus discussed the matter more openly than hitherto, and the marquis heard about it through a priest who had learned in secret how and when they meant to do the deed.

The marquis took counsel with the mayor, Dr. Velázquez, and his secretary, Antonio Picado. They calmed his fears, saying that there was no need to set any store by such wretched people who only said such things to calm their hunger and forget their misery. But the marquis had now changed his first idea and was afraid. He did not go to mass in the cathedral on St. John's day, 1541, which was the day they had fixed for his death, and he did not go the Sunday following, June 26, excusing himself on the grounds of ill health, though his real desire was to stay in the house for a few days and decide with his friends and advisers how best to put an end to the impudent boldness of his enemies, which now passed all bounds. The *vecinos* and chief gentlemen of the city called on the marquis after mass that Sunday, having noted his absence, and after seeing him, retired to their houses, leaving with him only Dr. Velásquez and Francisco de Chaves, who was his intimate friend.

The Chileans, aware that the marquis was now more suspicious than hitherto and that his supporters had visited him in such numbers, suspected that a plan was being arranged to kill them. Thus they grew alarmed, and like desperadoes that very Sunday, at the hour when all were

---

[14] An alternative meaning of a fig is "a contemptibly worthless trifle," according to *Webster's Dictionary.* I suspect that the fig combined with the slogan "for the Chileans" meant something like "I don't give a fig for you and your cowardice"—a strong insult of men who already feel that their honor has been impugned.

at dinner and the marquis himself had just dined, they all came out into the corner of the square to the left side of the cathedral church, where Don Diego de Almagro the younger and his chief followers lodged, and they crossed obliquely over the square, which is very long, to the marquis' house in the opposite corner. There were thirteen of them. Twelve are named by López de Gómara, though he does not say where they came from. They are Juan de Rada, who was leader of the rest; Martín de Bilbao; Diego Méndez; Cristóbal de Sosa; Martín Carrillo; Arbolancha; Hinojeros; Narváez; San Millán; Porras; Velázquez; Francisco Núñez; and Gómez Pérez, who was the one not mentioned by López de Gómara.

They crossed the whole square with their swords bared shouting: "Down with the traitor and tyrant who has killed the judge the emperor sent to punish him!" The reason why they came out so openly and made so much noise was to cause the people of the city to think that they must be very numerous, since they dared to do such a deed so publicly, and thus prevent them from coming out of their houses to help the marquis. The manner in which they did it was astonishingly bold and rash, but it was the marquis' misfortune that the partisans of Don Diego de Almagro should succeed in their aim under pretense of avenging their leader's death, as we shall see.

The Death of the Marquis and His Poor Funeral

[3:7] Hearing the noise made by the Chileans, some Indians in the marquis' service entered his room and warned him of their approach and their threatening appearance. The marquis was talking to the mayor, Dr. Velásquez, Captain Francisco Chavez, who acted as his deputy, and Francisco Martín de Alcántara, his half-brother, as well as twelve or thirteen of his servants, and he suspected what was afoot when the Indians brought the warning. He bade Francisco de Chavez shut the door of the room and the hall where they were, while he and his friends got their arms and prepared to defend themselves from the attackers.

Francisco de Chavez thought that the affair was a private quarrel by some soldiers and that his authority would be sufficient to stop it; and instead of shutting the door as he had been ordered, he went out to meet them and found them already climbing the stairs. Much disturbed at finding what he had not expected, he asked them: "What do you want?" One of them thrust at him with a sword for answer. Finding himself wounded, he laid his hand on his own sword, but they all attacked him and one struck him so hard in the neck that, as López de Gómara says in his chapter cxlv: "his head was smitten off and his body went rolling down the stairs." The marquis' servants who were in the room came out at the noise, but on

seeing Francisco Chaves lying dead, they turned back and fled like mercenaries, flinging themselves down from windows that gave onto a garden of
the house. These included Dr. Juan Velázquez, who had his wand of office
in his mouth so as to free his hands, and hoping apparently that the attackers would respect it. These last forced their way into the room, and finding
no one there, went on into the hall.

When the marquis realized they were so close, he went out half-armed
without having had time to tie the laces of a breastplate he had put on.
He had a shield on his arm and carried a sword in his hand. He was
accompanied by his brother Francisco Martin de Alcántara and two
pages, fully grown men, one called Juan de Vargas, the son of Gómez de
Tordoya, and the other Alonso Escandón. They wore no armor, for they
had no opportunity to get any. The marquis and his brother stood at the
door and defended it bravely for a long time without letting the attackers
pass. The marquis, full of spirit, told his brother: "Kill them, they are traitors!" Both sides fought hard, until the marquis' brother was killed, for he
had no armor. One of the pages took his place, and he and his master
defended the door so manfully that the enemy began to doubt whether
they could force a way through. So, fearing lest help would come for the
marquis and they would all be killed if the struggle went on long, Juan de
Rada and one of his companions seized Narváez and threw him through
the door, so as to keep the marquis busy while the rest of them got past.
So it fell out; for while the marquis received Narváez at the point of his
sword and dealt him several wounds of which he soon died, the rest came
in, and some attacked the marquis and others his pages, who fell fighting
like men, having severely wounded four of their opponents. When they
found the marquis alone, they all fell on him and surrounded him on all
sides. He defended himself like the great man he was for a long while,
leaping from side to side and wielding his sword with such force and skill
that three of his assailants were severely wounded. But as there were so
many of them, and he was more than seventy-five years old, he soon wea-
ried, and one of them approached and struck him in the throat with his
swords, whereupon he fell to the ground, shouting for confession. So
lying, he made a cross with his right hand, put his lips to it, and died kissing it.

This was the end of Don Francisco Pizarro, famous above all famous
men, who so enriched and extended and still does extend the crown of
Spain and the whole world with the riches of the empire he gained, as can
be seen and as we have often repeated. With all his greatness and wealth, he
was so wretched and poor when he died that there was no one to bury him.
In less than an hour fortune matched the favor and prosperity she had
shown him throughout his life with no less disfavor and misery. . . .

On the Customs and Qualities of the Marquis Don Francisco Pizarro and the Adelantado Don Diego de Almagro[15]

[3:8] "As the whole of this history and the discovery of the province of Peru with which it deals have their origin in the two captains of whom we have been speaking, the marquis Don Francisco Pizarro and the *adelantado* Don Diego de Almagro, it is fitting that we should write of their customs and qualities and compare them together, as Plutarch does when he writes of the deeds of two captains who have anything in common. And as we have said all that can be discovered of their lineages, we may add that in other respects both were full of courage and resolution, very patient of hardships and most virtuous men, both of them inclined to please everyone even though at their own expense. They bore a close resemblance to one another in their inclinations, especially in regard to their state of life, for neither of them married, though neither was under sixty-five when he died.

"Both were inclined to warfare, though the *adelantado* was fond of husbandry when there was no occasion for fighting.

"Both set out on the conquest of Peru at an advanced age, and both labored on it as we have said above, though the marquis suffered great dangers and many more than the *adelantado;* for while the former was engaged on the greater part of the discovery, the latter remained in Panama, providing whatever was necessary, in the manner we have described.

"Both were men of great spirit who always conceived high thoughts and strove to put them into execution, despite the great hardships they involved and notwithstanding their humanity and friendliness toward their followers. They were also liberal in giving, though in appearances the *adelantado* was the more so, for he very much liked his generosity to be published abroad and talked about. The marquis was rather the reverse, and was inclined to be annoyed if his liberality became public, and sought to hide it, being more concerned to meet the needs of those on whom he bestowed his gifts than to gain honor by them.

"Thus it happened that he heard that a soldier's horse had died and went down to the court for playing at ball in his house hoping to find the man, and carrying in his bosom a gold brick weighing ten pound which he meant to give him with his own hand. He did not find the man; meanwhile a game of ball was arranged and the marquis played without undressing so as not to show the brick, which he did not dare to remove from his bosom for above three hours, when the soldier who was to receive it arrived. Pizarro then secretly called him to a private room and gave it him saying that he would rather have presented him with three such bricks than

---

[15] This section reproduces Zárate's evaluation of the two leaders of the conquest of Peru.

have suffered the discomfort the man's delay had given him. Many other examples could be adduced of this quality. And it was extraordinarily rare for the marquis to give anything except by his own hand, and he always sought not to have it known.

"For this reason, the *adelantado* was always regarded as the more open-handed, for though he gave much he did it in such a way as to make it seem more. Yet with regard to the quality of magnificence, they may justly be matched with one another; for, as the marquis himself used to say, because of the conditions of their association with regard to all their property neither gave anything without the other contributing half.

"In this way the one who knowingly permitted the gift gave as much as the giver. This point of the comparison may be sufficiently illustrated by the fact that though the two of them were very wealthy men both in money and revenues in their lifetime, and either of them could give or hold more than many uncrowned princes in the past, yet both died so poor that not only is there no record of their having left any estates or wealth, but there was not even enough money found in their possession for their burial; the same is written of Cato, Sulla, and many other captains who received public funerals.

"Both were very devoted to the interests of their friends and followers, whom they enriched, promoted, and saved from danger. The marquis had this quality to excess, so much so that once in crossing a river called the Barranca, it happened that the great stream carried off a Yanacona Indian in his service, and the marquis threw himself in after him and drew him forth by the hair, exposing himself to great danger owing to the furious force of the stream, which none of his whole army, however young and bold, dared face. And when some of the captains rebuked him for his excessive boldness, he replied that they did not know what it was to be fond of a servant.

"Although the marquis governed longer and more peacefully, Don Diego was much the more ambitious and desirous of command and government. Both preserved old-fashioned ways and were so attached to them that they almost never changed the dress they wore in their youth. This was especially the case with the marquis who usually never dressed otherwise than in a black cassock with skirts down to the ankle and the waist halfway up his chest, and white deerskin shoes and a white hat, with his sword and dagger worn in the old-fashioned way.

"On some feast days, at the behest of his servants, he would put on a sable cloak the marquis del Valle[16] had sent him from New Spain, but as

---

[16] Hernan Cortés, the conqueror of Mexico.

soon as he came out of Mass he would cast it aside and remain in his house clothes. He usually had some napkins round his neck, for he spent most of the day in time of peace playing at bowls or at ball, and they served to wipe the sweat off his face.

"Both captains were very long suffering against toil and hunger, and the marquis was particularly so in the games we have mentioned, for there were few youths who could outlast him. He was much more inclined to all kinds of sport than the *adelantado,* so much so that sometimes he spent the whole day bowling, without caring who he played with, if it were a seaman or a miller, or without allowing others to hand him the ball or perform other courtesies due to his rank.

"There were few affairs for which he would break off his game, especially when he was losing, unless it were the news of some Indian disturbance. In this case he would at once don his armor and rush through the city with lance and shield to the place where the tumult was, without waiting for his followers, who afterwards caught up with him, running at all speed.

"These two captains were both so courageous and skilled in warfare with the Indians that either of them would have taken on a hundred Indian braves single-handed without the slightest hesitation. They had excellent judgment and were full of experience in all questions of warfare and government, particularly so as neither of them was well read: indeed they could not read or write or even sign their names, which was a great defect in persons of standing, apart from their need of it in business of such great consequence. Yet in all their qualities and pursuits they never appeared to be anything but noble, except in this matter alone which the learned men of old esteemed a mark of base birth.

"The marquis had such confidence in all his servants and friends that he delivered all his documents referring to questions of administration and the allocation of Indians by making two marks between which his secretary, Antonio Picado, signed the name of Francisco Pizarro.

"This may be excused as Ovid excused Romulus for being a bad astrologer, saying that he knew more of arms than of letters and was more concerned with conquering his neighbors. Both were simple and unpretentious among their followers and fellow citizens and went unescorted from house to house, visiting the *vecinos* and dining with whoever invited them. They were similarly abstinent and temperate, both in feeding and eating and in curbing their sensuality, especially as regards Castilian women; for they considered that they could not indulge themselves except to the detriment of the *vecinos* and their daughters and wives. Even as regards the Indian women of Peru, the *adelantado* was much the more temperate, for he was never known to have children by them or intercourse with them, though the marquis had a liaison with an Indian lady, a sister of Atahuallpa's by whom he left a son called Don Gonzalo, who died at fourteen, and a daughter called Doña Francisca. And he had a son called Don Francisco by another Indian of Cusco. The *adelantado* had the son who killed the marquis by an Indian woman of Panama.

"Both received favors from His Majesty, for Don Francisco Pizarro was given the title of marquis and governor of New Castile and awarded the habit of Santiago. And Don Diego de Almagro was given the governorship of New Toledo and made *adelantado*.

"The marquis in particular was much attached to His Majesty and fearful of his name, so much so that he abstained from doing many things which he had power to do, saying that he did not wish His Majesty to say that he was exceeding himself. Often when he was in the smelting house he would rise from his chair to pick up grains of gold and silver that fell from the chisel as the royal fifth was being cut, saying that the royal treasury must be gathered up with the mouth, if there was no other way. They resembled one another even in the manner of their death, for the marquis' brother killed the *adelantado* and the *adelantado's* son killed the marquis.

"The marquis was also very devoted to the development of Peru by improving its agriculture and buildings. He made some fine houses in Lima and left two sluices for mills in the river there, to the building of which he devoted all his idle moments, spurring on the workmen.

"He was very solicitous for the building of the cathedral of Lima and the monasteries of St. Dominic and the Mercedarians, and gave them allocations of Indians for their support and the repair of the building."

Thus Zárate. . . .

Almagro the Younger Has Himself Sworn in As Governor of Peru

[3:10] The Marquis died, as we have seen, through the overconfidence of Francisco de Chaves, who failed to shut the gates as he was bidden. If he had done so, those who were with the marquis would have had time to arm themselves while the attackers were breaking in, and would possibly have overcome the Almagrists. Since only four of them, the marquis, his brother and his two pages, all ill-armed, killed four of their assailants as the historians say, it may well be believed that if they had been better prepared these four and those who got away through the windows would have been sufficient to ward off their enemies and even to defeat them, for even though they themselves did not win the fray, help might have come in due course. But when misfortune occurs, it is hard to remedy it through human counsel.

The Negro López de Gómara mentions as being killed by the Chileans had heard the hubbub caused by the fight with the marquis and gone upstairs to help his master or die with him, but on reaching the door found him already dead. He tried to bolt it from the outside so as to shut the murderers in and call the justice, but as he was pulling the doors together, one of those within happened to come out, and realizing the slave's intention, attacked him and killed him with his sword. Seven of the marquis' followers died, including a servant of Francisco de Chaves. Then the Almagrists came out into the square with bloody swords, singing victory. Such was the end of the good marquis, due to the neglect and overconfidence of his friends rather than to the power of his enemies.

With the news of his death a great to-do was raised throughout the city. Some shouted: "Help in the king's name, they're killing the marquis!" Others cried: "The tyrant is dead and Don Diego de Almagro is avenged!" Amidst this shouting and confusion many came out to support either side, and there were many quarrels and frays in the square, resulting in dead and wounded on both sides. But when it became known for certain that the marquis was dead, his followers at once gave up. The Chileans now brought out Don Diego de Almagro the younger into the square, saying that there was no other king in Peru but he. Once the disturbances had settled down, he had himself sworn in by the city council as governor of Peru and nobody dared gainsay him, though all the members of the council were on the opposite side. Yet no one dared speak up or oppose the demands of the victors. The ministers of justice were removed and others of the winning side put in their stead. The richest and most powerful men in Lima were arrested because they were on the other side; and in short Almagro took possession of the whole city. He seized the royal fifths,[17] for which a very large sum was in store. The same was done with the property of the dead and absent. All this was needed to help the Almagrists, who were as poor as we have said. . . .

The messengers who took Almagro's powers and instructions to Cusco did not dare to commit any of the outrages that had taken place elsewhere; for though they had many partisans in the city, there were many more royalists, and these included the richest and most powerful inhabitants who had allocations of Indians, while Don Diego's party consisted of poor soldiers newly arrived in Peru who desired such disorders in order that they too might prosper. The *alcaldes*[18] of the city were then Diego de Silva, whom I have mentioned before, the son of Feliciano de Silva and a native of Ciudad Rodrigo, and Francisco de Carvajal, who was later commander

---

[17] According to Spanish law, one-fifth, or twenty percent, of all treasure went to the crown; that share was called the "royal fifth."

[18] An *alcalde* is a city or town magistrate.

under Gonzalo Pizarro. When these had seen the letters, they wished to avoid irritating the Almagrists and they and the whole council made reply neither obeying nor opposing, but saying that in a matter of such gravity it was necessary for Don Diego to send fuller powers than he had done; and when he did this, he would be accepted as governor. They said this not meaning to accept him but only to keep him waiting so that there should be time and opportunity for those who were on the Pizarrist side and were then absent to come to Cusco: most of them were out of the cities on their allocations or at their gold mines, which most of the allocations of Cusco have.

The Appointment in Spain of Vaca de Castro to Be Judge of the Events of Peru

[3:11] Gómez de Tordoya, who was one of the chief members of the city council of Cusco, was not in the city when Don Diego de Almagro's instructions and powers arrived. He had gone hunting seven or eight days before, and his retainers sent a messenger to warn him of what had happened. As soon as he read the letter he was so stricken with grief at the death of the marquis, of whom he was a close friend and servant, that he wrung the neck of his falcon, saying: "This is a time for fire and the sword rather than for hunting and pastimes." For, like an intelligent man, he realized that these events would lead to great disorders and cruel deaths. He then went to the city, which he entered by night, so as not to alarm his opponents, and spoke to the leading members of the council, telling them that they ought to summon people from Arequipa and Los Charcas and the whole region to the south of Cusco and bring in the Spaniards who were dispersed. Messengers should be sent to convey the news, and he offered himself as one of them. This done, he left the city the same night and went in search of Captain Nuño de Castro, who was fifteen or twenty leagues from the city, among his Indians. Both sent messengers to Pedro Ansúrez and Garcilaso de la Vega with orders to collect all His Majesty's servants and bid them rally to his service like loyal subjects.

After sending this message, Gómez de Tordoya went off in all haste in pursuit of Captain Pedro Alvarez Holguín, who had taken over a hundred Spaniards on an expedition to the east of the Collao to conquer some Indians in those parts who have still not been reduced even today. By making all haste he overtook him, and informed him of the marquis' death and of how Almagro the younger was claiming to be governor of the empire. He urged Holguín to shoulder the task and undertake so just a quest in the service of his God and king, begging him to act as leader of the forces that were being collected, and telling him, as a further inducement, that he offered himself as the first and least of his soldiers. Holguín, seeing the honor that was done him and the justice of the cause, accepted the task and at once raised His Majesty's flag and sent messengers to Los Charcas and Arequipa, to report his intentions and to say how he was going to march slowly with the forces he had toward Cusco so that those who came behind would catch up with him before he reached the city. The messengers found many coming from Arequipa and Los Charcas, for the whole country was already in an uproar at the confused news that rumor had spread about the marquis' death. The men from Arequipa and Los Charcas joined Holguín and marched to Cusco as a group of about two hundred men.

When the supporters of Don Diego who were in the city heard about this, they were afraid that they would be subjected to some rigorous punishment, and one night more than fifty of them fled in a band, meaning to join Almagro; there was no one of any prominence among them. Captain Nuño de Castro and Hernando Bachicao went out after them with twenty harquebusiers, and after a rapid night march captured them and brought them back to Cusco unharmed. Meanwhile Pedro Alvarez Holguín reached the city with his good company, which included many leading gentlemen. The council of Cusco received them with great content, and those in the city and the newcomers at once set about choosing a captain general, for Holguín resigned the post of captain on reaching the city. There was some delay and difference of opinion in making the choice, not because of passion but out of courtesy toward one another, for there were many gentlemen in the city who were equal in rank and merits and who deserved this office and other higher honors. But by the common consent of those who had newly come and those who were already in the city, Holguín was chosen and sworn as captain general and chief justice of Peru until His Majesty should decide otherwise. The citizens were within their rights in doing this; for in default of a governor appointed by His Majesty, the council of Cusco, as the capital city of the empire, was authorized to nominate officials for war and the administration of justice until His Majesty should make appointments. They elected Gómez de Tordoya as commander; Garcilaso de la Vega and Pedro Ansúrez as captains of cavalry; Nuño de Castro and Hernando Bachicao as captains of infantry; and Martín de Robles as bearer of the royal standard.

They publicly declared war on Don Diego de Almagro, and the *vecinos* of Cusco bound themselves to repay His Majesty all that Holguín might spend on the war from the royal treasury, if His Majesty did not approve the expense. In addition to guaranteeing the royal treasury in this way, the people of Cusco also offered their persons and property for the campaign, and those of Arequipa and Los Charcas did likewise. And everyone displayed such promptitude and willingness to serve His Majesty that in a short time more than 350 men were recruited, captains and picked soldiers. Of these 150 were horse, 100 harquebusiers, and the remaining 100 pikemen. Holguín had heard that Alonso de Alvarado had raised his flag for the emperor in Chachapoyas, and he and all his men rejoiced at it, for they had feared that the whole area from Lima to Quito was for Don Diego de Almagro. They also knew that Almagro was coming to Cusco to make war on them, bringing more than 800 men. When the captains had discussed this together, they considered that it would not be safe to wait for the enemy in Cusco, but that it would be best to join Alonso de Alvarado, taking the mountain road so as to avoid meeting Almagro and to collect the friends and servants of the marquis who had fled from Almagro to the mountains and fastnesses along the road. With this determination they left Cusco, leaving the old and sick behind so as to suggest that the city was still on their side. They also appointed a justice to govern it. They set out well equipped, with their scouts in front to explore the land and determined to fight Don Diego, if they could not capture him.

While these preparations were being made in Cusco, Don Diego de Almagro and his captains had not been idle in Lima. They had heard by secret letters from their friends what Holguín had done, and how he had decided to go across the mountains to join Alonso de Alvarado since he had too few men to resist the Almagrists. Then Don Diego decided, with the approval of his captains, to go forward and meet them. To this end he sent to summon his captain García de Alvarado to come back with all haste: he had gone down the coast below Trujillo and was gathering men, arms, and horses. When he received Don Diego's orders he obeyed, though he had previously resolved to go to the Chachapoyas against Alonso de Alvarado, thinking he was the stronger. When García de Alvarado arrived, Don Diego left Lima to go to Cusco against Holguín. He had 300 horses, all excellently equipped, 120 harquebusiers, and more than 160 pikemen, making nearly 600 in all, all picked men. Many noble and rich gentlemen went with them, having been taken by Don Diego when he killed the marquis.

On departing Almagro expelled the children of the marquis and of Gonzalo Pizarro so that none of his enemies should remain behind and the supporters of the marquis could not raise up one of his sons as their leader, as Almagro's men had raised him up. In order to find out if the marquis had left some secret treasure he had his secretary Antonio Picado severely tortured, and having got nothing out of him, hanged him, in payment of the medallion he had worn in his hat to mock the Chileans. This done, he marched on Cusco, taking all military precautions on the way.

We shall leave him on his journey, and Holguín on his, to return to say what His Imperial Majesty decided in Spain when news of the troubles in Peru up to the time of the death of Almagro the elder came to his ears. His

Majesty chose Licentiate Vaca de Castro, a member of his royal council, to go and obtain information about Almagro's death, but without making any alteration in the marquis' powers. However Vaca de Castro held a commission to become governor of Peru if the marquis should die in the meanwhile. This illustrious gentleman, as his works will prove him to be, was a native of the city of León, a member of the family of Vaca de Castro of Quiñones, very noble names among the many there are in that royal city.

He embarked in Seville for Peru, and after difficulties in the Northern Sea, reached Nombre de Dios[19] later than he had intended. He crossed thence to Panama, where he embarked for Peru in a ship that was but poorly equipped to speed the journey of one entrusted with so important and grave a mission. After sailing a few leagues, it pulled inshore because the wind was contrary. And it was so contrary that they lost an anchor, for lack of which the currents bore the ship away and carried it to the place called the Seno de la Gorgona, after the island of that name, a very difficult place for any ship that enters to leave, especially if it is sailing toward Peru. Therefore Vaca de Castro, after waiting to see if the mariners' efforts to get away would be successful and finding that they were all in vain, decided to go overland, as he could not progress by sea.

It was a long and very laborious journey, and took him longer than he would have wished because of the difficulty of the forests, the great rivers, and the rough mountains, which he crossed with some sickness and lack of supplies. His delay also gave Almagro the opportunity to hasten vengeance of his murdered father, since the king's punishment was postponed. With these difficulties, Vaca de Castro reached the confines of Quito where Pedro de Puelles was acting as deputy for Gonzalo Pizarro. As soon as he found himself in the territory over which he had jurisdiction and heard what had happened in Peru and the divisions that had appeared, he wrote to all concerned announcing his arrival and the powers he held from the emperor, so that they should all accept him as their governor. He sent commissions to all the cities of Peru, naming as judges those whom he was told were independent of the passions of the parties.

Vaca de Castro Is Accepted As Governor

[3:12] Among the instructions Licentiate Vaca de Castro sent out, that to Lima was addressed to Fray Tomás de San Martín, who was the provincial of the Order of St. Dominic, and to Francisco de Barrionuevo and Jerónimo

---

[19] Nombre de Dios is the name of the Spanish port on the east coast of the Isthmus of Panama from where travelers crossed the Isthmus to the Pacific, or South Sea, in order to sail south to Peru.

de Aliaga, who were to undertake the government of the city and those beyond it, until he himself should arrive. These dispatches were received in the convent of St. Dominic a few days after Don Diego had left the city. The provincial was away, for Don Diego had taken him with him in order to give his expedition the prestige that might be derived from his presence, but the council met by night and agreed unanimously to obey the instructions and receive the Licentiate Vaca de Castro as governor of the empire, and Jerónimo de Aliaga as his lieutenant, since the instructions were also addressed to him. This done the *vecinos* at once fled to Trujillo, for Don Diego was near and they were afraid. He, on hearing of this change in the city, was on the point of returning to sack it, burn it, and level it to the ground for so soon turning against him. But he did not dare to do this, lest Holguín should pass him in the meantime; for this was the prey he most desired to capture and the one of greatest importance to him. Because of this fear he went on in search of Holguín, but not without misgivings, for when it became known in his army that the emperor's governor had arrived in Peru, many of the leading men fled, including the provincial, Juan de Saavedra, the factor Illén Suárez de Carvajal, Diego de Agüero, and Gómez de Alvarado. . . .

When Vaca de Castro had sent out the messages we have mentioned, he went to the city of Quito in order to collect the men who were there. Lorenzo de Aldana, who was the marquis' deputy governor in Quito, came in to receive him, and so did Pedro de Puelles, who was deputy for Gonzalo Pizarro. Captain Pedro de Vergara, who was engaged in the conquest of the province called Pacamuru, which the Spaniards call Bracamoros, also came out to meet Licentiate Vaca de Castro, abandoning a village he had fortified to defend himself in case Almagro came or sent men against him. Before Vaca de Castro left Quito, he sent Pedro de Puelles on ahead to Trujillo so as to make the necessary preparations for war there. He also sent Gómez de Rojas, a native of the town of Cuéllar, with powers to repair posthaste to Cusco and try to get Vaca de Castro accepted as governor. He made such speed that he reached Cusco before Almagro, who had been held up at Jauja by the illness and death of Juan de Rada, which occurred there. Gómez de Rojas was well received in Cusco, and the governor's instructions were accepted and he was obeyed, for the people of the city had remained obedient to His Majesty, as Holguín had left them. Licentiate Vaca de Castro left Quito and went to Trujillo. On the way many noble gentlemen who had been scattered about Peru came out to greet him, as did many soldiers who desired to serve His Majesty. Holguín and his followers, who were now at Trujillo, decided to send two persons to offer, on behalf of all the rest, their obedience to His Majesty's governor, as we shall call him henceforward. Gómez de Tordoya and Garcilaso de la

Vega were appointed to undertake this mission. The governor was delighted to see them and to find his party growing from day to day, for with those he had collected when he reached Trujillo, he had more than two hundred soldiers, including those who had fled from Don Diego de Almagro, who were the provincial, Illén Suárez de Carvajal, Gómez de Alvarado, Juan de Saavedra, and Diego de Agüero, who were all leading men in the country, as well as many others who went with them. At Trujillo the governor was received with the military solemnity customary in wartime, with music and the sound of trumpets, fifes, and drums, and many salvos of harquebus fire, and not with the solemnities of peace, for it was not a time for laws, but for arms. . . .

After great suffering, Gonzalo Pizarro returns to Quito, where he is welcomed by those not absent in the war against Diego de Almagro the younger.

[3:15] . . . When Gonzalo Pizarro heard of the death of his brother the marquis and of the rising of Don Diego de Almagro, and his disobedience to His Majesty, and of the arrival of Vaca de Castro as governor of the empire and his expedition against Don Diego accompanied by all the friends and supporters of his brother the marquis, it seemed to him wrong that he should not serve His Majesty in the company of those gentlemen, most of whom had been his companions and comrades; he therefore wrote to the governor and reported on his journey and offered his person and his men to serve the governor as soldiers.

The governor replied acknowledging his goodwill and desire to serve the crown and thanked him in His Majesty's name, expressing his own great gratitude for the offer of his person and of men so experienced in military affairs. He begged him, however, and bade him in His Majesty's name to remain in Quito and rest from his past labors; and in due course he would advise him how he should serve His Majesty.

The governor did not want Gonzalo Pizarro to join his army since he was not without hope of coming to some agreement with Almagro and wished to avoid open conflict, fearing that, as the two parties were so impassioned, the struggle would lead to the destruction of both sides, and like a prudent man he wished to avoid so much bloodshed. He thought that if Gonzalo Pizarro were in his army, Almagro would not accept or even heed any offer of terms, or dare to place himself in his hands, fearing that Gonzalo Pizarro should wreak some cruel vengeance on him. He knew how popular Gonzalo was with everyone, and must necessarily be so with the whole army.

Such was the governor's intention. Some malicious persons thought it insufficient, and said that he was afraid that if Gonzalo came to the royal camp, he would be acclaimed general by common consent because of the universal affection for him and of his valor and authority and military experience.

Gonzalo obeyed the governor's orders and stayed in Quito till the end of the war. The governor also sent to instruct those who were in charge of the children of the marquis and of Gonzalo to keep them where they were in San Miguel and Trujillo and not bring them to Lima until they received new instructions. He said they would be safer at that distance than nearer at hand: his critics said he wanted to keep them away from him although they were only children.

When the governor had given these instructions, he traveled toward Huamanga, for he was told that Don Diego was already near that city and intending to enter it, as it was considered a stronghold, being surrounded on all sides by deep ravines and gorges and difficult of access. He sent Captain Castro ahead with his harquebusiers to hold a very steep hillside on the road, known to the Indians as Farcu and to the Spaniards as Parcos. On the way the governor heard that Almagro had already entered the city. This he greatly regretted, for the site was very favorable, and his own people had still not come up but were strung out along the road.

Alonso de Alvarado went back to collect them, and made such haste that they all reached the place where the governor was. Many of them had covered four leagues and some five or six in the course of that day, in order to arrive as soon as possible, and were very weary owing to the difficulty of the road. They spent the night drawn up in formation; for they had news that the enemy was two leagues away. But next day they heard from scouts that the news was wrong and that Don Diego was at a distance from the city. This calmed them and they went on to Huamanga. The governor did not stay there long, for he feared that if a battle was to be fought, as seemed likely, it would be disadvantageous to fight it there, since little use could be made of his horses in which he was superior to his enemy and which ought to tell very much in his favor. He therefore left the city and marched to some fields called Chupas, whence he sent two messengers to Don Diego, one called Francisco de Idiáquez and the other Diego Mercado, who told him that the governor offered him in His Majesty's name pardon for all that had happened if he would place himself under the royal standard and disband his army; he also offered rewards. Don Diego replied that he would accept the terms provided a general pardon was extended to all his followers and he were made governor of the new kingdom of Toledo and the gold mines and allocations of Indians his father had had.

Don Diego was inspired to make these excessive demands by a priest who had newly come from Panama and who had told him a few days before the terms were offered that he had heard in Panama that it was publicly said that His Majesty had pardoned him and awarded him the governorship of New Toledo, which included Cusco. The priest had asked for a reward for bringing the good news. He had also told Almagro that Vaca de Castro had few men, that they were ill armed and dissatisfied. Though this information was hard to believe Don Diego accepted it because it was favorable, and took such courage that he replied making these demands, supposing that the governor, being as weak as the report said, would grant any concession he asked for.

After Vaca de Castro had sent the above-mentioned messengers he also sent a soldier called Alonso García with official letters to many captains and leading gentlemen, promising them pardon for what had happened and great allocations of Indians. The messenger went disguised as an Indian and kept away from the road so as not to be stopped. He was unfortunate, for as it had recently snowed, Don Diego's scouts, who were very alert, found Alonso García's track in the snow, and followed it till they found him and brought him to Don Diego with all his dispatches. Almagro was furious at this double dealing as López de Gómara says in chapter cl and Zárate in Book IV, chapter xvi, and declared that it was not for gentlemen and imperial officials to make offers of peace on the one hand and attempts to bribe and spread mutiny among captains and soldiers on the other. Thus enraged, he ordered the messenger to be hanged, both for bringing the message and for appearing in disguise; and he then prepared his men for the coming battle in the presence of the governor's other messenger. He promised to give anyone who killed the owner of an allocation his Indians, his wife, and his property; and he told the governor that he had no intention of obeying him, so long as he was accompanied by his enemies, Pedro Alvarez Holguín, Alonso de Alvarado, Gómez de Tordoya, Juan de Saavedra, Garcilaso de la Vega, Illén Súarez de Carbajal, and Gómez de Alvarado, and all the other gentlemen who had been on the Pizarros' side. He gave this reply to break the governor's confidence in arriving at an agreement; for if he separated from those who had been on Pizarro's side, as Almagro asked, he would have been left alone. Almagro also sent to tell the governor that he need not count on anyone deserting; he had better set aside any hopes he might have entertained of this, for all his followers would do battle with great spirit and would hold their ground against the whole world, as he would prove by experience if he would but wait: he was setting off at once to meet him.

And Almagro did so, making his men ready and marching toward the governor's camp. Not only he but all his followers were anxious to offer battle, for they were all indignant at the attempt at double dealing. His followers were rather strengthened than shaken in their friendship and devotion to Almagro, saying that the governor would deal as falsely with them as he had with their leader and would not keep his promises. They therefore proposed to die fighting and hear no more terms. It was thought that but for this, and if there had been a pardon with His Majesty's signature, Almagro would have accepted any reasonable terms.

The Battle Begins

[3:16] The governor realized on receiving Almagro's reply that many of his own followers were hesitant about giving battle, for they said they were alarmed and perturbed that His Majesty should not have accepted the battle of Las Salinas, for he had thrown Hernando Pizarro into a dungeon for fighting it, and they were afraid of committing a similar misdeed. In order to remove this difficulty and to settle his followers' fears, the governor ordered a list of the crimes of Don Diego de Almagro to be drawn up, how he had killed the marquis and many other persons, had confiscated the property of others and assumed control of them, had allocated Indians without having a commission from His Majesty, and was at present leading an armed force against the royal standard and had challenged the governor to a pitched battle. In order to justify his action the governor signed this in the presence of them all, and pronounced sentence against Don Diego de Almagro, declaring him a traitor and rebel, and condemning him and all his followers to death and the confiscation of all their property. Having delivered sentence, he summoned all the captains and the whole army to aid and assist him to execute it as minister of His Majesty and governor of the empire.

Having issued this sentence, Vaca de Castro considered that there was no purpose in discussing terms any longer, in view of Almagro's desperate reply and pertinacity in his rebellion; he therefore prepared his forces for battle, knowing that Don Diego was now at hand.

He led his troops forth and delivered a harangue, bidding them remember who they were, whence they came, and why they fought. The possession of the empire depended on their strength and efforts: if they were defeated, neither they nor he could avoid death, and if they won, in addition to having fulfilled the obligations they owed their king as his loyal vassals, they would remain lords of their allocations and properties and enjoy them in peace and quiet. And to those who had no Indians he would give some in His Majesty's name, for it was precisely in order to reward those who had served him loyally that His Majesty wanted the land of Peru. He said that he realized that there was no need for him to exhort and encourage such noble gentlemen and brave soldiers: he indeed would rather take courage from them, which he did and would go ahead and break his lance before the rest. They all replied that they too would be cut to pieces and die rather than be defeated, and each of them regarded the quarrel as his own. The captains earnestly begged the governor not to take the van where there was such great danger, for the safety of the whole army depended on that of its general. Let him go to the rear with thirty horsemen, and wait there so as to lend help where it was most needed. On the earnest request of his captains the governor agreed to stay with the last, though he wished to be among the first. In this agreement they waited for Don Diego, who was two leagues away. On the following day two scouts arrived with news that Don Diego was less than half a league away and resolved to give battle.

The governor set out his men in formation. On the right of the infantry he set the royal standard, which was entrusted to Alonso de Alvarado and borne by Cristobal de Barrientos, a native of Ciudad Rodrigo and *vecino* of Trujillo, where he had an allocation of Indians. Pedro Alvarez Holguín and Gómez de Alvarado, Garcilaso de la Vega and Pero Ansúrez, the captains of the cavalry, were to the left of the infantry, and each, as Zárate says in his Book IV, chapter xviii, had his standard and company in good order and was himself stationed in the front line. Between the two squadrons of cavalry were Captains Pedro de Vergara and Juan Vélez de Guevara with the infantry. Nuño de Castro and his harquebusiers went ahead as an advance party to open the skirmishing and retire in due course upon the main formation. Vaca de Castro remained in the rear with his thirty horsemen, a little apart from the army, so that he could see where he was most needed in the battle and lend help, as he did.

These are Zárate's words. Holguín wore over his armor a doublet of slashed white damask, saying: "They usually aim at the mark, and few or none hit the white." In the above order the governor waited for Don Diego de Almagro, who reached the plain and occupied a mound at a distance from the royal formation and even beyond the range of artillery fire. His sergeant major, called Pedro Suárez, who had been a seasoned soldier in Italy and knew all about warfare, saw that the position was better than the enemy's and soon drew up the army on the same lines as theirs. He placed the cavalry on either side of the infantry, with the captain general Juan Balsa and his commander Pedro de Oñate, and Captains Juan Tello de Guzmán, Diego Méndez, Juan de Oña, Martín de Bilbao, Diego de Hojeda, and Malavez. They all had excellent companies and their men were keen to fight to win the empire and become lords of vassals. The sergeant major placed his artillery, with Pedro de Candía as its captain, in front of the squadrons, pointing toward the direction from which the enemy could attack. Having arranged the army in this fashion, he went to Don Diego, who was between the cavalry and infantry with a guard of eight or ten men, and said:

"Your Lordship has his army drawn up in order with so many advantages of position and artillery that the enemy can be defeated without running a lance or striking a blow with a sword, but merely by staying quietly here without budging. Wherever the enemy may attack, you can defeat him and cut him to pieces with the artillery before he comes within harquebus range."

By the time Don Diego had drawn up his battle array, it was already late, and less than two hours of daylight remained. Vaca de Castro's advisers disagreed whether they should fight that day or not. Francisco de Carvajal, his sergeant major, being a man of experience in such matters, said that they should by no means fail to give battle that day, even though it were necessary to fight in the dark, for otherwise they would encourage the enemy and discourage their own men, many of whom would go over to Don Diego on seeing a sign of weakness. The governor therefore determined to offer battle forthwith, and said he would be glad to have the power of Joshua to bid the sun stand still.

They marched toward Don Diego's position, and he ordered his artillery to fire in order to frighten them. Francisco de Carvajal perceived that if they advanced straight at the enemy they would suffer heavy losses from the artillery which was numerous and extremely good, and took another direction, where he was sheltered by the slope of a hill. Passing round this they came out into the open, where they stood in obvious danger from the artillery; but Pedro de Candía, who was captain of it, fired high and did no damage. When Don Diego saw this, he fell upon him and slew him with his lance over the cannon. He then sprang down from his horse, and was so furious at his captain's treachery that he leapt up onto one of the pieces, and standing near the mouth of the cannon, lowered it a point by the weight of his body and ordered it to be fired, as he stood on it. The ball was aimed at Vaca de Castro's formation and cut a lane in it from van to rear, as Zárate says in Book IV, chapter xix, and López de Gómara (chapter cl), though they do not mention the death of Candía or how many died from that cannon ball: it struck down seventeen men. Four more such balls would have won the day and made it unnecessary for Don Diego to fight, as his sergeant major Pedro Suárez had assured him; but owing to the treachery of his captain, he lost it. . . .

The Victory of the Governor and Flight of Don Diego

[3:17] When his Majesty's captains and his sergeant major Francisco de Carvajal saw their battle array cut open and their infantry in confusion, they filled the front of the lane cut by the cannon ball and closed ranks, encouraging their men and ordering them to attack with all possible ferocity, so as not to give the enemy the opportunity of firing any more cannon balls by further delay. In order to advance more rapidly, they forsook the artillery so as not to be held back by it.

Almagro's captains were ill advised about their own interests and not very experienced in such cases. When they saw the enemy advancing on them at all speed, they began to shout: "They are winning honor from us: they see us standing here quietly and think we are afraid of them, so they attack us as though we were cowards! Up and at them, for we can't stand such an insult!" They thus forced Don Diego to advance with his whole army, which they did with such little thought that they got in front of their own artillery.

When the sergeant major Pedro Suárez saw this, he went to Don Diego and shouted to him: "Sir, if Your Lordship had kept my order and followed my advice, we should have won the victory today. But you have taken other counsel, and we shall lose. I will not be defeated, and as Your Lordship won't let me win on your side, I'll do so on the other." So saying, he spurred his horse and rode over to Vaca de Castro, bidding him hasten to close with his enemies and telling him about the disorder they had produced among themselves.

Vaca de Castro took Pedro Suárez's good counsel and ordered his formation to march rapidly forward. Francisco de Carvajal considered himself victorious on hearing Pedro Suárez's account, and as if in triumph at the enemy's ignorance, he took off his coat of mail and a visor he was wearing, and threw it on the ground, telling his men not to be afraid of the artillery, for it would not hit him though he was as big as any two of them. . . .

Vaca de Castro's men hastened to the top of the hill and found that Don Diego's army had almost lost its original formation. His harquebusiers received them with a shower of bullets and did much execution against the infantry. Gómez de Tordoya, the commander of the army, was hit by three balls and died within two days. Captain Nuño de Castro was badly wounded, and many others killed. When Francisco de Carvajal saw this, he ordered the cavalry to attack, in which he had great confidence because they were much more numerous than Don Diego's. On receiving the command they fell on Don Diego's and fought a very fierce engagement which lasted a long while without advantage to either side. Captain Pedro Alvarez Holguín was killed by a shot from a harquebus, for as he was so clearly marked out by his white dress, and they knew who he was, all the most notable shotsmen wanted to try for him. On the other side, Vaca de Castro's infantry attacked and fought bravely till they captured the artillery which was idle because Don Diego's own men had shown so little military skill, or rather none at all, and placed themselves in front of it. Both sides fought so obstinately that though the sun had set and the night fallen, they still went on, only able to distinguish one another by their war cries, some shouting "Chile!" and others "Pachacámac!" instead of Almagros and Pizarros, for these names were also given to the two parties. The mortality of the cavalry was very great, for in addition to encounters with lances much damage was done among them with swords, clubs, and axes.

Their stake in the victory sharpened their cruelty toward one another, for they knew that the winners would enjoy the empire and its great riches and the losers would forfeit them and their lives too. It was now more than two hours after dark and four since the battle began. The governor with his thirty horse attacked Don Diego's formation from the left, where the men were still fresh, and the battle seemed to begin all over again. But at last the governor won the victory though ten or twelve of his men were killed, including Captain Jiménez, Mercado de Medina, and Nuño de Montalvo. Both sides sang victory, and the battle still went on though Don Diego's [men] were weakening. As he became aware of this, he attacked the enemy with the few men he had left, and made an inroad into them, performing marvels himself in the hope that he would be killed; but he was neither killed nor wounded, for he was well armed and not recognized. He fought, as López de Gómara says in his chapter cl, with courage.

It was now acknowledged that the governor had won the day; and some of Don Diego's leading supporters, on seeing this, shouted their names: "I am so-and-so, and I am so-and-so who killed the marquis." Thus they died fighting desperately and were cut to pieces. Many of Don Diego's men saved themselves by removing the white armlets they wore under cover of darkness, and putting on red ones taken from the dead on Vaca de Castro's side. Don Diego, on seeing that victory had slipped between his fingers and that death too avoided him, left the battle with six friends, who were Diego Méndez, Juan Rodríguez Barragán, and Juan de Guzmán, and three others whose names have been forgotten. He went to Cusco where he met with the death his enemies had not been able to give him at the hands of those he himself had made men of by granting them the administration of justice and military posts. As soon as they saw him coming back defeated, Rodrigo de Salazar, a native of Toledo, whom he had left as his deputy, and Antón Ruiz de Guevara whom he had made *alcalde ordinario* of the city, arrested him. They also arrested those who came with him so as to add to their cruelty. Of this Zárate says in his Book IV, chapter xix: "Thus ended the command and government of Don Diego, who in a day saw himself lord of Peru, and in the next was arrested by his own alcalde whom he himself had given authority. And this battle was fought on September 16, 1542."

Thus Zárate, who here finishes the chapter in question. . . .

The Good Government of Licentiate Vaca de Castro

[3:19] With the death of Don Diego de Almagro the younger and of the most prominent and guiltiest of his followers and the exile of the less guilty, peace and quiet settled on the empire of Peru, for the name and party of the Almagros was brought to an end. Licentiate Vaca de Castro, like a prudent man, governed with great rectitude and justice, to the general applause and satisfaction of Spaniards and Indians alike, for he made laws of great advantage to both. . . .

[3:19] Having cleared of soldiers[20] the whole length and breadth of Peru, which measures seven hundred leagues from Quito to Los Charcas, Vaca de Castro was left free of the importunities and troubles they caused him and governed in peace and quiet to the satisfaction of everyone. He made such laws as we have said, obtaining information from the old *curacas* and captains about the administration of the Inca kings, and choosing from these reports whatever seemed to him best adapted to the interests of the Spaniards and the improvement of the Indians' lot. He summoned Gonzalo Pizarro, who was still in Quito, and having thanked him on his own behalf for his past conquests and undertakings and rewarded him on His Majesty's behalf according to his merits, he sent to him to his home and his Indians in Los Charcas, bidding him go and rest and look to his health and his fortune. The Indians set to cultivating the land and producing a great abundance of food, now that they were free of the vexations and persecutions they had suffered during the recent wars; for both sides had waged the struggle at the expense of the lives and property of the Indians, and a million and a half of them had perished, as López de Gómara says at the end of his chapter cli. By the industry of the Spaniards who also enjoyed the peace and sought their own prosperity, very rich gold mines were found in many parts of Peru, but the richest were to the east of Cusco, in the province called Calahuaya, or by the Spaniards Caraya, where much very fine gold of 24 carats was extracted, and still is today, though not in such abundance. To the west of Cusco in the province called Quechua, which contains many tribes of the same name, in the region called Huallaripa, they found other mines of gold, less fine than those of Calahuaya, though they still reached 20 carats, more or less; but in such quantity that I remember seeing, nine or ten years after the discovery, one of the *vecinos* who had a share in them receive two thousand pesos in gold dust every Saturday from his Indians.

---

[20] Vaca de Castro sent out new expeditions, charged with exploration, thereby giving employment to potential malcontents.

We call gold dust the gold that is brought out in its natural state; it resembles the filings of blacksmiths, and there is another kind rather coarser like the bran from flour. In this they also find the grains called *pepitas* which are like the pips of melons or gourds and are worth three, four, six, or eight ducats, more or less, as they chance to be discovered. Of all this gold a very large quantity was retained at the melting works for His Majesty's fifth, which was an incalculable treasure, for he received one mark out of five, one peso out of five, and so on down to the last ha'penny. The volume of trade with Spain was in proportion to the amount of treasure found and extracted. With all this prosperity and the administration of a governor so Christian, so noble, so wise, so zealous in the service of our Lord God and his king, the empire flourished and improved from day to day. And what is most important, the teaching of our holy Catholic Faith was spread throughout the whole land with great care by the Spaniards, and the Indians accepted it with no less gladness and satisfaction, for they saw that much of what they were taught was what their Inca kings had taught them and bidden them observe under their natural law.

In the Majesty of the preaching of the holy Gospel and the prosperity of peace, quiet, and the enjoyment of spiritual and temporal goods that Indians and Spaniards alike then possessed, the Devil, that enemy of the human race, ordained that all these good things should be spoiled and reversed. He therefore roused his ministers—who are ambition, envy, covetousness, avarice, wrath, pride, discord, and tyranny—and bade each perform his functions and stop the preaching of the holy Gospel and the conversion of the gentiles to the Catholic Faith, which was what most distressed him, for he was losing the ascendancy he had established over those heathens. And our Lord God permitted him so to do, in His secret wisdom and for the chastisement of many, as we shall see.

Certain persons, showing themselves very zealous for the well-being of the Indians without considering the difficulties and the harm that would result to the very persons they wished to assist from their ill advice and folly, proposed in the Royal Council of the Indies[21] that new laws and ordinances ought to be adopted for the good government of the empires of Mexico and Peru. The one who most insisted in this was a friar called Fray Bartolomé de las Casas, who years before, as a secular priest, had traveled through the Windward Islands and Mexico, and after becoming a regular, put forward many proposals which he said were for the good of the Indians and their conversion to the Catholic Faith and to the advantage of the royal treasury. . . .

---

[21] The Royal Council of the Indies was a group of royal advisors, named by the crown, who advised the monarch on the affairs and government of the Spanish possessions in America, which was also called "the Indies."

New Laws and Ordinances Made in the Court of Spain

[3:20] In 1539 Fray Bartolomé de las Casas came from New Spain and arrived in Madrid, where the court then was, and in his sermons and private discourse he showed himself extremely zealous for the welfare of the Indians and spoke very warmly in their defense. He proposed reforms which, although they seemed good and holy, nevertheless proved very harsh and difficult to put to effect. He put them forward in the Supreme Council of the Indies where they were not well received, for the good cardinal of Seville Don García de Loaisa prudently rejected them. He was a member of the council and had been a governor in the Indies for many years, and knew more about them and what was necessary for their good than many of those who had conquered them and settled there; and with his discretion and good counsel he was never of the opinion that what Fray Bartolomé asked should be granted. The latter therefore suspended his claims until 1542, when the emperor Charles V returned to Spain after a long journey through France, Flanders, and Germany. His Majesty, being a very religious man, was easily persuaded to do as the friar wanted, for fear of the burden on his conscience if he failed to execute the new laws and ordinances that were necessary for the well-being of the Indians. His Imperial Majesty, having listened attentively to the friar, summoned his councils and various other grave lawyers, prelates, and religious. The case was put before them and discussed, and finally Fray Bartolomé's claims were approved, though against the opinion of the cardinal and president above-mentioned and of the bishop of Lugo, Don Juan Suárez de Carvajal (whom I knew); the *comendador mayor*[22] Francisco de los Cobos, His Majesty's secretary; Don Sebastián Ramírez, bishop of Cuenca and president of Valladolid, who had been president at Santo Domingo and Mexico; and Don García Manrique, count of Osorno and president of the Orders, who, as López de Gómara says, had dealt with affairs of the Indies for a long time in the absence of the cardinal Don García de Loaisa. All these, being men of experience in Indian affairs and having dealt with them for a long time, were opposed to the ordinances, which were forty in number.

The emperor signed them in Barcelona on November 20, 1542, as López de Gómara says in his chapter clii. The battle of Chupas between the licentiate Governor Vaca de Castro and Don Diego de Almagro the younger occurred on September 15 of the same year, two months and five days before the ordinances were signed. This clearly shows the diligence and solicitude of the Devil in preventing the preaching of the holy Gospel

---

[22] Commander or head of a military order.

in Peru, for scarcely had so great a fire as that been extinguished than he endeavored to kindle another and greater one, as we shall see from the results produced by the ordinances. We shall only mention four of these ordinances, though our authors say more of them, for these are germane to our history: they are as follows.

The first ordinance was that on the death of the conquerors and settlers who were *vecinos* in the Indies with allocations of Indians entrusted to them and placed under their control by His Majesty, their sons and wives should not succeed to them but they should come under the royal control and the children should be granted a sum drawn from their revenues, on which to maintain themselves.

No Indian was to be forced to labor except in places where no other solution was possible, but their work was to be remunerated. No Indians were to be forced to work in the mines or pearl fisheries, and the tribute they were to pay their master should be established and the personal service abolished.

The *encomiendas* and *repartimientos*[23] of Indians held by bishops, monasteries, and hospitals should be suppressed; those who were or had been governors, presidents, judges, magistrates, or their deputies, or officers of His Majesty's treasury should likewise be deprived of their Indians and be prohibited from having Indians even if they offered to resign their offices.

All the *encomenderos* of Peru, or those who had Indians, and had taken part in the disturbances and struggles between Don Francisco Pizarro and Don Diego de Almagro, should lose their Indians, on whichever side they had been.

This ordinance meant, as Diego Fernández says, that practically nobody in Peru could have Indians or estates, and none of the people of standing in New Spain or Peru could have them, under the third law; for all or nearly all of them had been corregidors, alcaldes, or justices or deputies or officials of the royal treasury; so that these two laws alone were like a sort of net that enclosed the whole of the Indies and excluded their owners.

For the better understanding of these ordinances we must say something of the motives of those who discussed and approved them. As to the first ordinance, we must explain that the conquerors of the Indies were awarded the allocations of Indians in return for their services, and were to enjoy them for two lives: their own and that of their eldest son, or daughter if they had no son. Later, when they were bidden to marry because it was thought that if they were married they would settle down and cultivate the land and live quietly on it instead of seeking changes, the award

---

[23] See p. 63.

of the Indians was extended to the wives of the conquerors, who would inherit them in default of children. The second ordinance which prevented them from forcing the Indians to work was adopted because of reports that the Indians were made to work without being paid. This was true of some conscienceless Spaniards, but not of all of them in general, for there were many who paid their Indians and treated them like their own children; and the Indians were and are prepared to work without pay, for they are like day laborers in Spain who hire themselves out to dig or reap and work for their food. To forbid Indians to work in this way was to do them much harm, for it deprived them of their right to earn. What should have been done was to order those who did not pay them to be very severely punished.

With regard to the law against putting Indians to work in the mines, I have no comment to offer, except to refer to the Indians who still today in 1611 work by order of the governors in the silver mines of the hill of Potosí and in the quicksilver mines in the province of Huanca: if they ceased to do so, neither the silver nor the gold of the empire would be brought every year to Spain.

And with regard to the regularization of the tributes to be paid to the *encomenderos,* this was a good law; and it was received with general approval when President Pedro de la Gasca established the norms in Peru, as I myself saw. As to the removal of personal service, I can only say that they must have been misinformed about this. Each *vecino* was given a number of Indians for service in his house as part of the tribute; for this purpose, in addition to the main allocation, they were allowed some villages of forty or fifty houses, or sixty at most, with obligation to provide what is called personal service, which entailed supplying the owner's house with fuel and water and fodder for his horses (for there was no hay in those days), and they paid no other tribute. In this fashion my father had three little villages in the valley of Cusco, one of which was called Caira, and many other *vecinos* of Cusco had them in the district round the city. And when there were no small villages to be awarded for personal service, the main allocation was required as part of its tribute to supply Indians for this service, which they did willingly and performed the tasks with ease and content. Thus as President la Gasca found this custom well established and accepted by both parties, he made no attempt to alter it, but left it as it was.

The third law, by which allocations of Indians were to be removed from bishops, monasteries, and hospitals wherever governors had awarded them to these, was acceptable to everyone. It was thought that no wrong was done in removing these Indians, for the intention of the governors in awarding them had not been to go beyond the powers conferred on them by His Majesty to allocate Indians for two lives and no more. As monasteries, prelacies, and hospitals are permanent, they were done no wrong by being made equal to the conquerors of the empire. The last and fourth ordinance which remains to be commented on will be discussed later in our discourse[24] on the objections raised by those who were deprived as a result of it.

---

[24] See pp. 173–4.

Chapter Four
Rebellion against the New Laws

The promulgation of the new ordinances leads to disturbances in Mexico that are eventually resolved by a judicious and cautious viceroy. However, there was no such skilled leader in Peru, only recently at peace after a major rebellion.

The Doings of Viceroy Blasco Núñez Vela on His Arrival

[4:1] . . . [W]e must now attempt to give an account of the misfortunes, bloodshed, and calamities in the empire of Peru, which arose from the severe, harsh, and uncompromising character of the viceroy Blasco Núñez Vela, who so resolutely persisted in putting these rigorous ordinances into force, against the opinion of the judges of his own *audiencia*[25] and without in the least considering what was in the best interest of his king. We should recall that the two fleets for Peru and Mexico separated in the Gulf of Las Damas. The viceroy sailed on and had fair weather till his arrival at Nombre de Dios on January 10, 1544, whence he went to Panama and at once released many of the Indians the Spaniards had brought there from Peru and ordered them to be sent back to their various provinces. Many were angered by the removal of these Indians from their masters, both because they had been trained for work and because they were now Christians; the release was also against the wishes of many of the Indians themselves. The viceroy was repeatedly addressed on this matter, and efforts were made to dissuade him on the ground that the step was contrary to the service of His Majesty and of God, since it was notorious that the chief object of the Spaniards was to make the Indians Christians and this could not be put into effect if they were under the control of the caciques. In particular it was obvious that if an Indian had become a Christian and then returned to his cacique's authority, he would be sacrificed to the Devil. Moreover, His Majesty's express command was that the Indians were to be set at liberty, and those who were in that province wanted to remain there, and it was against their own will that they were being sent to Peru, with moreover so little provisions that it was certain that many of them would die. The viceroy's reply to all this was that His Majesty had expressly ordered them to be

---

[25] The *audiencia* was a superior, or appeals, court that consisted of judges appointed by the crown and serving at its discretion.

sent, and he could and would do nothing else. He therefore bade the Spaniards who had Indians to send them off at their own expense.

About three hundred Indians were removed from private persons, and these were forthwith embarked and sent to Peru; most of them died for want of food or because they were abandoned on the coast. When the people who had advised the viceroy realized the great dangers which it was feared would follow the execution of the ordinances, they sought to prevent him from proceeding with it, adducing many arguments to bring these dangers home to him, and reminding him of the great wars that had taken place in Peru and of the dissatisfaction and unrest existing among the settlers. The viceroy listened to all this reluctantly, and replied sharply that as they were not within his jurisdiction he could not hang them all. In this way he raised a complete barrier against any persuasion as to what required to be done. He stayed twenty days in Panama, during which time the judges obtained information about many aspects of Peruvian affairs. In particular they realized two things: first, how deeply outraged the conquerors were by the ordinances, and second, the great danger of trying to put them into force so soon after Licentiate Vaca de Castro had fought Don Diego de Almagro the younger, and defeated and executed him with a loss of 350 men in the battle: as a result of which the survivors were all expecting to receive great favors for the real services they had done His Majesty. When the judges understood this, and considered the nature of the task and the character of the viceroy, they ceased to urge him, but thought that once they arrived in Peru, and he saw what the country and people were like, he would be more disposed to take their advice.

The viceroy, annoyed for little or no reason at what the judges had told him, resolved to leave before them and said that he had sworn to show them what sort of man he was by having the ordinances obeyed and executed by the time they arrived. As Licentiate Zárate was at the time ill and confined to bed, the viceroy paid him a visit before his departure. The licentiate said to him that, as he was determined to leave without them, he begged and prayed him to enter Peru gently and not try to execute any of the ordinances until the *audiencia* had been set up in Lima and he was in full control of the whole country. When this was so, he could put into execution whatever laws were necessary, both for His Majesty's conscience and the good government and well-being of the natives. With regard to the laws that were too harsh and any others that seemed inappropriate, it would be best to send His Majesty a report on them: then, if His Majesty again instructed him to carry them out, in spite of the information he was given, he would be in a better position to execute them, since he would have established himself more firmly in Peru and justices of his own choosing would have been appointed to all the towns and villages.

Licentiate Zárate said all this and more; but it was not to the viceroy's taste. On the contrary he was greatly annoyed by it, and replied with some asperity, swearing to carry out the ordinances according to the stipulations contained in them and to brook no delay or postponement: when the judges got to Peru, he would have done their work for them. With this he embarked alone, refusing to wait for all or any of the judges, though they begged him to do so. On March 4, he reached the port of Tumbes, where he landed, and continued his journey by land, executing the ordinances in each of the settlements he came to, assessing the Indians some of them had and depriving others of their Indians and placing them under the crown. In this way he passed through Piura and Trujillo, promulgating the new laws and refusing to accept any petitions, though the *vecinos* alleged that all this could not be done without a formal sentence, if the ordinances were to be applied, or until the *audiencia* had been set up, since these were His Majesty's express commands in one of the laws which stated that a viceroy and four judges were being sent to execute them. However, the viceroy intimidated and threatened those who persisted, spreading great distress and confusion in the hearts and minds of all of when they considered how harsh the laws were, embracing them all at large and sparing none. Even before this, as soon as the viceroy reached the coast of Peru, he had sent forward his credentials and instructions to Lima and Cusco with orders that he was to be acknowledged and obeyed and that Licentiate Vaca de Castro should lay down his authority, as he himself was now in the country as viceroy.

Some days before these messages were received in Lima, it had become known that His Majesty had appointed Blasco Núñez Vela, and a copy of all the ordinances had also been received. At this the city council had sent Don Antonio de Ribera and Juan Alonso Palomino to inform Licentiate Vaca de Castro, who was in Cusco. He too had had letters from Spain announcing the appointment of Blasco Núñez Vela and the dispatch of the ordinances. These letters were brought him by his servant Diego de Aller, who had gone to Spain and came hastening back with the news.

All this is from Diego Fernández of Palencia;[26] and the other historians say the same.

The Reaction to the Ordinances

[4:2] Governor Vaca de Castro, on hearing the news of the coming of Viceroy Blasco Núñez Vela and of the ordinances he was bringing, and how he was executing them without listening to anyone or admitting any appeal,

---

[26] Diego Fernández (el Palentino), *Primera y segunda parte de la historia del Peru* [1571], various editions.

thought that he had better cover himself by going to Lima and receiving the viceroy. He therefore refused to receive the embassy of Don Antonio Ribera and Juan Alonso Palomino from the council of Lima or to listen to the representatives of the municipality of Cusco and the *vecinos* who had come from other places. These all urged him not to receive the viceroy but to appeal against the severity of the ordinances in the name of all of them and against the viceroy's instructions on the ground of his harshness and incapacity for the office. They further suggested that they should not accept the viceroy as governor, since he had proved himself unworthy of the office by refusing a fair hearing to His Majesty's vassals and showing such obduracy in even the most trivial business. They told Vaca de Castro that if he did not undertake the task, there would be others in Peru who would. . . .

[4:4] Many other things were said about the ordinances, not only in Lima, but also throughout Peru. In order to explain these complaints and lamentations, we should mention that it was then the custom in both Mexico and Peru, and still was in 1560 when I left, that as offices were not held for life, four gentlemen of the greatest credit and trust should be elected in each Spanish settlement to act as officers of the royal treasury and keep the fifth of the gold and silver mined throughout the country: this was the first tribute the Catholic monarch laid on the whole of the New World. The officials of the royal treasury were the treasurer, accountant, factor, and inspector whose duty it also was to collect tribute from the Indians when a *vecino* died and they were placed under the control of the crown. In addition to these offices each Spanish settlement elected annually two ordinary alcaldes, a corregidor and his deputy, and six, eight, or ten *regidors,* in proportion to the size of the place; elections were also made to the other offices that were necessary for the good government of the republic.

Under the third ordinance, these officials were treated in the same way as governors, presidents, judges, and magistrates and their deputies. All who had held such offices or were now holding them were to lose their Indians under the new law. For this reason the victims said:

"We won this empire at our own cost and risk, and have augmented the crown of Castile with all the great kingdoms and dominions it now possesses. In payment for these services we were given the Indians we have, and we were given them for two lives, though they should have been perpetual as *seigniories*[27] in Spain are. The reason why our Indians are now being taken away is that we have been elected officials of the royal treasury, or magistrates, or *regidors.* If we perform these duties well and do no one any harm, why should we be deprived of our Indians because we have been elected as

---

[27] A *seignory* (or *seigniory*) is the lordship of a manor.

men of standing? Yet, they order us to keep our offices, which may be an excuse to deprive us of anything we may gain in the future on some other occasion. If this is what we have come to, we should have done better to be thieves, bandits, adulterers, and murderers, for the ordinances do not mention these, but only those of us who have been respectable citizens."

Those condemned under the fourth law spoke as freely, or more so. This laid down that all those who had taken part in the rivalries between Pizarros and Almagros should be deprived of their Indians: this law, as Diego Fernández says, meant that no one in all Peru could have Indians or estates.

To this they asked what blame attached to those who had obeyed His Majesty's governors, for both were legitimate governors and had ordered the settlers to do what they had done. Neither of them was against the royal crown, but had been drawn into rivalries and discord by the Devil over the question of the division of the two jurisdictions. If one party had done such wrong as to have their property confiscated, it was obvious that the others should remain free for their services to their king. But to condemn the two sides equally was more like the tyranny of Nero and other such oppressors than a desire to favor the vassals of the crown.

They also uttered iniquities and blasphemies against the authors of the ordinances who had persuaded and forced His Majesty to sign them and order them to be put rigorously into force by telling him that this was in his interest.

They said that if these people had been in the conquest of Peru and undergone the toils the conquerors had experienced they would certainly not have made such laws but would have opposed them. They bolstered up these statements and blasphemies with examples from ancient and modern history like the wars and hatred between Almagros and Pizarros. They said that if when there had been wars in Spain between the two kings Peter the Cruel and Henry, his brother, to whom the lords and landowners rallied, serving them until one died, if any succeeding king had ordered all the estates and properties to be taken away from both sides after the wars were over, what would the leading men in Spain have said or done? Similarly with the wars between Castile and Portugal over the inheritance of the so-called Beltraneja, who was twice sworn princess of Castile and was supported by many of the lords of Castile: when Queen Isabella spoke of these and called them traitors, the duke of Alba heard her and said: "Let Your Highness pray to God that we may win, for if they win we shall be the traitors."[28]

---

[28] Garcilaso here refers to the conflict that took place at the end of the fifteenth century between the partisans of Isabella of Castile, sister of King Henry IV, and those of Henry's daughter Juana, for control of the Crown of Castile. Isabella won, and succeeded to the throne in 1474, ruling with her husband and consort, Ferdinand of Aragon.

They argued from this that if the successor to the throne had taken away the estates of all the lords who had taken part in the war, what would they have done? They said a great many more shameful things, which we shall not write down lest we give offence to our readers: these roused their indignation till they came to the pass they later reached. . . .

During all this time the viceroy was traveling on, and wherever he passed he put any part of the ordinances that was applicable into execution; and though he was aware of the disturbances and complaints this was producing, he did not cease to do so, but daily displayed greater rigor so as to prove that he was not afraid of the settlers and was determined to be a good servant of the crown and do the king's bidding: he kept saying that he would respect the king and no one else. . . .

Disturbances Among the Spaniards about the Ordinances

[4:7] . . . The scandal and alarm was increased by the rigid character of the viceroy, his refusal to hear the petitions of any of the cities and his determination to apply the ordinances in their full rigor. The settlers in the four cities, Huamanga, Arequipa, Chuquisaca, and Cusco where the viceroy had not yet been acknowledged, decided that they would elect a procurator to represent them all and the whole kingdom: his election by Cusco, the head of the empire, was regarded as his election by the whole country, and it was hoped that this would remedy the calamity they all feared. The matter was discussed and letters were sent to and fro in an effort to select a person with the necessary qualifications for the undertaking.

With this intent they fixed their eyes on Gonzalo Pizarro, for there was no one else in the whole country who might more reasonably accept the office, principally because he was brother to the marquis Don Francisco Pizarro and had helped to win Peru and suffered all the toils and labors we have mentioned, though our account has fallen short of the truth. By nature he was full of nobility and virtue, and because of his character he was beloved and respected by everyone. For all these reasons even if he had not been appointed by the kingdom at large, he was bound to be the protector and defender of the Indians and Spaniards of the empire.

The councils of these four cities therefore wrote to Gonzalo Pizarro, who was at Los Charcas where his allocation was, begging him to come to Cusco to discuss a matter of general concern to all of them, and of no less interest to himself, for he was the principal loser, since apart from the loss of his Indians the viceroy had often said that he had His Majesty's orders to cut off Gonzalo's head. . . .

[4:8] On his election as procurator general of Peru, Pizarro decided to form a company of two hundred soldiers both to deal with a viceroy who had shown himself so uncompromising about the ordinances and to make himself safe from having his head cut off, as it was publicly reported the viceroy had repeatedly threatened to do. He did not raise his standard or appoint captains, for he did not wish his actions to smell of rebellion or resistance to the royal authority; he only wished to have a bodyguard. The *regidors* and the whole city addressed him on this point saying that it was not their intention or that of the empire to resist His Majesty's commands in his ordinances by force of arms, but to petition submissively since they felt their case was so strong that their prince and king would not deny them justice. He ought therefore to dismiss the men and go as procurator and not as captain, since their intention was to be obedient subjects, as they protested they were. He replied that they knew of the viceroy's character and how he had said he had special orders to cut off Gonzalo's head; how then could they send him to the slaughterhouse with his hands in his pockets, for he might be beheaded with no gain to them and without even being heard? If they wanted him to go to certain death, he would give up the office of procurator and return home, where he would wait and see what the viceroy tried to do with him: this would be better than irritating him into hastening his death and destruction. The councilor and the representatives of the other cities saw that Gonzalo was right, in view of the viceroy's character, conduct, and policy and allowed him to raise men for a bodyguard. They then produced the pretexts mentioned by our two authors[29] for appointing him captain, the chief of which was that he would have to pass through the forests in which Manco Inca had shut himself up. Having obtained permission to raise men, he increased their numbers till they reached the four hundred horse and foot mentioned by López de Gómara, and there were even many more. When the citizens saw this, they regretted having elected him, for it seemed more like a rebellion than a request for justice, and so the three López de Gómara mentions protested, and so did many others, as we shall see.

Pizarro took great care in preparing himself for his claim, urgently writing to all parts where he knew there were Spaniards, not only to the three cities, but also to the Indian villages and allocations, appealing to them with the best arguments he could think of and offering them his person and wealth for any contingency, either present or future. This aroused suspicions, and even the certainty, that he wanted to resume his claim to govern Peru; for, as all three historians say, he had powers from his brother the marquis, Don Francisco Pizarro, to govern after the marquis' death, under

---

[29] The two authors are Agustín de Zárate, author of *Historia del descubrimiento y conquista del Perú* [1543] (book 5, ch. 4) and Francisco López de Gomara, *Historia general de las indias* [1552] (ch. clvii).

a document of the emperor's when he was awarded the governorship for two lives, his own and a nominee's, just as the allocations of Indians had been for two lives. . . .

Both Gonzalo Pizarro and the viceroy raise an army and prepare for war. The viceroy's rages and his murder of a royal factor encourages his opponents as Gonzalo Pizarro's forces approach Lima.

[4:14] . . . The viceroy knew that the enemy was daily drawing closer, and that many of those about him openly showed their dissatisfaction at the execution of the ordinances, while those who concealed this feeling were very lukewarm in his service and were perceptibly discontented. As he pondered on this and saw the spirit of his men grow hourly more adverse, he decided to change his policy, though it was now late, and suspend the ordinances, supposing that by publishing this he could extinguish the fires that were raging, and that Gonzalo Pizarro would no longer have any excuse for acting as procurator general and would disband his army, after which the disorders would die down and the country would be pacified. So he announced the suspension of the ordinances, as Fernández says, until such time as His Majesty had been informed and had issued new instructions. . . . Though the suspension came very late, it would still have done much to settle things if it had contained any provision for negotiations and an avoidance of the open breech that followed. But as the news of the suspension was accompanied at once by that of the viceroy's protest and the report that he had acted under constraint and meant to apply the ordinances as soon as the country was at peace, the result was to anger everyone rather than to appease them. The incident clearly revealed the obstinacy of the viceroy in pursuing their common disadvantage. They were therefore more rebellious and more obstinate even than before, and they went on resolved to die in their quest. The viceroy was scandalized when he learnt this and found that a measure designed to appease them had only inflamed them. His own followers were dejected, and many of them inclined to Pizarro who had risked his neck for the sake of them all. The viceroy decided to shut himself up in the city, and not wait for the enemy in the open.

He therefore fortified the city, cleared the streets, made embrasures, and brought in supplies in case the siege should last. But as fresh news came in daily of the strength of Pizarro, he thought he had better not wait in Lima but withdraw to Trujillo, eighty leagues away. He planned to take the wives of the *vecinos* in ships while the army marched down the coast.

He thought of depopulating and destroying the city, breaking up the mills and taking away everything that could be of use to the enemy, and collecting all those coastal Indians and taking them inland, so that Gonzalo Pizarro would find no supplies or Indian serfs and have to disband his army and abandon his plans. He put these ideas before the judges, who when they saw his purpose opposed it openly. They said that the royal *audiencia* could not leave the city since His Majesty had ordered it to sit there: they could not accompany His Lordship or permit anyone to abandon his home. So the judges and the viceroy appeared in open conflict and the *vecinos* were more inclined to take the part of the judges than that of the viceroy, for the judges had spoken in favor of them and tried to prevent their wives and supporters from being taken away by soldiers and sailors. When the viceroy left his meeting with the judges, at which nothing was decided, he thought he would put into effect his plan of escape by sea, sending his brother by land with the soldiers. . . .

The viceroy is arrested; he is held on an offshore island. The vecinos of Lima try to intercede with Gonzalo Pizarro to save the life of the viceroy, but fail. The judges try to delay appointing Gonzalo governor as he demands, but give way, and Gonzalo Pizarro is named governor and enters Lima.

The Festivities and Rejoicings of the Pizarrists

[4:20] Gonzalo Pizarro and his captains displayed their rejoicing and satisfaction at becoming lords of Peru. They organized many solemn festivities with bullfights and games of canes and the ring. Some wrote very good poems on these, and others maliciously satirized them. They were so satirical that though I remember some of them, I thought it better not to include them here.

In the midst of the general rejoicings he had ordered the release of the gentlemen *vecinos* from Cusco who had fled from him when he left that city: all of them had been arrested by Carvajal as we have said. He declared a general pardon for all those who had not rallied to him, except Licentiate Carvajal, who had fled though Gonzalo had been such a friend of his, and Garcilaso de la Vega. Fernández mentions this in his Book I, chapter xxvii. We shall soon say how it happened, for these authors did not obtain a full account of this episode, and though he and Zárate touch on it they do not say how it came to pass. Gonzalo also forbade anyone to leave the city without his permission; and when Rodrigo Núñez and Pedro de Prado asked for it, it caused their death, for they raised suspicions about themselves and it was thought that they meant to escape. There were thus no rejoicings without executions and no executions without rejoicings on one side and mourning on the other, for all things are possible in civil wars. . . .

Gonzalo decides to send ambassadors to His Majesty to report on what has been done and beg him to confirm Pizarro's governorship; Vaca de Castro, who had been arrested by the viceroy, escapes with the help of a judge of the audiencia and flees to Quito, where he begins to raise an army to move against Gonzalo Pizarro. Gonzalo sends men north to Trujillo to hold the frontier against the viceroy, but they are taken and killed.

[4:24] ". . . When Pizarro had heard how his captains were worsted and how the viceroy was daily gathering strength, arms, and equipment, he decided to go with all possible haste and undo the viceroy and his army. He felt sure that more men from Spain and other parts of the Indies would arrive from day to day, and they must necessarily land at or near the port of Tumbes, where the viceroy was. He was also afraid that some dispatch might come from His Majesty in the viceroy's favor, which would have broken the spirits of his followers.

"With this thought he determined to take his army before things got worse and seek out his enemies, and bring matters to the test of arms, if the viceroy waited for him. He therefore instructed his captains, paid the men, and sent the horses and equipment on to Trujillo, while he and the chief men in his army remained alone, to follow on behind.

"A brigantine from Arequipa then arrived in Lima with a sum of over 100,000 castilians for Gonzalo Pizarro, and another came from Tierra Firme belonging to Gonzalo Martel de la Puente who was sending his wife and children to Cusco, where his house was. Gonzalo Pizarro and his friends were puffed up with pride at their good fortune with the ships, which they very much needed. Indeed they were so cock-a-hoop that they feared no one in all the world."

So Zárate[30]. . . .

The Pizarrists put a great many harquebuses, pikes, and other equipment and armor on the ships. They embarked more than 150 leading men, and took Licentiate Cepeda, the judge, and Juan de Cáceres, His Majesty's accountant, in order to give the expedition greater authority. Cepeda's departure dispersed the *audiencia*, for no judge was left in Lima but Licentiate Zárate. And to protect himself further from royal commands, Gonzalo carried the royal seal with him. Having to depart from Lima, a place so important to his plans, he thought that he should leave the city under the control of a man who would hold it for him come what might. For this purpose he chose Lorenzo de Aldana, a most prudent, discreet gentleman, well beloved by everyone and rich, for he had a great allocation in the city of

---

[30] *Historia,* ch. xvi [16].

Arequipa. Pizarro left him eighty men as a guard, which was sufficient for the security of the city, for all the *vecinos* who had Indians were going with him. He embarked in March 1545, going by sea to the port called Santa, fifteen leagues from Trujillo. Here he landed and spent Easter at Trujillo where he waited some days until the men he had sent to various places rejoined him. As there was some delay, he thought he had best take his army out of the Spanish town so as not to give too much annoyance with billeting, and went to the province called Collique, where he spent some days until the men he was expecting appeared. He held a review and found he had more than six hundred foot and horse. Though the number was not greatly in excess of the viceroy's, he was better armed and equipped; his soldiers were veterans and skilled in warfare, and had been in other battles and knew the country and its difficulties, being inured to military hardships in their previous battles from the time they had arrived to conquer the empire. The viceroy's men, on the contrary, had mostly come recently from Spain and were raw recruits unaccustomed to fighting, ill armed, and with poor powder and lacking many other things necessary for warfare. . . .

Gonzalo and his forces pursue the viceroy; the rumors of the viceroy's vengeance against any who fail to support him lead many of the conquerors to flee to Lima for safety. Because this is a civil war, with all of the hatred that engenders, there is much violence on both sides. Gonzalo tricks the viceroy into thinking that he can defeat Gonzalo on the road, thus tiring the viceroy's forces in a difficult march.

The Viceroy Is Defeated and Killed

[4:34] The viceroy entered the city of Quito. He found no resistance, but a woman told him that Pizarro was coming against him, at which he was astonished and perceived the deception that had been practiced on him. But Pizarro did not know the viceroy had reached Quito, imagining he was still in his camp until next morning when the scouts came near the tents and saw how little stir there was. They went into the camp and learnt from the Indians what was afoot and told Gonzalo. He hastily sent out scouts in all directions, and thus learnt that the viceroy was in Quito. So he struck camp with all speed, and marched in good order to give battle wherever he found the viceroy. The latter knew what was happening and that the enemy had the advantage over him, yet he had no remedy but to risk a decision, hoping that all His Majesty's servants would desert to him. He came out of the city to receive the enemy and encouraged his men with great vigor; and they all marched along as if victory was already assured; for despite Pizarro's advantage in numbers, the viceroy had very valiant captains and other noteworthy men. His captains of infantry were Sancho Sánchez de Avila and his cousin Juan Cabrera and Francisco Sánchez; of cavalry Adelantado Sebastián de Belalcázar, Cepeda, and Pedro de Bazán.

The armies came within sight of one another and advance parties of harquebusiers came out on both sides and skirmished. Pizarro's were much stronger than the viceroy's, because they were skilled from long practice and had plenty of good powder; the viceroy's were the opposite. The armies were so close that it was necessary to recall the skirmishers to the banner. On Gonzalo's side Captain Juan de Acosta went out to bring them in, accompanied by another good soldier called Páez de Sotomayor. Then Gonzalo ordered Licentiate Carvajal to attack the enemy's right with his company. He placed himself in front of the cavalry, but the captains would not consent to his exposing himself and put him with seven or eight companions on one side of the infantry so that he could direct the battle. The viceroy's cavalry, some 140 men, seeing that Carvajal's were attacking, went out to meet them, and all rushed forward without any sense of order or timing, so that, as Zárate says, when they reached the enemy they were already half discomfited. A picket of harquebusiers awaiting them on one side did much execution among them, and Licentiate Carvajal and his men handled them severely. Although Carvajal's were few, they had the advantage over the viceroy, for they and their horses were fresh and strong, and his were weak and weary. Many were unseated by lances in the charge, and all of them came to close quarters and fought with swords, axes, and clubs. The battle grew very hot. Gonzalo's standard now moved forward with a hundred horsemen, and finding the enemy already worsted, easily completed their confusion. On the other hand the infantry fought hard, and there was such shouting and noise that the forces engaged seemed much larger than they were. At the first shots Captain Juan Cabrera was killed, and soon after Captain Sancho Sánchez, who had fought valiantly with a broadsword and cut his way through several of the enemy's ranks.

But Pizarro's army was so much more numerous and better armed that they overwhelmed their opponents, surrounding them on all sides and killing their captains and most of the men. The viceroy fought along with his cavalry and performed many brave feats. In the first encounter he felled Alonso de Montalvo and engaged others with courage and vigor. He was disguised, wearing an Indian shirt over his arms, and this was the cause of his death. Seeing that his men were lost, he tried to retire but could not, for a *vecino* of Arequipa called Hernando de Torres engaged him without recognizing him, dealt him a two-handed blow on the head with a battle axe, which felled and stunned him. Here Zárate (Book V, chapter xxxv) says as follows: "The viceroy and his horse were so tired from their labors the night before, when they had not stopped or rested or eaten, that he was easily brought down. Although the battle was still raging between the infantry, at the sight of the viceroy's fall, his followers, who recognized him, weakened and were defeated, and many of them were killed."

So Zárate. If Hernando de Torres had recognized the viceroy by the habit of Santiago worn openly on his breast, he would certainly not have struck to kill, but have tried to capture him with the help of his comrades. But because of the Indian dress he took the viceroy for a private person, and even a poor soldier, and so did as he did and caused his death. The viceroy was blamed for going in disguise, but his purpose was to avoid being taken prisoner if he were worsted. He wished to be unrecognized so that he should not be accorded the honors of a viceroy, but treated like a private soldier: and this was the cause of his misfortune.

Licentiate Carvajal saw that the enemy was beaten and scoured the field in search of the viceroy, wishing to satisfy his anger at the death of his brother. He found Pedro de Puelles about to kill him, though he was nearly dead from his fall and a harquebus shot he had received. One of the viceroy's soldiers revealed his identity to Puelles, who otherwise would never have recognized him in his disguise. Licentiate Carvajal was about to dismount and finish him off, but Puelles stopped him, saying that it was an unworthy act to lay hands on a man who was nearly dead. Then the Licentiate ordered a Negro to cut his head off. This was done and it was taken to Quito and placed on the gibbet, where it was exposed for a short time, until Gonzalo Pizarro found out about it. He was very angry, and had it removed and put with the body for burial. . . .

Such was the end of this good gentleman, who had persisted so in the application of laws that were not in the king's interest, nor in that of Peru, causing the death and destruction of Spaniards and Indians we have described and shall describe in our history. But he was not so much to blame as has been said, for he had explicit orders to do what he did, as we shall see from the historians and as he himself often said.

On the Question of Gonzalo Becoming King of Peru

[4:40] . . . Carvajal gave much thought to Pizarro's affairs, considering how he might perpetuate his rule over the empire, not only as governor in the emperor's name, but as its absolute master, since he and his brothers had won it. He wrote him a long letter urging him to take the title of king, which Fernández mentions (chapter xil). But when he met Gonzalo in Lima, he said (though this is out of its proper place):[31]

---

[31] There is no historical record of Carvajal writing the letter Garcilaso describes here. The letter and its contents appear to be an example of Garcilaso's literary technique of expressing ideas of his own through statements expressed by his subjects.

"Sir, when a viceroy is killed in a pitched battle and his head is cut off and placed on a gibbet, and the battle was against the royal standard, and there were as many deaths and as much looting as there have been since, there's no pardon to be hoped for and no compromises to be made, even though Your Lordship makes ample excuses and proves himself to be more innocent than a suckling or babe. Nor can you trust their words or promises, whatever assurances they give, unless you declare yourself king; and take the government yourself without waiting for another to give it you, and put a crown on your head; and allocate whatever land is unoccupied among your friends and supporters; and as what the king gives is temporary for two lives, you give it as a perpetual title and make dukes and marquises and counts, such as there are in all the countries of the world, so that they will defend Your Lordship in order to defend their own estates.

"Set up military orders with the same names and titles as those in Spain and other saints as patrons and such insignia as you think fit. Give the knights of the orders revenues and pensions to keep themselves and live at ease, as military knights do everywhere. With all this I have said in brief Your Lordship will attract to your service all the Spanish chivalry and nobility in this empire, fully rewarding all those who conquered it and who have served Your Lordship, which is not now the case. And to attract the Indians and make them so devoted that they will die for Your Lordship as they would for their Inca kings, take one of their princesses, whichever is closest to the royal line, to wife, and send ambassadors to the forests where the heir to the Inca is and bid him to come forth and recover his lost majesty and state, asking him to offer you as your wife any daughter or sister he may have. You know how much this prince will esteem kinship or friendship with you, and you will gain the universal love of all the Indians by restoring their Inca and at the same time make them genuinely willing to do whatever their king orders them on your behalf, such as bringing supplies, abandoning the villages, holding the roads against your enemies—in short all the Indians will be on your side, and if they do not help your enemies with supplies and porters, no one can prevail against you in Peru. Their prince will be satisfied with the title of king and the fact that his vassals obey him as they used to do; and he will govern his Indians in peace as they did in the past, while Your Lordship and your officials and captains govern the Spaniards and have charge of military affairs, requiring the Inca to tell the Indians to do whatever you command. Thus you will be sure that the Indians do not deceive you or act as double spies, as they do now, serving first one side and then the other.

"In addition, Your Lordship will receive from the Inca not only all the gold and silver the Indians produce in this empire, for they do not regard it as treasure or wealth, but also all the treasure of the kings their ancestors which they have hidden, as is well known. All this will be given and delivered to Your Lordship both on account of your relationship with the Inca and because of his restoration to his former majesty. With all the gold and silver they were reputed to have Your Lordship can buy the whole world, if you want to be master of it. And pay no attention if they say you are a traitor to the king of Spain; you are not, for as the saying goes, no king is a traitor. This land belonged to the Incas, its natural lords, and if it is not restored to them, you have more right to it than the king of Castile, for you won it at your expense and risk, together with your brothers. Now, by restoring it to the Inca, you are simply doing what you should by natural law; and in seeking to govern it yourself as its conqueror and not as the vassal and subject of another, you are doing what you owe to your reputation, for anyone who can become king by the strength of his arm should not remain a serf for lack of spirit. It all depends on the first step and the first declaration. I beg Your Lordship carefully to consider the import of what I have said about ruling this empire in perpetuity, so that all those who live and shall live here may follow you. Finally I urge you whatever may happen to crown yourself and call yourself king, for no other name befits one who has won an empire by his strength and courage. Die a king. I repeat many times, die a king and not a vassal, for whoever lets a wrong be put on him deserves worse." . . .

Gonzalo Pizarro Returns to Lima

[4:41] Gonzalo wished to avoid a decision about assuming the title of king, for his natural respect for his prince was stronger than the pleas of his friends, and he never lost hope that His Imperial Majesty would grant him the confirmation of his governorship of Peru, on the grounds that he and his brothers had won it, and in return for his personal services, realizing that he knew all those who had served His Majesty in Peru and was in the best position to reward them. All these things were arguments in favor of the award of the governorship, in addition to the fact that the emperor had issued a grant to the marquis his brother by which he could appoint his successor as governor and he had in fact appointed Gonzalo. In the late conflict with the viceroy it was thought that he had sufficient justification because of the viceroy's severity in applying the ordinances without heeding the kingdom or its procurators, wherefore the whole of Peru had elected Pizarro its procurator general. In any case the judges, not Pizarro, had arrested the viceroy and sent him to Spain. In the light of all this, Pizarro thought that he not only deserved a pardon for the past, but the award of the governorship anew; for it is a natural habit among men of war to esteem their own deeds, even if they are guilty ones. As Pizarro had not dared to venture on an undertaking so much to his advantage, as his friends maintained, the common people attributed it to lack of sense, and not to excess of respect toward the king. They regarded him as mean-spirited and mocked his lack of judgment. The historians have respected this, because they were given a distorted version, and do not say what really happened. For it was the common opinion of those nearest to Gonzalo Pizarro who knew him best that he was a man of good judgment, who never caviled or deceived or made false promises or spoke evasively. He was simple, sincere, noble, and good, and trusted in his friends, who destroyed him, as the historians themselves say. . . .

Gonzalo Pizarro resolved to leave Quito for Lima and reside there, as it was in the middle of the empire and he could move north or south as the affairs of peace or war required. He left Pedro de Puelles as his lieutenant and captain general in Quito, with 300 soldiers. He had great confidence in Puelles who had served him so loyally and rallied to him when he would otherwise have been lost. On reaching San Miguel, he heard that there were many Indians in the district on a war footing, and sent Captain Mercadillo with 130 men to conquer them. He founded the city now called Loja. He sent Captain Porcel with 60 men to his former conquest of Pacamuru, and ordered Licentiate Carvajal to go by sea with the party of soldiers Palomino had brought from Nicaragua, executing his instructions in each of the ports up the coast. Carvajal carried this out fully and went as far as Trujillo, while Gonzalo reached the same place by land; on joining forces they made arrangements for the journey to Lima. Gonzalo left Trujillo with 200 picked soldiers, including Licentiate Carvajal, Juan de Acosta, Juan de la Torre, Licentiate Cepeda, Hernando Bachicao, Diego Guillén, and other noble people. He advanced on Lima.

On his arrival his friends differed about the manner of his entry. Some said it should be under a canopy as a king, for such he was and would soon be crowned: those who said this were of course those who had urged him to call himself king. Others spoke more moderately, and said that he ought to make a new gate and street in one of the quarters of the city in memory of his entry, as they did in Rome when the emperors entered in triumph after their great victories. Both parties were obstinate in their views and tried to get their own way, but Gonzalo refused to accept either of them but agreed to what Licentiate Carvajal might decide. He then arranged for Gonzalo to enter on horseback with his captains walking in front of him and their horses led before them, the infantry following behind drawn up in ranks. The cavalry was also to enter on foot, along with the infantry, since it seemed that if the captains went on foot the men should not ride. Pizarro rode after his comrades on a splendid horse. He was flanked by four bishops: on his right the archbishop of Lima with the bishop of Quito by his side, on his left the bishop of Cusco and the bishop of Bogotá, who had come to Peru to be consecrated by the other three prelates. After them came another band of soldiers on foot, forming as it were a rearguard for Pizarro, though none of them carried arms such as pikes or harquebuses or wore armor, so as to avoid appearing as if they were going to war. They had only swords and daggers, as in time of peace. Behind these came Lorenzo de Aldana, as Pizarro's deputy, with the city council the *vecinos,* and the other citizens, who had come out to receive the governor and congratulated him with great acclamations and thanksgivings by each and all, in return for what he had done in saving their property and for having undergone such privations and risking his life for them all. So Gonzalo made his entry, and went to the cathedral to worship the Blessed Sacrament. There was much music in the streets, with singing, trumpets, and excellent minstrels he had: the bells of the cathedral and the convents rang out joyfully through the city. After adoring the host Gonzalo went to his house, which had belonged to the marquis, his brother. The historians say that he now lived with much greater pomp and pride than before. One says he had a guard of eighty halberdiers[32] and that no one now sat in his presence; another says he gave his hand to be kissed by everyone. This is said partly as a form of flattery by slandering an enemy, and partly to shock the reader. Most of what they say about this gentleman and his officials is in the same slanderous strain; but I can swear as a Christian that I am telling the truth when I say that I never saw a halberdier in his guard or heard tell that he had one. I have already mentioned that when the marquis entered Peru he had an edict from His Majesty permitting him to raise twenty-four halberdiers as his bodyguard, but this was impossible as no one, except two men I knew, wanted to be a halberdier, which was regarded as a low sort of employment. I do not know how it was possible to find eighty of them later when people were prouder and more presumptuous. Our historians themselves have said that the Spaniards in Peru pride themselves on their free-handedness and will not even take pay from the king in time of war. Possibly this was a printing error and the author put halberdiers instead of harquebusiers (as another writer has it), being unaware of the pride of the Peruvian Spaniards and not realizing that a bodyguard could be of harquebusiers and not halberdiers. They also say that he used poison to kill whomever he wished. This is certainly false witness, for no such thought ever entered his head. If anything of the sort had happened, I would have

---

[32] A "halberd" was a weapon that consisted of an axe blade mounted on a pike and was used by a guard or "halberdier." "Halberdiers" were originally Swiss mercenaries who fought on foot, and their massed detachments proved to be capable of defeating mounted knights in the field.

heard about it then or later, as they did; such wickedness would have caused him to be hated by everyone, yet the historians often said he was greatly loved. I hope I may be permitted to say truly without offending anyone what I saw, for my only purpose is always to tell plainly what happened without hatred or flattery, since I have no motive for either. . . .

Chapter Five
The Restoration of Order in Peru

The Selection of Licentiate Pedro de la Gasca

[5:1] While these events were taking place in Peru, Diego Alvárez Cueto and Francisco Maldonado reached Spain, the first representing the viceroy and the second Gonzalo Pizarro. They went to Valladolid where the court was residing and Prince Philip was governing in the absence in Germany of his father the emperor, who was then personally conducting the war he was waging as a Catholic prince to reduce the Lutherans to the service of the Holy Mother Church of Rome.[33] Each of the ambassadors informed His Highness and the Royal Council of the Indies as best he could of events in Peru up to the time of their departure, when the death of the viceroy had still not taken place. The news of the disturbances caused great regret, and the prince ordered the wisest and most experienced advisers in his court to discuss the situation and recommend a solution. These were Cardinal Don Juan Tavera, archbishop of Toledo; Cardinal Don Fray García de Loaisa, archbishop of Seville; Don Fernando de Valdés, president of the royal council and bishop of Sigüenza; the duke of Alva; the count of Osorno; the *comendador mayor* of León, Francisco de los Cobos; and the same of Castile, Don Juan de Zúñiga; Licentiate Ramírez, bishop of Cuenca and president of the royal *audiencia* of Valladolid; the judges of the Royal Council of the Indies, and other persons of authority.

All these and the court in general were astonished that the laws and ordinances framed for the universal welfare of Spaniards and Indians in Peru should have gone so awry as to cause the destruction of both and bring the kingdom to such a pass that the emperor was in danger of losing it. In this mood they held many meetings to decide how to remedy the evident danger of losing the empire, of which they were so conscious. There were divergent opinions. Some proposed that it should be reconquered by force of arms with the dispatch of an army led by experienced captains. But the difficulty of raising so many men, arms, horses, munitions, and supplies, and sailing them so far over two seas forced them to drop the idea. Other opinions held by less warlike people and cooler heads were that as

---

[33] Garcilaso refers here to the religious wars during the first half of the sixteenth century between Charles V, King of Castile and Holy Roman Emperor, and the Protestant princes of Germany.

the trouble had sprung from the severity of the laws and the harsh character of the viceroy, it would be best to remedy it with antidotes: annulling
the former laws, and making new and contrary ones, and sending out a
gentle, kindly, prudent, experienced, astute, and resourceful person who
would be able to conduct peaceful affairs, or warlike ones if necessary. They
selected Licentiate Pedro de la Gasca, a priest of the Council of the Inquisition, who they were satisfied possessed all the qualities they required; and
so they wrote to His Majesty asking him to approve their choice.

The Arrival of Licentiate la Gasca and His Reception

[5:2] Adding what this author[34] omits about the powers taken by Licentiate la Gasca—for although he says the emperor gave him what he asked for,
he does not say what it was—we should explain that he asked for absolute
power in all matters, to the full extent of His Majesty's authority in the
Indies, so that he could raise men, arms, horses, money, ships, and supplies
anywhere he needed them. He asked for the revocation of the ordinances
the viceroy had taken with him, and a pardon for all past criminal offenses
with a bar against the starting of proceedings either by the crown or by private parties; a guarantee of unmolested possession of property; power to
send the viceroy back to Spain if this seemed necessary for the peace of
Peru; the right to draw on the royal treasury for any expense needed for
reducing Peru, and for its government and the administration of justice;
and liberty to award all the vacant allocation of Indians and any that might
fall vacant, and to appoint the officials of the whole empire, governors to
the parts that had been discovered, and conquerors to what remained to be
discovered. For himself he asked to have no salary, but only a royal treasurer to spend whatever he required and give account to the officials of the
exchequer afterwards.

Licentiate la Gasca asked for all this, wisely looking to the past and to
the future, so that it should not be said that he had been induced to face
the enormous difficulties and dangers that lay ahead in the hope of reward,
but that he was moved by zeal for the king's service for which he sacrificed
rest, peace of mind, and life itself, etcetera.

And in explanation of López de Gómara's remark that his abilities
greatly surpassed his appearance, the fact is that he was very small and
oddly built, being as large as a tall man from the waist down and barely a
third of a yard from the waist to the shoulder. On horseback he looked
even smaller than he was, for he was all legs. His face was very ugly. But

---

[34] López de Gómara, *Historia*, ch. clxxx.

what nature had denied him in physical gifts, she had doubled in his mind and spirit, since he had all the qualities this author says and more, and reduced an empire so lost as Peru was to the king's service. I knew him, and in particular watched him all one afternoon when he was on the balcony of my father's house overlooking the square, where many solemn festivities were being held in his honor.

The president watched the bull running and jousting from this balcony, and was lodged in the house that belonged to Tomás Vázquez and now belongs to his son Pedro Vázquez, where Gonzalo Pizarro also lodged. This house is to the west, opposite the convent of Our Lady of the Mercies, and although it has a corner in the square with a large window from which Licentiate la Gasca could have watched the festivities, he preferred to see them from my father's balcony which gives onto the middle of the square.

Now we must proceed to tell of his deeds, which, though they were not affairs of the sword and lance, were yet so full of wisdom and prudence that he took all the measures necessary to end the war and secure his object, after which he left the country free and unoppressed. It required great patience and restraint to suffer the labors that presented themselves and put up with the shameless disrespect of the military people. It needed much astuteness, discretion, and skill to penetrate and foil the stratagems of his enemy, who showed great ingenuity. The proof is that he succeeded in a way that would seem incredible to anyone who considers what a state the empire was in when he accepted the task. We shall omit the voyage of the president (as we shall call him from now on) to Nombre de Dios, which Fernández describes, and say only what happened after.

At Santa Marta the president learned of the death of the viceroy from Licentiate Almendárez, then governor of that province and of New Granada. Licentiate la Gasca and all his friends were deeply distressed, thinking that it would be impossible to reduce people who had committed so great a villainy against their king as to kill a viceroy in pitched battle. But the president disguised his emotions so as not to cause greater alarm, and in order to seek a solution spoke very openly to the effect that his powers enabled him to pardon as much and even more, if there could be more to pardon. His powers had been signed after the deed had been committed, so there was no doubt that it was covered by the general pardon. He also realized that the disappearance of the viceroy would contribute greatly toward reducing the empire to His Majesty's service, by removing the general hatred he had inspired by his harshness. In addition it avoided the obstacle that would have been created if it had become necessary to expel the viceroy from Peru in order to pacify it, for he might have resisted, saying that it was an outrage after he had served his king so zealously against rebels who had defied his commands. . . .

Gonzalo Learns of the President's Arrival

[5: 3] . . . When Gonzalo's hopes of becoming permanent governor of Peru were at their highest pitch, he received letters from his general Pedro de Hinojosa with news of the president's arrival. This set off a great dispute among his followers, and at a council attended by the captains and *vecinos* they all aired many conflicting opinions. Finally, they reduced them to two—some said that he should publicly or privately have the president killed; others that he should be brought to Peru, for when he came and they had seen his powers it would be easy to get him to concede all they wanted. If this did not succeed they could delay him for a long time by saying that they had to collect all the cities of Peru at Lima, so that their procurators could decide whether to receive him or not: as the places were so far apart, the meeting could be delayed more than two years, and meanwhile they could keep the president waiting on the island of Puna under a reliable guard so that he could not write to His Majesty and accuse them of disobedience. Others said that the best and quickest thing would be to send him back to Spain with a good supply of money and comforts for the journey, to show that he had been treated as a minister of the crown.

They spent many days in this confusion of ideas; and at last by common consent they decided that procurators should be sent to His Majesty to take whatever steps were necessary for the empire, and giving an account of the latest events, especially justifying the battle of Quito and the killing of the viceroy, laying the blame on him as the aggressor, and saying that he had forced them to kill him by attacking them and that they had done so in battle in self-defense. At the same time they begged His Majesty to appoint Gonzalo governor of the empire because he had conquered it and deserved the office for many reasons, and had His Majesty's engagement to the marquis that the latter should appoint the next governor to succeed him. The procurators were to ask the president in Panama not to come to Peru until His Majesty was informed and sent new instructions about what should be done.

This done, they began to select the ambassadors to go to Spain, and in order to give the mission greater authority, they begged Don Fray Jerónimo de Loaisa, archbishop of Lima, to accept the leadership, for as prelate, father, and pastor of the city he would command more attention in Spain. They also asked the bishop of Santa Marta and Fray Tomás de San Martín, provincial of the Order of St. Dominic, and sent Lorenzo de Aldana and Gómez de Solís to accompany these three. They were given money for the journey so that they could spend what was necessary; and Gómez de Solís, who was Pizarro's chamberlain, was also given thirty thousand pesos for Hinojosa's expenses in Panama. Lorenzo de Aldana was earnestly requested, as a friend and fellow countryman, to send rapid and reliable news of the outcome of the journey and whatever he could find out in Panama about the president's powers. So they sailed in October 1546 with the title of ambassadors of the empire of Peru to His Majesty. . . .

The ambassadors reach Panama and repudiate Gonzalo, delivering their fleet to the president, who offers to repudiate the ordinances in exchange for Gonzalo's surrender. Gonzalo rejects the offer and the two sides prepare for war. The rebels argue among themselves, and some begin to go over to the side of la Gasca. Gonzalo insists on an oath of loyalty from his followers, but as la Gasca moves south, more and more important men desert Gonzalo. Lorenzo de Aldana, one of Gonzalo's ambassadors to la Gasca, goes over to the president, who put him in charge of promising in la Gasca's name a general amnesty to those who come over to the side of the royal forces under la Gasca's authority.

Lima Declares for His Majesty

[5:15] Ill fortune was not content to dog Gonzalo with all these defections from his army, reducing it from the thousand soldiers with whom he had left Lima a few days earlier to no more than two hundred. It also ordained that those he had left in Lima as his most trustworthy friends, both because of pledges they had given him and their ties of kinship, should now turn against him and go over to the king's side. Two days after Gonzalo's departure for Arequipa, Don Antonio de Ribera, who had remained as his deputy in Lima, and the alcaldes Martín Pizarro and Antonio León, and other *vecinos* who, on grounds of old age or illness, more feigned than real, had obtained permission to stay behind on condition that they exchanged their arms and horses for their persons—these old and sick men, finding the enemy twelve or fifteen leagues away, took the city flag out into the public square, called together the people, and raised it in His Majesty's name, announcing the president's bidding and the general pardon.

Fernández says that this was done by order of Gonzalo, who had left instructions to this effect so that those who had forsaken him should get no credit for going over to the king. However, Fernández himself contradicts this, saying that it must be a malicious invention. But it was in fact the case; for Gonzalo did give such instructions: and it was for this reason that he left as his deputy Don Antonio de Ribera, to whom he was so attached both on account of their kinship and of Ribera's service to the marquis, his brother, and himself. He realized that by getting the city to declare for His Majesty (after his own departure) Ribera would gain credit and honor in the eyes of President la Gasca; for Gonzalo was well aware that as soon as he was out of sight, the people in the city would turn against him as the other captains and deputies had done in various parts of Peru, and he thought that it was better that this should be done by his orders, even if they had to be kept secret. This would assist Don Antonio de Ribera; moreover his niece, the marquis' daughter, Doña Francisca Pizarro, remained in Ribera's hands.

When the city had risen against Pizarro, Aldana was informed of the fact. He celebrated the event with incredible delight, for he had not expected those within to come over so easily, and was some distance out at sea, where he was cautiously collecting all those who came over to him. Captain Juan Alonso Palomino was on the shore for this purpose and had fifty men with him. Boats were kept ready so that they could retire if necessary, for it was feared that Gonzalo would return to the city when he knew what had taken place there. In order to learn immediately of Pizarro's approach, if he did return, twelve horsemen were stationed on the road: these were men who had fled to Aldana, and were therefore regarded as more loyal than those who had simply declared for him, since they had turned their backs on Gonzalo. Captain Illanes was sent in a frigate to sail southwards and where possible to land a religious and a soldier who were to convey the president's dispatches to Centeno and others to well-known men who were with Acosta; the Indians would spread them throughout the country and so they would reach their destinations. The letters did Acosta a great deal of harm, as we shall see.

Captain Aldana, whom I knew and of whom I shall later make special mention, took the above measures on shipboard, still not daring to land; for as both elements were disturbed, he feared that some might try to kill him and then desert to Gonzalo Pizarro. In addition to the many who went over to the king, there were some who left the king and came over to Gonzalo; and the historians give their names. Aldana was afraid that one of these might attempt to perform some striking act such as killing him. Because of these fears he stayed quietly out at sea until he knew that Gonzalo was 80 leagues from Lima; and by the time the news arrived he was 110 leagues away. Then Aldana and all his followers landed. Everyone in the city, captains, soldiers—though there were few of these—even children, came out solemnly to receive him. He left the fleet in charge of the *alcalde ordinario* Juan Fernández after the necessary ceremonies of handing it over. He then entered the city and sought out such arms and munitions as there were.

Meanwhile it was reported that Gonzalo was returning to the city, and though this was so impossible that the news should have been disregarded, fear made them insecure and they believed it and even supposed that the enemy was four leagues away. They thought that they were not strong enough to resist him, and those who had no horses to escape by land went out to sea to seek refuge in the ships, while those who had mounts rode to Trujillo by the royal highway. Others who were unable to take such precautions scattered and hid in secret places, such as canebrakes and farmsteads or wherever they could. They thought they were lost for a day and a night, until they received assurances that the news was false. . . .

La Gasca and his army move south from Trujillo toward Lima, receiving news of Gonzalo's actions from the men who continually desert Gonzalo and report to him. La Gasca's commander moves his army to Jauja to meet Gonzalo, who is moving from Arequipa to Cusco, and the two armies engage at Huarina. Gonzalo's forces win the battle, but with many wounded.

Licentiate Cepeda and Others Try to Persuade Gonzalo Pizarro to Ask for Peace

[5:27] Having done his duty toward the dead, Gonzalo Pizarro intended to go to Cusco, but he could not do this for many days, as he was greatly impeded by the many wounded he had with him. He and his officers were much troubled by them, for they could travel only in short stages. On the way Licentiate Cepeda reminded Gonzalo Pizarro of a promise he had made him earlier that he would discuss terms of peace with President la Gasca when a favorable opportunity presented itself. Cepeda said that now was the most suitable moment to get good conditions. Many others agreed with Cepeda, for the affair was discussed at a meeting of the leaders, and most of them desired peace and quiet. They were so insistent that Gonzalo grew angry, as López de Gómara says in his chapter clxxxiii:

> "At Pucarán Pizarro and Cepeda disputed over the question of coming to terms with la Gasca, Cepeda saying that that was the best opportunity and reminding him that he had promised to take it at Arequipa. Pizarro, following the views of others and influenced by his good fortune, said that it was a bad policy, for if he began negotiations it would be regarded as weakness and all his followers would desert, and many of his friends who were with la Gasca would fail him. Garcilaso de la Vega and some others were of Cepeda's opinion."

So López de Gómara.

Gonzalo turned down Cepeda's advice, which would have been advantageous, and took that which was later given him by Captains Juan de Acosta, Diego Guillén, Hernando Bachicao, and Juan de la Torre, who were young and bold, and thought themselves invincible after the great victory of Huarina, and had no wish to negotiate, for they would not be satisfied with less than the whole empire of Peru. Two days after this meeting the commander, Francisco de Carvajal, returned from his journey to Arequipa, and two days later he had Captain Hernando Bachicao strangled for having gone over to Centeno at Huarina. Carvajal had known about this on the day of the battle, but he postponed the punishment, not wishing to spoil so great a victory as he had won by killing a captain who had been so long in his service and was so committed to his party as Bachicao. After this, Gonzalo and his army reached Cusco, still harassed by the number of wounded.

Captain Juan de la Torre had arranged a solemn reception with many triumphal arches in the streets down which Pizarro would pass. They were made of many different flowers of various pretty colors, as the Indians used to make them in the time of the Inca kings. The infantry came first, each company separately with its banners raised, the men marching in order, three in each rank, preceded by their captains. Next came the cavalry in the same order. Long after the army had been billeted, Gonzalo Pizarro entered, attended only by his servants and the *vecinos* who were with him. He had not wished to enter with the soldiers, lest it should be said that he was exulting over his enemies. On his entry the bells of the cathedral and convents were rung, though there were few of them at that time. The Indians in the city appeared in the square from their various quarters and in their tribal groups, and acclaimed him with loud shouts, calling him Inca and giving him other royal titles which they used in the triumphs of their own kings. They had been ordered by Captain Juan de la Torre to celebrate as they did in Inca times. There was music of trumpets and minstrels, for Gonzalo had excellent musicians. He entered the church of the Mercedarians to worship the Blessed Sacrament and the image of his mother, our Lady the Virgin. Then he walked to his lodgings in the house belonging to his deputy and commander Alonso de Toro, opposite the Mercedarian convent.

I entered the city with them, for the day before I had gone out as far as Quespicancha, three leagues from Cusco, to receive my father. I walked part of the way, and was borne part of it on the backs of Indians who took turns to carry me. For the return I was given a horse and a man to lead it, and I saw all I have described, and could still say in which house each captain was lodged, for I knew them all and remember the houses, though it is nearly sixty years since all this happened. Memory retains what is seen in childhood better than what happens in later years.

As soon as Gonzalo and his army had entered Cusco, Francisco de Carvajal began to take the necessary steps for the continuance of the war. He sought to make up the number of weapons lost in the battle of Huarina, and made much gunpowder and collected plenty of lead. The spare harquebuses, which were numerous, for he had collected all that Centeno's men had left on the battlefield when they were killed or fled, were put in order. This was done with great care and attention, for he esteemed harquebuses above all other weapons of offense and said that it was not in vain that the pagans had armed their god Jupiter with this weapon which wounds and kills from a distance as it does near at hand. He had pikes made, though not of ash, which is not found in Peru, but of other woods, equally good and stronger. He collected plenty of cotton or wicks, and left no detail, however small, unprepared for its proper time and season. He saw to everything himself, and never trusted to his subordinates to see to it, for he was afraid of negligence on their part. He was so solicitous and painstaking in all these tasks that he was never idle, and it seemed as if he never ate or slept.

He always rode a big mule of a color between dun and red: I never saw him on any other mount during the whole time he was in Cusco before the battle of Sacsahuana. He was so single-minded in seeing to all his army's needs that his soldiers came across him at all hours of the day and night doing his own duty and other people's. Carvajal thought they would criticize his earnestness, and as he passed by with his hat in his hand, instead of saying: "I kiss your hands," he would say: "What you can do today, don't put off till tomorrow." This phrase he had constantly in his mouth. When they asked him, when he ate and when he slept, he would say: "Those who have work to do find time for everything." In the midst of all this activity Francisco de Carvajal did not forget to keep his followers up to the mark, and committed a characteristic act in having a noble woman of Arequipa strangled, because after the battle she had railed womanishly against Gonzalo Pizarro, saying that his tyranny would be put down like that of others more powerful than he, who had won greater victories than Huarina but had still lost in the end. She quoted instances from the ancient Greeks and Romans, and said it all in public so often and so fearlessly that Carvajal hanged her from a window in her dwelling after she had been strangled.

Following his defeat at Huarina, la Gasca remains in the Jauja Valley, in Antahuailla, recovering and rebuilding his forces.

The Army Leaves Antahuailla

[5:30] After the fury of the winter had passed, the president decided to leave Antahuailla and go in search of Gonzalo Pizarro, who was at Cusco. He traveled with his army as far as the river Amáncay, which the Spaniards call Abáncay, and which is twenty leagues from the city. They found the bridge badly burnt, for then, as we have said, all the bridges in the empire were made of osier cables. They began to repair it, which was not difficult, as the river is particularly narrow at the point where the bridge is attached. After crossing it, they held a council about where they should cross the Apurimac, which was more difficult. They were doubtful about crossing it by the royal highway, for the river is very broad there, and though the bridge is made across the narrowest point, it is still two hundred paces across. There was also another obstacle, namely that there are few Indian villages on the road and these poor, so that they would find no food. It was therefore decided that the army should cross by one of three bridges, which would be built upriver where it passes through wild mountains and has a narrow channel over which the bridges could more easily be built. One of the three places chosen was Cotapampa; the second, higher up, Huacachaca; and the third Accha. The road to all three places was very difficult, and almost impassable for an army in formation owing to the steepness of the mountains, which would be incredible to anyone who had not seen them. Nevertheless they decided to pass through them, as there was no other road. . . .

As soon as the president had left Antahuailla with his army on the way to Cusco, Pizarro knew about it, for he was informed hourly where the enemy was and what he was doing. In time of war the common Indians cannot be relied on to keep any secret, for they act as double spies, and not knowing which side will win, try to please both of them, warning each of what the other is doing so that the victors will not afterwards harm them for not having done so. I believe we have mentioned this before, but we repeat it here, because one of the historians greatly emphasizes the secrecy that the president enjoined on Indians and Spaniards. Though Gonzalo knew that the president was approaching, he made no attempt to cut the roads or bar the difficult places, which were so numerous. He simply remained still, quite unperturbedly waiting to give battle, and confident in the result after the many victories he and his army had won in that war.

His commander Francisco de Carvajal did not rest by day or night, studying means to make Gonzalo Pizarro master of the whole empire after the great things they had already done to that end. But seeing that Pizarro now thought of nothing at all but the coming battle, he went to him and begged him to consider carefully what he was about to propose, saying: "Sir, considering what has passed and our present situation, and remembering that in every battle there is a risk of losing or winning, it seems to me that Your Lordship should avoid an issue but try to delay and draw out the fighting until your success is assured. Now I'll make a speech that might be made before either army, so that Your Lordship won't deny that what I have to say is for your good, and is necessary to achieve your aims and what we all desire.

"In order to obtain victory over your enemies, Your Lordship must go out of this city and leave it without a single inhabitant, breaking the mills, taking away all the food, banishing the inhabitants, removing their merchandise, and burning everything you can't take with you, so that the enemy find nothing of the slightest use to them. Your Lordship has two thousand men coming against you: one thousand are seamen and ship's boys and such people and they'll all arrive naked, shoeless, and starving. All their hopes are set on getting to this city to repair their hunger and nakedness. If they find it as I've described, they'll be utterly discouraged. The president won't be able to maintain them, and he'll be forced to dismiss them as useless people.

"Your Lordship shall also dismiss Centeno's men: for they've been defeated and will never make good friends. You can take more than five hundred men with you, for many soldiers have joined our army since the battle of Huarina to enjoy your success. They'll be picked men, and not one of them will fail you or deny you in any emergency. You'll set two [detachments] of fifty harquebusiers apiece on either side of the road, and they'll be twenty or thirty leagues from your army, bringing in sheep and any supplies they find. What they can't carry they'll burn or destroy so that it won't be of any use to the enemy. Your Lordship's men will be eating kids and calves and Peruvian lambs and all the best there is in the provinces in front of us. Your enemies can't follow you with their present army of two thousand, because it's too cumbersome and half the men are useless. The thousand who could follow you will be starving because they'll find no food on the road. Any they do get will come from a hundred leagues and more away, for they too will have used up all the supplies in the provinces they've come through, and every day they'll be further away from them.

"They won't be able to follow you with a thousand men. If they do try to follow, they'll have to divide in two. Your Lordship can fight either half with advantage, and if you don't want to fight, you can travel at leisure from province to province, spinning out the war and taking it easy, until you tire out the enemy and force him to surrender or offer very advantageous terms."

Gonzalo rejected this very profitable advice, saying that it would be cowardice to retreat from the enemy when he did not appear to have any marked advantage, and that they would besmirch and disgrace their past victories and surrender and destroy the fame and honor they had won.

Carvajal answered: "You'll not lose honor, you'll add to it; for great captains who are skilled in warfare should know how to spin it out with true military ingenuity until they weaken and break their enemy without risking a battle in which there is no certainty whatever of victory, as you can see from the many battles that have been fought all over the world. The battle of Huarina is good proof of this, for Your Lordship won it quite against the expectations of the enemy, since they'd ordered their servants to prepare double rations for the prisoners they thought they'd take from us. Remember that that victory was won more by the special grace of God than by any human force or skill, and it's wrong to tempt God to perform miracles like that at every touch and turn."

Pizarro still said that he thought it looked ill to turn their backs on the enemy. He wanted to wait and try his fortune: it had given him many victories and never allowed him to be defeated and it wouldn't deny him this final victory. So their conversation ended, to the great regret of Carvajal that Pizarro would not accept his good advice. Fernández (chapter lxxxviii), telling part of this conversation, attributes the following among other things to Carvajal: "Let Your Worship do as I say, and we'll give a lance apiece of Centeno's to Centeno's men and let them go. They'll never make good friends, and we'll withdraw better without them."

All these words are from Diego Fernández, and they are clearly Carvajal's, for that remarkable man, never sufficiently praised by his own followers or others, had some such saying for every occasion. The reason why Gonzalo Pizarro did not take Carvajal's excellent advice, or other similar suggestions we shall mention later, was that the commander had lost credit in the general's eyes since the day in Lima when Gonzalo and his captains held the council about whether to receive President la Gasca or not. Carvajal then said the letters were good bulls, and he thought they should take them and enjoy them until they saw exactly what powers the president had. These words sowed the suspicion in Gonzalo's mind that Carvajal was playing a double game, for the advice was not to his liking and counter to his ambitions: Gonzalo did not want anyone to advise him that there should be any other governor, since he regarded himself alone as entitled to the office. As it is natural for those in command not to brook rivals or equals, this quite unfounded suspicion was sufficient to undermine Carvajal's credit and to cause Gonzalo to believe a thing so contrary to Carvajal's character and record. Neither the miracles Carvajal performed in his service, nor the victory at Huarina were sufficient to restore him to his former position. And this suspicion did cruel harm to Pizarro himself, who was ruined the sooner for his refusal to believe Carvajal or take his advice: if he had done so, he might have proved more fortunate, as those who knew these secrets affirmed. . . .

The Two Armies Approach Each Other

[5:33] When Pizarro saw that Acosta's expedition had borne little or no fruit, he decided to go out and receive the president and do battle with him, for he staked all his hopes on this, on account of the victories he had invariably won over both Indians and Spaniards. He had it announced that everyone was to be ready on the fourth day to go to Sacsahuana, four leagues from the city, which was done without consulting Carvajal.

When the latter knew of it, he was very angry, and went to Gonzalo and said: "It's quite the wrong plan to go out and receive the enemy, for if Your Lordship does you'll merely lighten his task and simplify things for him, and at the same time complicate them for yourself instead of adding to his difficulties. I beg Your Lordship to believe this and have a little confidence in me."

Pizarro replied that he had chosen a certain position at Sacsahuana as the place of battle, where the enemy could only attack from in front, and he hoped to defeat them with the artillery, without coming to grips.

Carvajal replied: "Sir, there are plenty of such strong places in this country, and if Your Lordship bids me, I'll find one that'll assure us of victory. What I suggest is that instead of going out four leagues to meet the enemy, you withdraw the same distance and wait for him at Orcos five leagues away. Give the enemy this distance to march and you'll see what confusion and straits he'll get into, and how difficult it will be for him to follow you. When you've seen this, you can choose whichever seems the best policy, either give battle as you wish or continue to withdraw, as I beg you. And I beg you again to retire instead of waiting to receive them. Do this, if it is only to avoid spurning the advantages and countenancing the disadvantages of a horoscope the astrologers have cast for Your Lordship.

"It is well known that they've said you run great danger of losing your life in such and such a year, but that if you survive it, you'll live long and very happily. The year in which Your Lordship's life is in danger is this present year, and the crucial point is not many months, maybe weeks, ahead. Now, as the horoscope is just as unfavorable as it is favorable, you should take the course that is most likely to save your life, and avoid and abominate anything that may threaten it, at least until the year's out. Otherwise you may have cause to blame yourself and your present and future adherents will weep for pity that you didn't set such store by these things as you should have done; for although there's not enough certainty in horoscopes for us to believe them, it seems to me that we should always wait for the period they mention to expire, in order to see if they're true or false. There's nothing to force Your Lordship to give battle, and plenty of reasons for obliging you to put it off and get more advantages than you now have. Who obliges us to risk what we can make quite sure of by marching quietly from place to place at our own ease and comfort and with a great deal of trouble to our enemy, at least until this astrological year, at once so promising and so threatening, is out?"

Pizarro's reply was brief. He said that no one was to advise him to retreat near or far, much or little, for the only thing that befitted his fame and honor was to follow his fortune and finish his resolve, which was to await the enemy at Sacsahuana and give battle without looking at the moon or the stars. So their conversation ended, and Carvajal came away very distressed, telling his friends that their lord the governor had made a fatal decision at the end of his days. Everyone else thought so too, when they realized how precipitately he was delivering himself into his enemy's hands without regard for his safety and authority. They said that it was not for lack of understanding, for he had no lack of that; but it must be the excessive influence of signs and planets that had blinded him and obliged him to place his throat under the knife, since he refused to accept such wholesome advice as his commander had offered.

Returning to the president, for we must frequently move from one side to the other like a weaver, since both sides make the cloth, we should say that on the withdrawal of Acosta, the way lay open for the royal army to advance without fear of its adversaries. But it was so encumbered by artillery, munitions, and supplies that it could not leave that place until the fourth day; for it took three to bring the whole of the baggage train up the hill from the river to the place where the army was. The president then ordered the army to advance in good order; but despite the efforts of the officers the impedimenta were so great that they could not move as fast as they wished. The longest day they were capable of was of two leagues, and most were only one; and after each day they had to stop a day or two for the rearguard to catch up.

Meanwhile Gonzalo was hastening to get his followers from Cusco to Sacsahuana where he was to await the enemy and offer battle. His captains were all young and bold, and thought of nothing but their own bravery, in which they were full of confidence. They therefore hastened to march forward and conclude the campaign imagining themselves already as masters of Peru. Carvajal and those who sided with him and shared his views—and these were the most esteemed and practiced members of the army—were very critical of the policy of going out to meet the enemy, especially as they had many men to whom they could not trust their lives and fortunes as Gonzalo trusted his own followers; for they had more than three hundred followers of Diego Centeno, people who had surrendered to them so recently that many of them still had plasters on their wounds. These men were enemies and therefore more likely to seek their destruction than to desire their success; and on the day of the battle they were to flee instead of fighting, thus dispiriting and discouraging those who were Gonzalo's faithful friends.

They were therefore very discontented, and Carvajal continued whenever opportunity offered to try to dissuade Gonzalo and see if he could not make him reverse his decision and so avoid the evident destruction of his life and honor and everything else that was his. But God had ordained, as his rivals used to say, that Gonzalo's crimes should lead him to the punishment he deserved, and he refused to follow any advice but his own. This so angered his adherents that they prepared in their hearts to repudiate him when they could. On this point I can affirm that after the battle of Sacsahuana when peace had been restored, I heard some of Gonzalo's leading supporters, who were talking of these events, state that if he had retired as his commander had advised him, they would have died rather than deny him; for they regarded Carvajal as an oracle, and on account of his wisdom and long experience expected his military recommendations to bring them success and prosperity.

Gonzalo Pizarro, obdurate in his own destruction, left the city of Cusco at the end of March 1548 and reached Sacsahuana, less than four leagues away, in two days. He took so long because he too was encumbered with artillery, supplies, and baggage, wishing to have everything necessary to avoid hunger and meet all kinds of needs in case the enemy were delayed. And although he undertook this journey against the advice of most of his friends, as we have said, they did not dare to oppose him, for they saw that he was quite determined on it. So almost all of them were confirmed in their resolve to look to their own particular interests, in other words to repudiate Gonzalo Pizarro, who was clearly surrendering himself to death, which now called him at the best and most successful moment of his life. He was forty-two years of age, and had won every battle he had fought against Indians and Spaniards, and less than six months before had obtained the victory of Huarina, which raised him above all the famous captains of the New World. All this prosperity and his hopes of the future, and his life to boot, were buried in the valley of Sacsahuana.

The Armies Prepare for Battle

[5:34] . . . The night before the battle, Acosta decided to take four hundred harquebusiers and attack the royal army, to see if he could do something to repair his negligence and the failure of his recent expedition. The soldiers who had gone with him grumbled loud and long at his carelessness and lack of military skill. And when Carvajal knew how things stood, he wept his ill fortune that had deprived him in his old age of the greatest deed that would have crowned his whole career. When Acosta was ready for the attack, it was found that one of Centeno's soldiers had escaped; and suspecting that he would have given warning of Acosta's attack, they abandoned it. Gonzalo Pizarro was not sorry, for he thought that the safest way to obtain a victory was to fight a pitched battle, and not to try alarms and night attacks. López de Gómara here says that he told Acosta: "Juan, as we've as good as won, don't let us risk it," which "was fatal arrogance and blindness."

So López de Gómara. The arrogance and blindness of Pizarro and his captains lay in supposing that the whole army would fight as well as themselves, in which case they could not have failed to win. But this was not so: neither those who thought themselves valiant, nor those reputed cowards fought.

The soldier who deserted warned the royal army that Juan de Acosta and his men were ready to make a surprise attack by night and offer battle. This obliged the president and his army to pass the whole night drawn up in formation; they were so cold that, as López de Gómara and Zárate say, their lances fell from their hands, which were too numb to hold them. At daybreak, April 9, 1548, the royal army resumed its formation after recovering a little from the previous night. The infantry was placed together, under the captains we have already named, with [detachments] of harquebusiers on either side. To the left of the infantry they stationed 200 horses, under Diego de Mora, Juan de Saavedra, Rodrigo de Salazar, and Francisco Hernández Girón (whom Zárate calls Aldana). To the right were Captains Gómez de Alvarado, Don Pedro Cabrera, and Alonso Mercadillo, with 200 more horse forming a guard for the royal standard carried by Licentiate Carvajal, the ensign general, who accompanied these captains. To their right, at a good distance, was Captain Alonso de Mendoza. He was accompanied by Diego Centeno, and they had a company of 60 horse, most or almost all of whom had escaped from the battle of Huarina. As companions in their past reverses and hardships they wanted no other captain but Mendoza. These were stationed near the river to help those who might flee to the royal army on that side: they were well aware that there were men everywhere who would desert to the royalists, and such fugitives would run the greatest danger at that point. Captain Gabriel de Rojas strove to bring the artillery down to the plain, which was done with great difficulty owing to the steepness of the mountainside. General Pedro de Hinojosa, Commander Alonso de Alvarado, Sergeant Major Pedro de Villavicencio, and Governor Pedro de Valdivia disposed the squadrons. Behind them all was the president with the three bishops of Lima, Cusco, and Quito, and the provincials of the order of Preachers and the Mercedarians, as well as a great many other priests and friars who had come with the army. In their rear there were 50 horsemen to protect them in case some impudent wretch attacked them.

The Events of the Battle of Sacsahuana

[5:35] On the other side, Gonzalo Pizarro sounded the call to arms as soon as it grew light and ordered his men up to the plain between the ravine and the mountain where they were to draw up. The artillery was brought up and placed on an eminence. Licentiate Cepeda, as López de Gómara says, was instructed to arrange the troops, for Francisco de Carvajal refused to perform his usual duty as commander that day out of pique that Gonzalo Pizarro should have refused to follow his advice. He thought the day was already lost, and placed himself as an infantry captain at the head of his company. Thus the historians make no mention of him in describing the disposition of the troops.

While they were all busily taking up their stations, my lord Garcilaso left them, and on the pretense that the Indian who should have brought him his lance had not done so, he went down to the river shouting for the man. As soon as he was covered by the ravine, he went toward the royal standard, and having crossed a small bog between the two armies, he went down to the river, climbed up the side of the ravine and presented himself to the president in full view of both armies. The latter welcomed him and embraced him with great satisfaction, saying: "My lord Garcilaso, I always expected your honor would render His Majesty such a service."

My lord Garcilaso then replied: "Sir, as a prisoner deprived of his liberty, I have not been able to serve His Majesty or Your Lordship hitherto, though I have never lacked the desire to do so." . . .

Gonzalo's army was drawn up, as seemed best to Licentiate Cepeda. On the side toward the mountain there came forth a [detachment] of harquebusiers to skirmish with the royalists. Captains Hernán Mejía de Guzmán and Juan Alonso Palomino came out against them with their companies of harquebusiers and drove them back without loss to either side. Meanwhile, the artillery of both armies was fired. Gonzalo's did no damage because the president's army was stationed in a hollow like a cup, and the balls passed over their heads. The president's artillery was very well placed, for it dominated the opposing camp, in which it landed many balls, according to the historians, killing two men. This is the truth; and one of them was a page to Gonzalo Pizarro.

Licentiate Cepeda, who was arranging the troops in order of battle and desired to go over to the royalists, pretended to go and look for a better position than that which the army was occupying, and as soon as he was at a little distance, spurred his horse. This was a very handsome animal, a dark chestnut with its neck, breast, and rump covered in handsomely decorated black cowhide, an original and singular trapping which was unique in those days and which I have never seen since I left Peru. Nevertheless the splendid covering harmed both horse and rider, for while they were still running and had already gone some distance from Pizarro's lines, Pedro Martín de Don Benito came out in pursuit on a big, long horse as thin as a rake, which I also knew: it was a chestnut and covered more ground in a single stride than others in three or four. He overtook Cepeda as he was entering the small bog near the royalist camp; and lanced the horse in the rump (bringing it down in the mire) and its rider in the thigh. He would have killed him if four of Mendoza's company had not come to the rescue: as we have mentioned, they were stationed there for this purpose. The covering impeded Cepeda's horse, for without it would have run more freely and avoided Pedro Martín de Don Benito, who was a big old man, hard and tanned. After performing this feat, he hastened back to his own lines, and Cepeda as a result of the timely aid he had received, was able to get out of the bog and go and kiss the president's hand. He received him with great joy, as López de Gómara says (chapter clxxxvi): "la Gasca embraced Cepeda and kissed him on the cheek, though he was all muddy. He regarded Pizarro as beaten without him." So López de Gómara.

Meanwhile many other soldiers came over at various points, both horse and foot. One of them happened to be Martín de Arbieto, whom we mentioned in the battle of Huarina and promised to say something of his doings. Here we shall insert one of them. He was riding a good horse with a long-stirruped harness and a lance on a rest, such as were and are rarely seen in Peru. With him was a soldier called Pedro de Arenas, a native of Colmenar de Arenas, a small, neat man, very honest and a good soldier: I knew him later. He had a fine sorrel and white pied mare, small in size like its master, and more suitable for riding through city streets than for the battlefield. Martín de Arbieto reined in his horse so as not to forsake one who had placed himself under his protection. Pedro Martín de Don Benito had lanced four or five foot, and seeing these two riding away, set off after them to lance them too. Martín de Arbieto, who was riding in front of his companion, easily cleared the bog, but Pedro de Arenas' mare became stuck and in floundering threw its rider into the mud, for his saddle was a long-stirruped one and the girths were loose. Arbieto, on seeing this, went back through the marsh and rode straight at Pedro Martín de Don Benito to prevent him from killing his friend. When Pedro Martín saw that Arbieto meant to fight him, he pulled up and stood waiting. Arbieto called to him: "Come on, you rogue; we'll see who sucked the better milk!" But his opponent refused the challenge and returned to his own ranks without saying a word.

On one of these excursions Pedro Martín was hit by a stray shot which pierced his right hand and made him drop his lance. Having lost it, he went to Gonzalo Pizarro and said, "I'm of no use to Your Lordship now," and so saying joined the rear rank of the horse. While this was going on both horse and foot continued to desert to the royalists. Francisco de Carvajal, seeing that they were losing because Gonzalo had not paid any attention to him, began to sing aloud:

> "Mother, my little hairs are gone away
> Gone two by two with the wind away."[35]

And he went on singing this song in mockery of those who had rejected his counsel, until there was not a soldier left on his side. Thirty-two harquebusiers left the [detachment] to the right of Gonzalo's formation, pretending to be going to skirmish with the enemy, as though they were still quite loyal. But when they were some distance away, they ran helter-skelter for the royal lines. They and those who had already fled advised the royalist general and his officers not to come forward to fight, but to stay where they were, for very soon all Pizarro's men would abandon him and leave him alone. And so it turned out, for Gonzalo sent thirty horse to follow the harquebusiers and stop them, which they did so dutifully that they too delivered themselves up to the president. Another forty of the harquebusiers who were on Pizarro's left deserted, and no one dared pursue them as they withdrew in good order, facing their former companions and showing signs of firing on anyone who tried to resist them. They also ceased the pursuit because Mendoza and Centeno with their sixty horse had crossed the bog and come nearer to help the deserters. When the pikemen saw that the harquebusiers on both wings had fled and that they themselves could not pretend that they were going to skirmish with the enemy, they dropped their pikes as one man, and began to flee in all directions, thus completing the dispersal of Gonzalo Pizarro's army.

Such was the battle of Sacsahuana, if it can be called a battle, for there was no more fighting than we have said, not a sword thrust, nor a clash with lances, nor a harquebus shot between the two sides. Gonzalo's defeat was so rapid that it will have taken longer to read this chapter than he took to suffer the reverses we have described. On his side ten or twelve were killed, as López de Gómara says. They died at the hands of Pedro Martín de Don Benito and others who were trying to stop the deserters: the president's men did not kill one of their enemies. Although the historians say that the two armies were within harquebus shot, it was a very long shot, for there were more than five hundred paces between them. On the royalist side only one was killed, shot by the carelessness of one of his companions.

---

[35] *Cabellicos:* "little hairs," a pun on *caballicos,* "little horses."

Gonzalo Pizarro Surrenders; the Capture of Francisco de Carvajal

[5:36] The last straw in Gonzalo's destruction was the action of the pikemen dropping their pikes and taking to their heels. This left him and his officers aghast, for they had not imagined such a thing to be possible. Gonzalo turned to Acosta, who was nearby, and said: "What shall we do, brother Juan?"

Acosta, showing more valor than discretion, replied: "Sir, let's attack and die like the ancient Romans!"

Pizarro said: "It's better to die like Christians."

Here López de Gómara comments (chapter clxxxvi): "It was the word of a Christian and of a brave man: he preferred to surrender rather than flee, for no enemy ever saw his back," etcetera. A little further on he adds: "He was very gallant on his powerful chestnut horse, and wore a coat of mail and a rich breast guard with a surtunic of crushed velvet and a golden casque on his head with a gold chin guard," etcetera. Thus López de Gómara. Zárate adds that the tunic he wore over his arms was of yellow velvet covered almost all over with gold plates, and that he said to Acosta: "Well, as they've all gone to the king, I'll do the same," etcetera.

So he rode toward the royal army with such captains as wished to follow him: Juan de Acosta, Maldonado, and Juan Vélez de Guevara. Diego Guillén had already gone over to the president. On the way Gonzalo came upon Pedro de Villavicencio and seeing that he was well attended, asked him who he was. On learning that he was the sergeant major, he said: "I am Gonzalo Pizarro, and I surrender to the emperor." So saying he handed him a sword he was carrying in his hand; for he had broken his lance on his own men as they fled, as Zárate mentions. Villavicencio was delighted at his good fortune; and he therefore courteously thanked Pizarro for the honor he did him by surrendering to him. In recognition of this he refused to accept his sword and dagger, which were of great value, for the hilt and guard were of gold.

A little later they met Diego Centeno who went up to Gonzalo Pizarro and said: "I am very sorry to see Your Lordship in this case."

Gonzalo smiled somewhat, and said: "There's no use in talking of that, Captain Centeno. I have finished today: tomorrow you'll weep for me." And without saying any more they went to the president. . . .

When Gonzalo Pizarro reached the president, he found him alone with the marshal, the magnates having withdrawn to a distance, so as to avoid seeing the leader they had abandoned and sold. Pizarro greeted the president on horseback without alighting, for they were all mounted. The president did the same and asked him if he thought it right to have stirred up

Peru against the emperor and to have made himself governor of it against His Majesty's will, and to have killed his viceroy in pitched battle. He replied that he had not made himself governor, but that the judges, at the behest of all the cities of Peru, had bidden him become it and had authorized it in the light of the power vested by His Majesty in his brother the marquis to appoint his successor as governor. His brother had appointed him, as everyone knew, and there was nothing surprising in the conqueror of Peru becoming its governor. As to the viceroy, the judges had also ordered him to be expelled from Peru, saying that it behove His Majesty's service and the peace and quiet of the empire. He had not killed the viceroy: what had happened was that the viceroy had caused so many wrongs and deaths by his precipitate and unjustifiable actions that the relatives of the dead had been forced to seek revenge. If the messengers he had sent to report to His Majesty (who were those who had sold him and caused him to be called a traitor) had been allowed to pass, His Majesty would have regarded himself as well served and have acted in quite a different manner; for everything Pizarro had done then and since had been at the instance of the *vecinos* and procurators of the cities of the whole of Peru, and had been approved by all the lawyers in the country.

The president then said that he had shown himself very ungrateful for the grants His Majesty had made to his brother. This had enriched them all, though they had been so poor before, and had raised them from the dust; and in any case Gonzalo Pizarro had played no part in the discovery of Peru. Gonzalo answered: "My brother alone was enough to discover the country; but all four brothers were necessary, and the rest of our relatives and friends, to conquer it, as we did at our own risk and expense. The only honor His Majesty did my brother was to confer on him the title of marquis: if he did more, tell me what it was. He did not lift us up from the dust, for we have been noblemen and gentlemen with our own estates since the Goths came to Spain. Those who are not may very well be raised from the dust by His Majesty's offices and commissions. If we were poor, that was why we ventured out into the world, and won this empire, and gave it to His Majesty, though we might have kept it ourselves, as many others who have won new lands have done."

This angered the president, and he twice shouted: "Take him away; take him away. He's as much of a rebel today as he was yesterday." Then Centeno led him away, having requested the president for the privilege. The other captains were sent to various places where they could be safely guarded. . . .

The Captains Are Executed and Their
Heads Taken to Various Parts of Peru

[5:39] . . . The following day Gonzalo Pizarro and his commander and captains who had been captured on the day of the battle were executed. As López de Gómara says (chapter clxxxvii), they were Juan de Acosta, Francisco Maldonado, Juan Vélez de Guevara, Dionisio de Bobadilla, and Gonzalo de los Nidos. He mentions that in the case of the last of these they pulled his tongue out through the back of his neck, though he does not say why: it was because he uttered great blasphemies against the Imperial Majesty. All these and many others were hanged, and though they were gentlemen their privileges were not respected since they were traitors to the king. After being hanged, their heads were cut off and sent to various cities in Peru. Juan de Acosta's and Francisco Maldonado's were placed on the gibbet in the main square of Cusco, each in an iron cage: I saw them there, though one of the historians, Fernández (chapter xci), says that Acosta's was taken to Lima. Dionisio de Bobadilla's and that of one other were taken to Arequipa, thus fulfilling the prophecy the good Juana de Leitão made to Bobadilla himself when he brought Lope de Mendoza's head to the city: her words were that it would soon be taken down and his own set up in the same place. This thus came about, exactly as she said. Gonzalo Pizarro and his officers were executed in haste, for, as the authors say, it was feared that the country would not be safe while he was alive. They sentenced Pizarro to be beheaded as a traitor; his houses in Cusco were pulled down and the site sown with salt, and a stone pillar was erected with an inscription reading: "This is the house of the traitor Gonzalo Pizarro," etcetera.

I saw all this carried out. The houses were those granted to him in the allocations of Cusco, when he and his brothers conquered the city. The place is called Coracora, or "meadow," in the Indian tongue. Pizarro spent the day of his arrest in the tent of Captain Centeno, where he was treated with the same respect as during his greatest prosperity and power. He refused to eat that day though he was invited to do so. He spent almost the whole time walking up and down alone, brooding. Late at night he called to Centeno: "Sir, are we safe tonight?" He meant would they kill him that night or wait till next day, for he well knew that each hour was a year for his rivals until they had killed him.

When Centeno understood him, he said: "Your Lordship can sleep safely; there's no need to brood over that." And after midnight he lay down a little on the bed, and slept about an hour. Then he resumed his pacing up and down till daylight. At dawn he asked for a confessor, and lingered with him till midday, where we shall leave him to return to Francisco de Carvajal, and say how he spent the day.

Carvajal did not behave so extravagantly as one of the authors says, but very differently. I shall recount this, not because I have any obligation for having received anything from him: on the contrary, he wanted to kill my father after the battle of Huarina, and tried to find reasons for this drawn from his own suspicions and imaginations. For this reason I might be expected to speak ill of him rather than seek to defend his honor. But the obligation of one who writes the history of those times for the information of the whole world binds me, and even forces me, if I may put it so, to tell the truth about what happened without passion for or against. And I swear as a Christian that I have clipped and cut short many passages so as not to seem to speak with passion against the versions of the historians, especially Fernández, who must have gone to Peru very late and have heard many fables invented according to the party passions of their authors. What I have said above, and other details I shall give of these days, I heard as a child from people who were talking of those things: at that time and for many years after there was no theme of conversation among noble people which did not touch to some extent on these matters. Later, when I was older, I heard them from a person or persons who were on guard over Francisco de Carvajal and Gonzalo Pizarro, for the tents they were in were very close together and the soldiers on guard, all eminent men, went between them relieving one another; so they saw everything and described all the details as eye witnesses.

How Gonzalo Pizarro Was Beheaded; His Character and Good Qualities

[5:43] It remains to speak of the pitiful death of Gonzalo Pizarro. He spent the whole day confessing as we have already noted, and we left him confessing until midday. He continued after the priests had dined, though he himself refused to eat and remained alone until the confessor returned: he stayed with him until very late. The ministers of justice came and went and tried to speed the execution. One of the gravest of them, annoyed at the delay, called out: "Come, haven't you finished with the man yet?" All the soldiers who heard this were offended at this disrespect, and uttered a thousand insults: although I remember many of them and knew the man, it would not be proper for me to set them down here or to mention his name. He went off without saying a word before anyone laid hands on him, as it was feared they would, on account of the indignation and wrath the soldiers displayed at his uncalled-for remark.

Soon after Gonzalo Pizarro appeared, and mounted a mule which was ready saddled. He was covered with a cloak, and though one author says his hands were bound, this was not so. A rope's end was hung over the mule's neck in compliance with the law. He carried in his hands an image of Our Lady, to whom he was most devoted. He begged her to intercede for his soul. After going halfway he asked for a crucifix. One of the ten or twelve priests who accompanied him happened to have one and gave it to him. Gonzalo took it and gave the priest the image of Our Lady, kissing the hem of the image's robe with great devotion. With his gaze fixed on the crucifix in his hands, he went to the platform that had been prepared for his execution and mounted it, standing on one corner of it, and talked with the spectators, who included all the soldiers and *vecinos* of Peru: only the magnates who had denied him were missing, and even some of them were there in disguise or muffled in their cloaks. He said aloud: "Gentlemen, you know that my brothers and I won this empire. Many of you have allocations of Indians the marquis my brother gave you. Others have allocations I gave you. Moreover many of you owe me money I lent you. Others have received money not as a loan but as gifts. I die so poor that even the garment I wear belongs to the executioner who is to cut off my head. I have nothing with which to seek the good of my soul. I therefore beg those of you who owe me money to give this money, and those of you who do not owe me any to give your own money as charity for as many masses as possible to be said for my soul, for I trust to God that, through the blood and passion of our Lord Jesus Christ His Son and through the charity you will give, he will have compassion on me and forgive my sins. God be with you all."

He had not finished this speech when a general wail went up, with groans and sobs and the shedding of many tears, when such pathetic words were heard. Gonzalo Pizarro knelt before the crucifix he had brought, which was placed on a table on the platform. The executioner, called Juan Enríquez, placed a bandage over his eyes. Gonzalo said: "It's not necessary. Leave it." When he saw the man draw his scimitar to cut off his head, he said: "Do your task well, Brother Juan." He meant that he was to do it generously and not torture him, as often happens.

The executioner replied: "I promise Your Lordship." So saying, with his left hand he lifted his beard, a long one about a palm long and round, for in those days they were worn full and untrimmed. Then with a single stroke he cut off the head as easily as if it were a leaf of lettuce, and remained with it in his hand; the body took some time to fall to the ground.

Such was the end of this good gentleman. The executioner wished to exercise his rights and denude him, so as to enjoy the spoils. But Diego Centeno, who had come to recover Gonzalo's body, ordered him not to touch it and promised him a good sum of money in exchange for the clothes. So they carried him to Cusco and buried him in his clothes, for no one offered to give him a shroud. He was buried in the convent of the Mercedarians, in the same chapel in which the two Almagros, father and son, lay, so that they were equals and companions in everything—in their conquest of Peru and in all being beheaded and buried by charity all three in a single grave, as though there was not even enough earth to cover them. They were made equal in everything by fortune, lest any should presume over the others or over the marquis Don Francisco Pizarro, the brother of one and companion of the other, who was killed as we have said and also buried by charity: thus all four were as brothers and companions in everything and for everything. It is the usual reward of the world to those who serve it best, as those who saw these things dispassionately observed; for those who finished thus had conquered the empire called Peru.

None of the three authors speak of Gonzalo Pizarro's appeal for charity at the hour of his death, despite the fact that he spoke as publicly as we have said. This must have been so as not to distress their hearers. I set out to tell simply what happened, and this is what I have done.

Once the storm of war was passed, all the *vecinos* of the empire, each in the city where he lived, had many masses said for Gonzalo's soul, both because he himself had asked for them as charity, and because of their general and common obligation toward him, since he had died for them. His head and that of Carvajal were taken to Lima, which his brother the marquis Don Francisco Pizarro had founded and settled. They were placed on the pillar in the square there, each in an iron cage. . . .

Chapter Six
La Gasca Reallocates the
Indians and Restores Order

Measures for the Punishment of the Rebels

[6:1] . . . The president at the same time announced a general pardon from blame and sentence for all who had followed the royal standard in the battle of Sacsahuana. This was to apply to any crimes committed during Gonzalo Pizarro's rebellion, even though they had taken part in the death of the Viceroy Blasco Núñez Vela and others of His Majesty's officials. The pardon covered only crimes: civil suits and the disposal of property were referred to legal process, according to the president's commission, as Agustín de Zárate says (Book VII, chapter viii), it being considered that Gonzalo de Pizarro had canceled criminal charges against his followers by his death.

Even though he had attained victory and had executed his enemies, the president, in this period of peace and calm, was more downcast, troubled, and distressed than he had been during the war, for then he had found many to assist him in bearing the burden of his military responsibilities, but now that peace was restored he was called upon to suffer the importunities, demands, and woes of 2,500 men who claimed pay and reward for their services. Not a single one of them, however little he had done, failed to think himself worthy of the best allocation of Indians in all Peru. And the persons who had been of most assistance to the president in time of war were precisely those who molested him most with their petitions and demands now that peace was declared. They were so tenacious and troublesome that in order to avoid their importunities to some extent, he decided to go to the valley called Apurimac, twelve leagues from the city, to attend to the allocating of the Indians more calmly. He took with him the archbishop of Lima, Don Jerónimo de Loaisa, and his secretary, Pedro López de Cazalla, and left instructions that no *vecino* or soldier, or any other person, was to follow him or disturb him in his task. He also ordered that no *vecino* in all Peru should go home until the distribution of the Indians had been completed, for he imagined that by keeping them together he could ensure against any attempt at revolt on the part of the common people. His wish and concern was to spread the soldiers over various parts of the kingdom, or to send them to make new conquests and win new lands, as those who

212

had won the empire had done. But he dispersed very few of them, for he was in a great hurry to get away from the country before there should be some rising among the many people who were dissatisfied, as he imagined, some having reason for their complaints and others none. . . .

The president ignores the complaints of those who did not receive an allocation of Indians or feel that they have received too little. There is great dissatisfaction among the Spaniards.

The Preoccupations and Labors of President la Gasca

[6:7] Having set up the *audiencia* in the city of Lima, the president applied himself to the pacification of the empire and the indoctrination and instruction of the natives. He ordered a general visitation to be made, and an assessment to be made of the tribute the Indians were to pay their masters, the result being set down in writing for each allocation, so that the Indians should not be required to pay more than was just. To this end Licentiate Cianca, as His Majesty's judge, went to the city of Lima, after having lightly punished a certain rising that took place in Cusco as a result of the past distribution.

He hanged one soldier and banished three others, but avoided pressing the punishment or investigating further for fear of causing a scandal and disturbances. For the same reason the president raised the sentence of banishment before any of those who had been sentenced craved pardon, for he saw that it was better to appease people who were full of grievances—and many with justification—with softness and suavity rather than provoke them with stern and harsh treatment. Licentiate Cianca, obeying President la Gasca's instructions, left as *corregidor* in Cusco one Juan de Saavedra, a very noble knight from Seville, who had Indians in the city.

The president sent the commander Alonso de Alvarado to the "New Town" with a commission as *corregidor*, enjoining him to pay particular attention to the settlement of the city of La Paz: the city had both names at first. He had an allocation of Indians near the city.

Meanwhile citizens came from all parts of the empire to the city of Lima to kiss the president's hand and thank him for the many great allocations he had bestowed on them. A great many of the leading soldiers who had served the king also appeared to ask for rewards for their services and satisfaction for their grievances, since the pay that was due to them had been given to others who deserved rather to be punished and executed for having betrayed His Imperial Majesty. News arrived of the deaths of Diego Centeno, Gabriel de Rojas, Licentiate Carvajal, and other citizens, and although the president was aware of the news, it was duly communicated to him with urgent and passionate demands that he should revise the past allocations, and rearrange them in such a way that all might have the wherewithal to eat, instead of their starving while those who had done most for the rebel leader died of apoplexy and surfeit. This is confirmed by López de Gómara, in chapter clxxxiv, which I have already cited, in these words: "Lastly they discussed a request to President la Gasca that he should revise the allocations, so that all should have a share, and either divide the greater ones or award them pensions payable from them. Otherwise they would seize them themselves, etcetera." These are López de Gómara's words.

The president was very distressed and exhausted because of his inability to satisfy so many claimants with so little to award and divide among them, they being so presumptuous about their merits and services that if the whole of Peru had suddenly become disposable, it would have seemed little in relation to the overweening arrogance with which they put forward their deserts. But the president, discreet, prudent, astute, and ingenious, held them off for the year and a half he was in the city. During this time several shameless and disgraceful incidents occurred, as the historians mention, but the good president suffered them with prudence and discretion. He did more than conquer and win all the empire: he conquered himself, as will be seen from some incidents I heard at the time and later since I came to Spain. . . .

Some of the angry rebels attack la Gasca's fleet on its way back to Spain, to no avail. In Cusco, violence grows as the malcontents grow in number and begin preying on the citizens of the city.

The Arrival and Death of the Viceroy and the Scandals That Follow

[6:17] At this time there arrived in Peru as viceroy, governor, and captain general of the empire Don Antonio de Mendoza, second son of the house of the marquis of Mondéjar and count of Tendilla, who, as we have said in the *Florida del Inca,* was viceroy in the empire of Mexico, a saintly and religious man with all the good qualities of a Christian and a gentleman. The city of Lima received him with due solemnity and festivities. . . .

[6:19] We have mentioned the arrival of the good viceroy Don Antonio de Mendoza at the city of Lima. He lived there a very short time, and in such sickness and pain that he seemed more dead than alive. There is therefore little to say of his viceroyalty. As soon as he reached the city, many citizens from all parts of the empire from Quito to Los Charcas gathered to kiss his hand and congratulate him on his arrival. One of them kissed his hand with great affection and many compliments, and ended: "I pray, Your Excellency, that God may take many days from your life and add them to mine."

The viceroy replied: "I am afraid they will be few and unprofitable."

The citizen, realizing that he had put his foot in it, said: "I beg pardon sir. I did not mean what I said, but the opposite. May God take many days from my life and add them to yours."

The viceroy answered: "That was what I understood you to mean, and there is nothing to beg pardon for in that." He then dismissed the visitor to the amusement of those who remained.

A few days later a captain, well known in our history, came in for the purpose of tendering to the viceroy advice which he thought essential to the security and good government of the empire. Among other points, the most important he made was this: "Sir, Your Excellency really must take action in the case of two soldiers who live in such-and-such an allocation. They live among the natives. They have guns and live off what they kill. All this shooting ruins the country. What is more, they make their own powder and shot, which is a very serious matter in this country. The whole of Peru is scandalized! There have been serious disturbances here, and it's high time they were punished. The least they deserve is to be dismissed from Peru."

The viceroy asked if they ill-treated the Indians, or sold powder and shot, or committed other serious wrongs, and when the captain replied that all they had done was what he had said, the viceroy gave his reply: "The crimes you mention are things to be grateful for, not things to punish. If two Spaniards live among the Indians, and eat what they shoot themselves, and make their own powder and don't sell it, I don't see what harm they are doing. On the contrary, it sounds a very good example for others to follow. Now good-bye, but don't let you or anyone else come back with this sort of tittle-tattle, for I don't like to hear it. The men you mention must be saints, if their life is what you describe as criminal." The captain went off, well rewarded for his charitable intentions.

The viceroy governed the empire gently and well in the little time he lived. Perhaps my country did not deserve such goodness: he was soon taken off to heaven. While he was sick, the judges ordered the serfdom of the Indians to be abolished, and it was published in the city of Lima, Cusco, and other places with such rigorous conditions that another disturbance was caused. A gentleman called Luis de Vargas was beheaded as ringleader, but the punishment of the affair was not pressed forward for fear of inciting and scandalizing many others, since the investigation cast suspicion of responsibility on General Pedro de Hinojosa, three witnesses having accused him in their statements, though not directly. The judges elected him *corregidor* and chief justice in Los Charcas, to make an honest man of him, as Fernández says in Book II, chapter iii, for they had news that many soldiers were out of hand. Although the general at first refused the office, the senior of the judges, Dr. Saravia, spoke to him and persuaded him to accept, which in effect he did. The blame attributed to him was a question of suspicion rather than of fact. The soldiers themselves said that he held out hopes, some said certain hopes, others vague ones, that on getting to Charcas he would do what they wanted: let them go there and he would provide for them as best he could. Although the words were vague, the soldiers, who were in favor of any rebellion, took them and explained them according to their own taste and wishes. Whether the general intended to rebel or not was not then made clear, though signs were not lacking that he was ill rather than well disposed. All the soldiers in Lima who could went off to Charcas and wrote to their friends in various parts of the kingdom to follow them. . . .

Francisco Hernández de Girón, a vecino *of Cusco, scandalized by the severe punishment of the men who rebelled against the royal authority in Charcas, rises in revolt. Despite victories at the beginning, the revolt is eventually defeated, with much loss of life among rebels and loyalists alike, ending the last important rising against royal authority.*

The End of This History

[8:21] Having begun this history with the commencement and origins of the Inca kings in Peru, and having noticed at length their conquests and generous deeds, their lives, their government in peace and war, and the idolatrous religion they had in heathen times—all of which were performed at length in the first part of these *Commentaries,* with divine aid— we fulfilled the obligation we felt toward our mother country and our maternal stock. In the Second Part, as we have seen, a long account was given of the deeds and heroic actions that the brave and valiant Spaniards performed in conquering that wealthy empire, wherein we have fulfilled, even though not completely, our paternal obligations, which we owe to our father and his illustrious and generous companions. It now seems to me proper to conclude this work, as I now do, at the end of the succession of the Inca kings, who numbered thirteen from their first possession of the empire until the arrival of the Spaniards, until the unfortunate Huascar Inca. Five others succeeded later, Manco Inca and his two sons, Don Diego and Don Felipe, and his two grandchildren, who never possessed any part of the kingdom except the right to it. There were thus in all eighteen successors in the direct male line from the first Inca Manco Capac to the last of these children, whose name I do not know. The Inca Atahuallpa is not included by the Indians as one of their kings, for they describe him as *auca.*[36]

With regard to the descendents of these kings not in the direct line, in the last chapter of the First Part of these *Commentaries* we mentioned how many descendants there were of each of the past kings. As I stated there, they themselves sent me a document in the name of all of them with power of attorney in favor of Don Melchor Carlos, Don Alonso de Mesa, and myself, so that any of the three of us could present it on their behalf to His Catholic Majesty and the Supreme Royal Council of the Indies. This document requested that, as descendants of kings, they should be relieved of the vexations they suffered. I sent the petition and the accompanying papers (which were addressed to me) to the capital directed to the said Don Melchor Carlos and Don Alonso de Mesa, but the former, though his own claims were of the same nature and based on the same legal and natural arguments as those of the Incas, was unwilling to present the papers so as not to reveal how many persons there were of the royal blood, thinking that if he did reveal this, he would lose many of the grants and honors he claimed and hoped to receive. He was therefore reluctant to raise his voice on his kinsmen's behalf; and he died, as has been said, without receiving anything for himself or his friends. I have mentioned this in order to clear myself and so that my relatives, wherever they may be, shall know what happened and not accuse me of neglect or ill will in not having done what they bade and requested me. I would indeed have been glad to have devoted my life to the service of people who so greatly deserved it, but I have not been able to do more, as I have been engaged in writing this history, which I hope will have been as great a service to the Spaniards who won the empire as to the Incas who formally possessed it.

The Divine Majesty, Father, Son, and Holy Ghost, three persons and one single true God, be praised *per omnia saecula saeculorum,*[37] who has granted me the great mercy of allowing me to reach this place. May it be to the glory and honor of His holy name, whose divine mercy, through the blood of our Lord Jesus Christ and the intercession of the ever Virgin Mary, His mother, and of all of His heavenly host, be my favor and protection, now and at the hour of my death, amen, Jesus, a hundred thousand times Jesus.

Laus Deo

---

[36] *Auca,* " meaning "enemy" or "traitor." Diego González Holguín, *Vocabulario de la lengua Quechua* [1583] p. 38.

[37] Forever and ever.

Index